LOUIS VUITTON

HOME RUN.
THE ALL-ELECTRIC BMW i3.

THE PLAYERS

A FILM FOR DIOR HOMME

WWW.DIORHOMME.COM/THEPLAYERS

p039—046

p097—103

PHOTOGRAPHER: *Henning Bock*
MODEL: *Michael Wagner*
HUSKY: *Tess*
GROOMING: *Christopher Sweeney*

MICHAEL WEARS: COAT by
Canada Goose, JUMPER by
Brioni, BINOCULARS by
Swarovski Optik

CONTENTS
— *November 2013*

CONTENTS
— November 2013

p123—128

p163—167

p266—267

PANERAI.COM

Mediterranean Sea.
"Gamma" men in training.
The diver emerging from the water
is wearing a Panerai compass on his wrist.

HISTORY AND HEROES.

RADIOMIR 1940 3 DAYS (REF. 514)
AVAILABLE IN STEEL AND RED GOLD

PANERAI
LABORATORIO DI IDEE.

Exclusively at Panerai boutiques and select authorized watch specialists.

ONLINE CONTENTS
—*monocle.com*

On *monocle.com* you can watch our short documentary films and slideshows for free. Some of the films expand upon the printed story, while others provide completely fresh content brought to you by our editors and correspondents around the world. Browse our films covering the A to E sections and, if you are a subscriber, access our magazine back catalogue online.

Art of the Arctic FILM: MONOCLE's culture editor Robert Bound heads into the blizzards to investigate the artistic allure of the Arctic at Copenhagen's Louisiana Museum of Modern Art.

Alaska ferries SLIDESHOW: Our transport editor Tristan McAllister spends three days aboard an Alaskan state ferry to discover the colourful people and machines that keep Alaska moving.

Turin design FILM: Turin is known for its design talent – especially during Paratissima, an international festival proudly showcasing the work of emerging designers. MONOCLE captures the new work on film.

Architecture Film Festival Rotterdam FILM: The city as "time machine" is the theme of AFFR 2013. We talk to the filmmakers and featured architects to explore the cinematic ideas premiered at this year's festival.

THE MONOCLE SHOP

At *monocle.com*'s online store you can buy all of our product collaborations as well as back issues and subscriptions.

Monochan toy NEW PRODUCT: MONOCLE's loveable mascot has been brought to life – in wool – by craft specialist Makers & Brothers and Irish textile designer Claire-Anne O'Brien. A wise choice for children or keen MONOCLE readers.

Cardigan by ESK NEW PRODUCT: Made with the finest cashmere and extra-fine merino, this cardigan is brought to us from ESK's woollen mills in Scotland. Details include a pencil pocket and real horn buttons.

Jambox NEW PRODUCT: San Francisco-based Jawbone has created this compact, portable speaker for us. It boasts crisp, high-quality sound at any volume and Bluetooth connectivity – so it can come with you as the party migrates from room to room.

EXTRAORDINARY CRAFTSMANSHIP
The new Vertu Constellation

Finished with luxury calf leather in a range of exquisite colours, sourced from a tannery with over 150 years' experience. A screen of virtually scratchproof sapphire crystal. And every extraordinary phone handmade and individually signed by a single craftsman in Church Crookham, England. Discover more at vertu.com

VERTU

HANDMADE IN ENGLAND

M24 RADIO CONTENTS

Fresh conversation, culture, business, design and great music at monocle.com/radio

WEEKDAYS 06.00 UK TIME

NEWS AND COMMENT FROM EUROPE, THE MIDDLE EAST AND BEYOND

The Globalist DAILY: MONOCLE's take on the world with our editors, correspondents and guests. Plus, The Globalist Asia, weekdays 20.00 BST, focusing on Asia and Oceania.

WEEKDAYS 08.00 UK TIME

THE AGENDA FROM MONOCLE'S EDITORS AND CORRESPONDENTS

Midori House DAILY: We reflect on the day's news and look ahead at the stories about to break, with live guests and cultural chat from the heart of MONOCLE HQ.

WEEKDAYS 12.00 UK TIME

NEWS FROM AROUND THE WORLD, ANALYSIS AND DEBATE

The Briefing DAILY: A mix of news and comment. The Briefing also greets those waking up on the US East Coast and in Latin America.

WEEKDAYS 18.00 UK TIME

DISCUSSION, DEBATE & DISPATCHES

Aperitivo DAILY: A perfect way to digest the day's events with discussion, analysis and interviews. Broadcasts live from Midori House and from the Monocle Café.

WEEKDAYS 22.00 UK TIME

NEWS FROM EUROPE AND THE AMERICAS

The Monocle Daily DAILY: Our evening news show looks at what's setting the agenda for a new day in Asia. Plus, we check in with the US and enjoy live studio discussion.

PREMIERES MONDAYS 19.00 UK TIME

A GLOBAL DIGEST OF MUSIC, ART, FILM AND MEDIA

Culture WEEKLY PREMIERE: MONOCLE culture editor Robert Bound presents the best of music, art, film and media – with live band sessions, new finds and plenty of debate.

PREMIERES TUESDAYS 19.00 UK TIME

A REVIEW OF DESIGN, ARCHITECTURE AND CRAFT

Section D WEEKLY PREMIERE: MONOCLE's weekly show about the design world puts the spotlight on the worlds of fashion, architecture and even font making.

PREMIERES WEDNESDAYS 19.00 UK TIME

INNOVATIVE BUSINESSES AND INSPIRING START-UPS

The Entrepreneurs WEEKLY PREMIERE: Hosted by Sophie Grove, this is the show for anyone who runs their own business – or wants to.

PREMIERES THURSDAYS 19.00 UK TIME

WHAT MAKES CITIES TICK, FROM CITY HALL TO THE SUBURBS

The Urbanist WEEKLY PREMIERE: Each week, Andrew Tuck looks at what makes a great city, from inspiring civic leaders to fresh technology – and even a bit of grit.

PREMIERES FRIDAYS 19.00 UK TIME

MONOCLE'S GUIDE TO FOOD, DRINK AND ENTERTAINING

The Menu WEEKLY PREMIERE: The show bringing the best of food and drink from Japanese baristas to South African caterpillar snacks, hosted ably by Markus Hippi.

PREMIERES SATURDAYS 09.00 UK TIME

THE BEST OF THE WEEK ON MONOCLE 24

The Curator SATURDAY: The highlights of MONOCLE 24 selected from the past seven days of programming. A fast-paced digest of a week in radio at Midori House.

PREMIERES SATURDAYS 10.00 UK TIME

THE PEOPLE AND PLAYERS SHAPING THE FUTURE OF PRINT MEDIA

The Stack SATURDAY: Hosted by our editor-in-chief, Tyler Brûlé, this show looks at the stories behind the world's best newspapers and magazines.

PREMIERES SATURDAYS 12.00 UK TIME

A LOOK AT LITERATURE, THEATRE, GALLERIES AND TELEVISION

The Review SATURDAY: Each week we look at the books, music and films you need to have on your agenda with regular hosts Gillian Dobias and Emma Nelson.

PREMIERES SUNDAYS 12.00 UK TIME

NEWS FROM EUROPE AND THE AMERICAS

The Monocle Weekly SUNDAY: Our original Sunday broadcast includes Tom Edwards' news preview, some great authors and thinkers – and some bad jokes.

Entrepreneurs are very good at spotting ideas. And advisers.

Asset Management
Wealth Management
Asset Services

Geneva Lausanne Zurich Basel Luxembourg London
Amsterdam Brussels Paris Frankfurt Madrid Barcelona
Turin Milan Florence Rome Tel Aviv Dubai Nassau
Montreal Hong Kong Singapore Taipei Osaka Tokyo
www.pictet.com

PICTET
1805

MESURE ET DÉMESURE*

TONDA 1950
Rose gold
Ultra-thin automatic movement
Hermès alligator strap

Made in Switzerland

lwww.parmigiani.ch

PARMIGIANI
FLEURIER

* Exact and Exultant

Monocle's network of bureaux stretches from Toronto to Tokyo, allowing us to deliver daily news and in-depth surveys in print, on radio and online.

+ Istanbul coming soon

PUBLISHING

Publishing Director
Pamela Mullinger
pm@monocle.com

Advertising Director
Anders Braso
ab@monocle.com

Advertising Executive
Rory Gallard
rpg@monocle.com

Advertising Executive
Tommy Seres
tse@monocle.com

Promotions Executive
Danielle Hinan
dh@monocle.com

Advertising Sales Coordinator
Nina Akbari
na@monocle.com

Advertising Assistant
Aya Monteverde
aim@monocle.com

Publishing Coordinator
Jessica Harris
jh@monocle.com

ADVERTISING OFFICES

Milan (ITALY)
Carina Negrone
carina@negrone.it

Zürich (SWITZERLAND/AUSTRIA)
Hans Otto
otto.hans@guj.de

Bangkok (THAILAND)
Nartnittha Jirarayapong
noo@njintermedia.com

Taipei (TAIWAN)
Keith Lee
leekh@ms4.hinet.net

PUBLIC RELATIONS

PR & Events Manager
Emily Smith
es@monocle.com

DISTRIBUTION & RETAIL

Retail & Distribution Director
Helen Leech
hl@monocle.com

Retail Operations Manager
Ian Hammond
ih@monocle.com

Subscriptions & E-commerce Coordinator
Ethan Hawkes-Pippen
ehp@monocle.com

Merchandise Coordinator
Edwin Lee
el@monocle.com

Customer Service Assistants
Javier Benito
jmb@monocle.com

Abigail Carlin
aca@monocle.com

Intern
Cenlang Wu

FINANCE

Chief Operating Officer
Sabine Vandenbroucke
sv@monocle.com

Financial Controller
Pauline Ho
pho@monocle.com

Accountant
Peter Pisani
pp@monocle.com

Accounts Assistant
Kyle Shin
ks@monocle.com

Intern
Joe Woodward

THE BOARD

Directors
Richard Atkinson
Tyler Brûlé
José Caireta
Sabine Vandenbroucke

Chairman
Tyler Brûlé

HEAD OFFICE

Monocle
Midori House
1 Dorset Street
London W1U 4EG
TEL: +44 (0) 20 7725 4388
FAX: +44 (0) 20 7725 5711
info@monocle.com
customerservice@monocle.com

Front of House
Edward Lucas
etl@monocle.com

Marie-Sophie Schwarzer
mss@monocle.com

BUREAUX

New York
611 Broadway - Suite 632
New York, NY 10012
TEL: +1 212 673 7374

Toronto
776 College Street
Toronto, ON M6G 1C6
TEL: +1 647 694 2619

Tokyo
Omotesando Hills
Zelkova Terrace W305
4-12-20 Jingumae
Shibuya-ku, Tokyo 150-0001
TEL: +81 3 5771 6065

Hong Kong
Shop 1, Bo Fung Mansion
1–4 St Francis Yard
Wanchai, Hong Kong
TEL: +852 280 42626

Zürich
Nordstrasse 18
CH-8006, Zürich
TEL: +41 44 368 7000

SHOPS

London
2A George Street
Marylebone
London W1U 3QS
TEL: +44 20 7486 8770
londonshop@monocle.com

Hyatt Regency London –
The Churchill
30 Portman Square
London W1H 7BH
TEL: +44 (0) 207 299 2370
hyattshop@monocle.com

Hong Kong
Shop 1, Bo Fung Mansion
1– 4 St Francis Yard
Wanchai, Hong Kong
TEL: +852 280 42626
hkshop@monocle.com

New York
535 Hudson Street
(at Charles Street)
New York City, NY 10014
TEL: +1 212 229 1120
nyshop@monocle.com

Toronto
776 College Street
Toronto, ON M6G 1C6
Tel: +1 647 694 2626
torontoshop@monocle.com

MONOCLE CAFÉS

London
18 Chiltern Street
London W1U 7QA
Tel: +44 20 7135 2040

Tokyo
B1F Hankyu Men's Tokyo
2-5-1 Yurakucho
Chiyoda-ku
Tel: +81 (0)3 6252 5285

Monocle (ISSN 1753-2434) is published 10 times a year by Winkontent Limited, Midori House, 1 Dorset Street, London, W1U 4EG. Registered no. 05265119 England. Printed by Southernprint Ltd, 17-21 Factory Rd, Upton Industrial Estate, Poole, Dorset BH16 5SN. Colour reproduction by Tag Response, 3-4 Bakers Yard, Bakers Row EC1R 3DD. All rights reserved. Reproduction in whole or part without written permission is strictly prohibited. All prices correct at the time of going to press, but subject to change. Monocle subscriptions: monocle.com email: subscriptions@monocle. com. Distributed by Seymour, 2 East Poultry Avenue, London EC1A 9PT, +44 (0) 20 7429 4000. All paper used in the production of this magazine comes from well managed sources. Subscription price £80/$128 based on current exchange rate. Periodicals postage paid at Dover, NJ 07801. Postmaster please send address changes to Airport World, 19 Route 10 East Bldg 2 Unit 24, Succasunna, NJ 07876.

VINTAGE ONLY

Dom Pérignon

ROSÉ VINTAGE 2003
A LIMITED EDITION BY JEFF KOONS

MONOCLE
—*Contributors*

In this edition of Monocle we look north to the Arctic Circle. So we asked our writers, photographers and illustrators how they cope in the cold.

Andrew Mueller
WRITER

London-based Mueller's latest book, *It's Too Late To Die Young Now*, is out now in his native Australia. For MONOCLE, he returns to Albania – a nation he first visited 10 years ago – to find many of those he met before are now running the country.
— AFFAIRS *p89*
If it's cold out?
"I stay in and set fire to things. Which is easier since I moved to a house with a fireplace."

Elna Nykänen Andersson
WRITER

Andersson is MONOCLE's Stockholm correspondent and a news presenter for Sweden's national broadcaster SVT. For us, she visits Greenland to investigate its quest for independence.
— AFFAIRS *p39*
If it's cold out?
"There's nothing better than a crisp, cold, sunny morning. It's the darkness that gets me."

Sam Island
ILLUSTRATOR

Island is an award-winning freelance illustrator based in Toronto where he shares a studio with his wife and dog. For this edition of MONOCLE, he depicts urban renewal in Australia on the Oceania briefing page.
— AFFAIRS *p72*
If it's cold out?
"Be prepared. I start growing my beard in mid-September for extra insulation."

Clare Dowdy
WRITER

Dowdy has been covering design and architecture from London for the past two decades and writes a fortnightly column in *The Financial Times*. For MONOCLE, she reports on the revival of London tray and trolley specialists Kaymet.
— DESIGN DIRECTORY *p202*
If it's cold out?
"I use a hot-water bottle – for eight months of the year."

Simon Bajada
PHOTOGRAPHER

Originally from Melbourne and now residing in Stockholm, Bajada photographs food and travel stories for editorial and commercial projects. For this edition of MONOCLE, he visits his current home city's thriving markets and restaurants.
— EDITS *p266*
If it's cold out?
"Dry cold and snow – yes. Wet cold and puddles – no."

Debbie Pappyn
WRITER

When not in Antwerp, travel writer Pappyn lives out of her Rimowa suitcase 80 per cent of the year writing for international publications and updating her own site, *classetouriste.com*. Among stories for MONOCLE this month, she camps on frozen sea ice near Baffin Island.
— EDITS *p256*
If it's cold out?
"Dress like the locals."

Sarah Vanbelle
ILLUSTRATOR

Vanbelle is an Antwerp-based illustrator and graphic designer who, after stints in Poland and the Netherlands, now works across exhibitions, print titles, concerts and non-profits. Her work flavours a story about cookies in this month's business briefing.
— BUSINESS *p118*
If it's cold out?
"If I can ride a sleigh from time to time, I'm happy."

Kristian Helgesen
PHOTOGRAPHER

Helgesen grew up in Stjørdal, Norway. After gaining a degree in documentary photography in the UK, he now lives in Oslo working for newspapers and magazines. For MONOCLE, he photographs properties in Bergen on Norway's west coast.
— DESIGN *p260*
If it's cold out?
"Here in Norway you don't really have a choice."

Lee Suckling
WRITER

Cutting his journalism teeth in Sydney and London, New Zealand writer Suckling now brings Kiwi stories to the wider world and also works for an animal health non-profit. For MONOCLE, he explains how to bring a NZ brand to the Chinese market.
— BUSINESS *p118*
If it's cold out?
"Think like Kevin Spacey and binge on Netflix."

Bragi Thor Jósefsson
PHOTOGRAPHER

Jósefsson has shot editorial, commercial, architectural and interior photography for over 25 years in his native Iceland. This month for MONOCLE, he visits the picturesque Sundlaugin recording studio in Reykjavík.
— CULTURE *p133*
If it's cold out?
"I put on my long johns."

Key to writers:

(TAB) Timothy Anscombe-Bell
(JB) Justin Bergman
(SB) Steve Bloomfield
(SEB) Steven Bodzin
(MB) Michael Booth
(RB) Robert Bound
(IC) Ivan Carvalho
(EC) Emma Chiu
(CC) Carole Corm
(AC) Adrian Craddock
(ADC) Alexandra De Cramer
(DD) Daphnée Denis
(PAE) Pauline Eiferman
(SFG) Simon Farrell-Green
(JAF) Josh Fehnert
(AVF) Alexa Firmenich
(NG) Nelly Gocheva
(SG) Sophie Grove
(TH) Tom Hall
(SK) Sahar Khan
(MDL) Michael Di Leo
(JZL) Jason Li
(VL) Vivien Lu
(ETL) Edward Lucas
(GSL) Gaia Lutz
(TMA) Tristan McAllister
(TMC) Tristan McConnell
(DM) David Michon
(ANM) Anastasia Moloney
(TM) Tom Morris
(AM) Andrew Mueller
(ENA) Elna Nykänen Andersson
(DEP) Debbie Pappyn
(PTP) Patrick Pittman
(GR) Gwen Robinson
(AES) Aisha Speirs
(LS) Lee Suckling
(SRT) Santiago Rodríguez Tarditi
(JT) Junichi Toyofuku
(BW) Ben Williams
(FW) Fiona Wilson

She's a fan.

MANDARIN ORIENTAL
THE HOTEL GROUP

50
YEARS OF PASSION
AND INNOVATION
DASSAULT FALCON

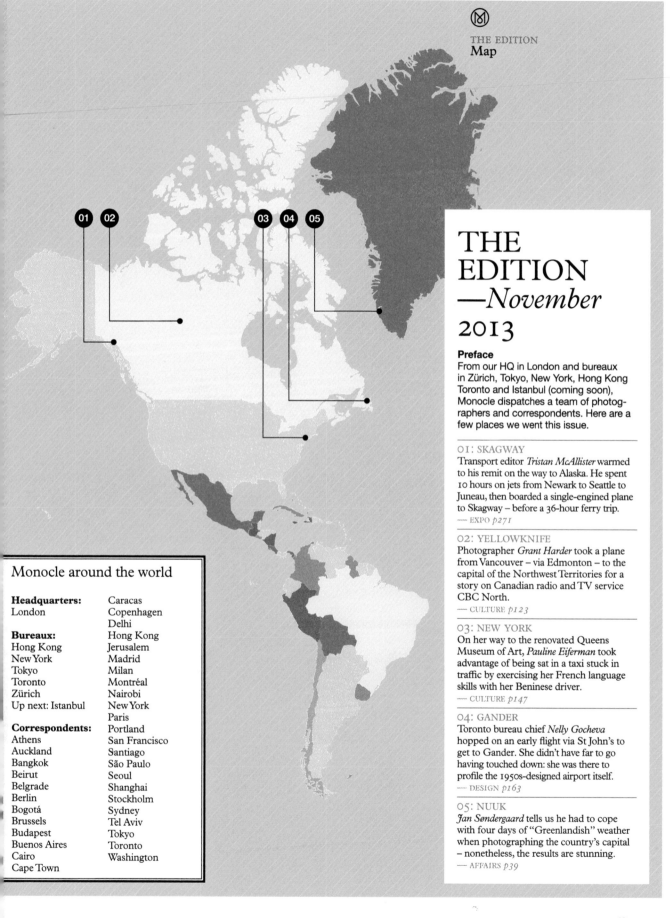

THE EDITION
—*November* 2013

Preface
From our HQ in London and bureaux in Zürich, Tokyo, New York, Hong Kong Toronto and Istanbul (coming soon), Monocle dispatches a team of photographers and correspondents. Here are a few places we went this issue.

01: SKAGWAY
Transport editor *Tristan McAllister* warmed to his remit on the way to Alaska. He spent 10 hours on jets from Newark to Seattle to Juneau, then boarded a single-engined plane to Skagway – before a 36-hour ferry trip.
— EXPO *p271*

02: YELLOWKNIFE
Photographer *Grant Harder* took a plane from Vancouver – via Edmonton – to the capital of the Northwest Territories for a story on Canadian radio and TV service CBC North.
— CULTURE *p123*

03: NEW YORK
On her way to the renovated Queens Museum of Art, *Pauline Eiferman* took advantage of being sat in a taxi stuck in traffic by exercising her French language skills with her Beninese driver.
— CULTURE *p147*

04: GANDER
Toronto bureau chief *Nelly Gocheva* hopped on an early flight via St John's to get to Gander. She didn't have far to go having touched down: she was there to profile the 1950s-designed airport itself.
— DESIGN *p163*

05: NUUK
Jan Søndergaard tells us he had to cope with four days of "Greenlandish" weather when photographing the country's capital – nonetheless, the results are stunning.
— AFFAIRS *p39*

Monocle around the world

Headquarters:
London

Bureaux:
Hong Kong
New York
Tokyo
Toronto
Zürich
Up next: Istanbul

Correspondents:
Athens
Auckland
Bangkok
Beirut
Belgrade
Berlin
Bogotá
Brussels
Budapest
Buenos Aires
Cairo
Cape Town

Caracas
Copenhagen
Delhi
Hong Kong
Jerusalem
Madrid
Milan
Montréal
Nairobi
New York
Paris
Portland
San Francisco
Santiago
São Paulo
Seoul
Shanghai
Stockholm
Sydney
Tel Aviv
Tokyo
Toronto
Washington

What does a car mean to you?

live brilliant

NEW THINKING.
NEW POSSIBILITIES.

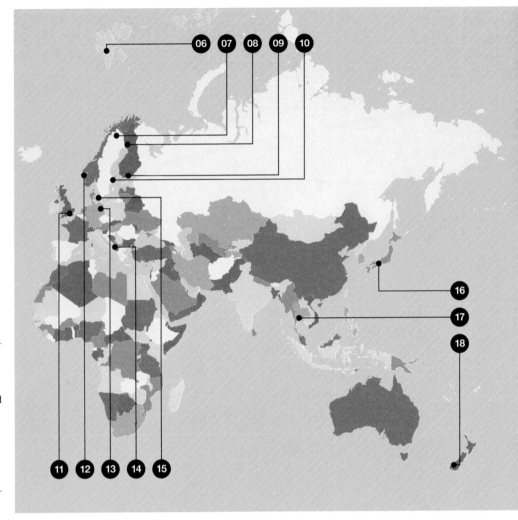

06: LONGYEARBYEN
Design editor *Tom Morris* made a three-legged journey to Svalbard's administrative centre, starting in London and taking in Oslo and Tromsø. On the shoot, Tom looked out for polar bears while the photographer took pictures. He didn't see any.
— DESIGN *p155*

07: KIRUNA
Following a one-hour flight from Stockholm, photographer *Lina Haskel*'s plane landed in Kiruna through heavy fog. Said fog lasted for the whole assignment, allied to the presence of a never-setting midnight sun. In such conditions, Lina did her best to ignore all thoughts of horror films for the duration of her stay.
— AFFAIRS *p51*

08: ROVANIEMI
"It's been a bit of a weird one to organise – I've been sending emails that begin 'Dear Santa'." Foreign editor *Steve Bloomfield* flew to Rovaniemi (by plane; the sleigh was being repaired) to interview Lapland's most famous resident for this issue's National Icon feature.
— AFFAIRS *p94*

09: HELSINKI
MONOCLE researcher *Josh Fehnert* flew from London to check out Finland's booming prefabricated housing scene. After a rainy morning of house hunting he headed to the leafy suburb of Käpylä to see why the neighbourhood is the perfect place to start a family.
— DESIGN DIRECTORY *p181, p184*

10: STOCKHOLM
Writer *Gabriel Leigh* navigated his way around Stockholm on the Tunnelbana (metro) for a special report on the capital's enticing culinary scene. "The tragic part of it was being surrounded by so much good food and having to leave most of it behind," he told us, not a little wistfully.
— EDITS *p266*

11: LONDON
It's not every day a photographer is required to climb aboard a cherry-picker platform but that's exactly what was asked of *Mark Sanders* for one of this issue's fashion shoots. The glamorous location that required multilevel manoeuvres? Midori House.
— DESIGN *p244*

12: BERGEN
The Kings of Convenience are Bergen's most popular cultural export – or they are if you speak to managing editor *David Michon*, anyway. For this issue's Property Prospectus, David took the opportunity to interview one of the band's duo – who, conveniently, is also an architectural psychologist – about the historic wooden homes of Nordnes. We believe some sneaky record signing may also have taken place.
— EDITS *p260*

13: BERLIN
Berlin correspondent *Kimberly Bradley* lives a mere three-block bike ride away from Monohaus, an all-concrete residential building that she was dispatched to report on. Because said building isn't quite finished, Kimberly was thrilled by the chance to wear a hard hat. Who knew head protection could be so exciting?
— DESIGN DIRECTORY *p194*

14: TIRANA
Photographer *Heiko Prigge* flew to Albania from London on the same plane as writer *Andrew Mueller* (we would like to think they sat next to each other and watched a film together but were unable to verify this before going to press). They were off to meet Edi Rama, the new prime minister of Albania, and find out how he intends to tackle his bulging in-tray.
— AFFAIRS *p87*

15: COPENHAGEN
MONOCLE's man in Denmark *Michael Booth* put his beaten-up Audi through its paces to get to the Royal Copenhagen porcelain factory for our Master & Apprentice feature.
— BUSINESS *p120*

16: OSAKA
Asia bureau chief *Fiona Wilson* enjoyed a beautiful view of Mount Fuji on the Shinkansen from Tokyo Station. She was on her way to Osaka to meet Yosaku Tsutsumi, founder of architecture firm Arbol. "After chatting with Tsutsumi I went to see Food Worker Funaki, a lunch place he's designed nearby," she says. "Great bento lunches and I loved the interior – communal tables and piles of homemade jam."
— DESIGN DIRECTORY *p192*

17: BANGKOK
Bangkok-based photographer *Christopher Wise* took the Skytrain and navigated some traditional Thai backstreets to profile the desirable neighbourhood of Soi Langsuan.
— DESIGN DIRECTORY *p176*

18: QUEENSTOWN
Auckland correspondent *Simon Farrell-Green* interviewed Queenstown residents for our report on perfect neighbourhoods – and now wants to move there.
— DESIGN DIRECTORY *p182*

Life is for

BEING CARED FOR

On board Finnair we take good care of you, so you can take care of your business. We provide personal, multilingual service, and make sure that you'll arrive at your destination refreshed and ready for the day ahead. Find a new way to fly at **finnair.com**

Get the full experience

FINNAIR

SHAPING SPACES

MONTHS OF
INNOVATING

WEEKS OF CRAFTING

Artist Richard Hawkins

COMME des GARÇONS SHIRT

IN FROM
THE COLD
—*Arctic Circle*

Preface
The Arctic Circle is fast
becoming a focal point for
business, global energy
needs and a few ambitious
diplomats too. Monocle
finds out why its people are
feeling on top of the world.

WRITER
Steve Bloomfield

The Earth looks like a very different place
when you are on top of the world. With
the North Pole at its heart, the map un-
furls towards Canada, Russia, the US and
the Nordic nations – a swirl of blues and
whites, with places we know in positions
we do not recognise. The phrase "Here
Be Monsters" may never have actually
been scrawled upon a map but it easily
comes to mind when faced with the vast
cartographic emptiness of the Arctic.

For those of us living far below the
High North, the Arctic Circle retains an
air of mystery and magic but as the ice
caps melt and life at the top of the world
begins to change, so too does our understanding. It is no longer merely the land
of the Northern Lights, Santa Claus and
polar bears, it is also a place of uranium
mining, oil drilling and shipping.

Arctic communities, and the nations
they form part of, are not the only ones
adjusting to the new realities. At the most
recent summit of the Arctic Council, China
was one of four Asian nations successfully bidding to become official observers. It describes itself as a "near-Arctic"

country (which is a little like describing
Belgium as an "almost tropical" nation)
but its desire to take advantage of the
changes in the region cannot be under-
estimated. China has already signed a
bilateral trade agreement with Iceland
and as Stockholm-based Elna Nykänen
Andersson discovers in our lead story (*see
page 39*), Greenlanders believe it is only a
matter of time before Chinese miners are
trudging through the snow in Nuuk.

Arctic politicians, in public at least,
welcome China's interest but then Arctic
diplomacy has always been warmer than
the name suggests. In a joint interview
with the Swedish foreign minister and
his outgoing Norwegian counterpart, we
hear how the Arctic Council can show the
rest of the world that delicate diplomacy
still works (*see page 51*).

The most dramatic example of
change in the Arctic is the opening up
of the Northern Sea Route, a feared and
once impassable channel that arcs over
the top of Russia and the Nordic nations.
The number of ships passing through
each year has risen from dozens to

hundreds since 2010, increasing the need for a new generation of icebreakers, such as those engineered by Finnish firm Aker in Helsinki (*see page 97*).

There are other consequences too. Once sleepy, snow-confined towns will have the chance to develop into truly global cities. MONOCLE's design editor Tom Morris heads to one such place, Svalbard, to meet the builders working out how to construct homes in the cold. A new port in the Norwegian archipelago could make it the Arctic's most important hub.

While you may never visit the Arctic, the Arctic is coming to you. Its changing climate will have a profound effect on all of us, the new energy possibilities raise questions for all of us, the new technologies created there will lead to changes for all of us. None of this is news to one particular Arctic figure who has been coming down south for rather a long time though. This wouldn't be a truly Arctic issue unless we met the region's one and only icon: a certain gentleman dressed in red who is gearing up for his busiest time of year (*page 94*). — (M)

Why the Arctic matters

01 The potential importance of the Northern Sea Route cannot be overestimated. While the number of ships currently using the route is still minute compared to the Suez Canal, it is rising fast. It's a more dangerous trip but that journey from Yokohama to Rotterdam just got a lot quicker.

02 There is a reason China is so interested in the Arctic and it's not just because of the new shipping route. Minerals and oil, once far beyond the reach of drillers and diggers, suddenly appear to be available as the ice caps melt.

03 Drilling and excavating brings its own set of problems, particularly in an area already damaged by climate change. The threat of oil tankers colliding with icebergs cannot be ignored; nor can the environmental harm caused by quarries and mines tearing through the sides of mountains.

04 The Arctic is one of the few remaining places on Earth where indigenous communities are able to maintain their way of life. There are threats but the political consensus – at least in everywhere except Russia – is far more progressive than elsewhere.

The best of
2 worlds perfectly aligned.

Introducing a whole new world of interactive comfort
and convenience with the all-new Royal Silk Class
from THAI. With an upgraded entertainment system
and device-charging working station that lets you ease
between work and play seamlessly, you'll make
more use of in-flight time. Or you can opt for rest
with our 180-degree full-flat seats, increased pitch,
and extra-private staggered seat layout.*
However you make time, we'll make it easy on THAI.

THAI
Smooth as silk

When combining leading-edge technology
with legendary service from THAI,
your journey is simply smooth as silk.

thaiairways.com

*Staggered seating on selected flights only.

THE ORIGINAL - THE LUGGAGE WITH THE GROOVES

In 1950, RIMOWA issued the first suitcase with the unmistakable grooves. Since then, it has evolved into a cult object in its own right. To this day, the original RIMOWA luggage has lost none of its fascination. It remains the luggage of choice for all those who seek the extraordinary – including models Alessandra Ambrosio and Johannes Huebl.

www.rimowa.com

Germany since 1898

The Slowear family of brands offers you the best
in terms of fitting, fabrics and finishings.
Slowear clothes are designed to live longer.

Enjoy Slowear.

The Slowear brands

SHOCK AND ORE
—*Nuuk*

ARCTIC SPECIAL
Greenland

Preface
What lies beneath the surface of Greenland could bring enormous wealth to the island. But it threatens both the traditional way of life and the centuries-old link to Denmark.

WRITER
Elna Nykänen Andersson

PHOTOGRAPHER
Jan Søndergaard

01 Telecommunications
   mast at Tele Greenland
02 Aleqa Hammond at her
   home in Nuuk
03 An exhibition stand at
   the Greenland Institute
   of Natural Resources
   in Nuuk
04 A wedding party in
   traditional Greenlandic
   costumes
05 Polaroil is a major
   oil-supply company
   in Greenland

From the windows of the prime minister's residence, an imposing wooden house in the picturesque colonial harbour of Nuuk, two possible futures for Greenland can be seen. The view from the living room shows large chunks of turquoise ice floating down Nuup Kangerlua, the Nuuk fjord. Boats return home carrying seals, redfish and whale. At Kalaalimineerniarfik – the cutting house – a few blocks away, workers wait for the fishermen and listen to the Sunday church service on the radio. This is traditional Greenland, an economy reliant on fishing and bolstered by Danish aid.

From the back of the house, the new Nuuk skyline, made up of grey and white high-rises dotted seemingly at random along the coast, stands against a majestic backdrop of snowcapped mountains. Beneath those mountains and beyond lie mineral riches and the possibility of a new Greenland.

This vast island of just 57,000 people is at a crossroads. With the ice caps melting, Greenland's once inaccessible natural resources are suddenly attracting investors. Mining and oil could bring great wealth to the island but they could also put the age-old Inuit lifestyle at risk and break the formal link with Denmark.

Aleqa Hammond, Greenland's new prime minister, knows exactly which direction she wants to take the island. Greenland needs independence – and mining. "If we want economic independence from Denmark, our economy can't be based on fisheries alone," she says.

The election in March came down to two interlinked questions: should Greenland allow foreign mining companies to start digging in its ground, and should the companies be forced to pay higher royalties to the local community if they find riches under the ice? Hammond says yes to both – and her country backs her.

In recent years, every Greenlander has come to know that the island, roughly 80 per cent of which is still covered with ice, holds some of the most coveted natural resources in the world. Scientists have identified several major sites that contain valuable rare earth metals, used in computers, flat-screen televisions and smartphones. At least one site contains large

01

02   03

04

05

01

quantities of iron ore and off the coast companies are drilling to find oil and gas. While all of these opportunities are currently only just that – opportunities – they are the best chance Greenland has ever had of becoming economically and politically independent from Denmark.

The promise of money is an attractive one in a country that doesn't produce enough of anything to support its population. Greenland, an autonomous country within the kingdom of Denmark, receives an annual subsidy of nearly DKK3.4bn (€456m) from Copenhagen that makes up about half of the government's overall budget.

But while many Greenlanders dream of a wealthy future, a host of problems still remain. With no roads connecting the towns and only small harbours, Greenland is a logistical nightmare – and with a tiny, poorly educated population, it hasn't got the workforce to operate state-of-the-art mines and oil rigs. Workers would have to be brought in from abroad and that would change the nature of this sparsely populated Inuit community.

Hammond has been living in the official residence since March, when she was elected prime minister. Originally from a small fishing village but educated as a teacher in Canada, she considers herself to represent "the new generation of Greenlanders". Her politics is certainly new. She is the first prime minister in the country to have introduced the idea of lifting Greenland's zero-tolerance policy on uranium – a question of crucial importance to Greenland's mining hopes. At one of the major rare earth sites, the metals are mixed with uranium, and unless the ban is lifted, mining companies can't start digging.

MONOCLE meets the prime minister on a Sunday, when she's just back from a brunch with the family at Nipisa, a restaurant that uses only Greenlandic ingredients in its cooking. It's her last free weekend with her three children before the autumn session kicks off at the Inatsisartut, Greenland's parliament; but her mind is already on her opening speech. "Usually, the prime ministers

The view from Copenhagen

There is weekly hand wringing in the Danish media and in parliament about the exploitation of Greenland's minerals. It is understandably galling for the Danes to watch as a former colony – one which consumes billions of kroner of their public money, as it has done for many decades – discovers the riches of Croesus beneath its soil and it's unlikely the Danes will share in the bonanza.

However, the Danes are wracked with post-colonial guilt and reluctant to interfere in internal matters, despite the fact Denmark still controls Greenland's international relations and defence. There are also the environmental issues awakened by the Greenlandic mineral rush: the Danes are vigorous finger-waggers about such matters. Also perhaps, they can't bear to see all that wealth slipping through those same fingers. "China doesn't love you for who you are," the spurned lovers in Denmark warn Greenland. "They just want to use you up and run off with your savings."

Uranium is the latest talking point, a potential by-product of the Kvanefjeld open mine in the south. It is illegal to mine uranium in Greenland but the deposits are of such a scale that they could single-handedly rescue Greenland's economy.

In the wake of Fukushima the price of uranium has plummeted. Greenland, and Denmark, are looking closely to see how Japan deals with its nuclear dilemma. — MB

02

Greenland: the facts

Greenland was discovered by Inuits more than 4,500 years ago. It was colonised by the Danes in 1721 and granted home rule in 1979, later replaced by the Self Rule Act in 2009.

Greenland is the world's largest island but despite the way it looks on the map it is 14 times smaller than Africa. Blame Mercator for that one.

Greenland has its own flag and issues its own stamps, featuring – and this won't surprise you – pictures of icebergs and scenes from the country's mining history.

Average life expectancy in Greenland has risen from 50 in the 1950s to 67 today but it's still far below Denmark's 78.

The ice cap covers around 80 per cent of Greenland and is up to 3km thick.

Greenlanders make their own ice cream and sorbet, using the inland ice.

Greenland boasts 14 airports, 37 heliports and seven ports. Not many roads though.

01 Nuuk is surrounded by spectacular natural scenery – Sermitsiaq mountain is in the background
02 Nuuk airport

have addressed the members of the parliament but I'm going to do it differently. I want to address the people. I want to talk about nation building," she says.

Hammond's bullish stance on mining, while popular, has prompted debate throughout the island. Some think lifting the uranium ban is going too far and putting Greenland's unique nature, along with its people, at risk. Others worry that the demand for higher royalties might scare off international mining companies such as London Mining, a UK-based company that has long had plans to open a large iron-ore mine in Isua right at the edge of the ice cap, just 150km northeast of Nuuk.

Hammond disagrees. "Royalties are the natural way to go. Some people say we shouldn't demand so much of the companies if we want their investments. But the owners of these resources are the people of Greenland."

London Mining's financiers have been said to include Chinese investors, which has caused worry among some Greenlanders. Even if the company itself says that it's too early to talk about the nationality of any investors or construction workers, rumours run wild from the southern tip of the island to the iciest north, with locals imagining armies of Chinese workers working in Greenland under Chinese wages and conditions. Hammond believes there is no need for concern.

"We're only 56,000 people. I know half of them by name. If mining companies come here, they will need foreign labour. But whether they're Chinese, Polish or Danish, they need to obey the law. Our labour unions will be included in the wage negotiations," she says.

Hammond herself seems to be more occupied with Denmark's possible involvement in Greenland's new plans. She doesn't want the politicians in Copenhagen standing in the way of lifting the uranium ban. While the autonomous Greenland has the right to decide on almost all its own matters, the Danish government still retains control of foreign affairs, security and the justice system.

"Denmark says that the question of uranium goes under Danish jurisdiction. I say no, it doesn't. All natural resource

01 Ice floating in the Nuuk fjord
02 Aqqaluk Lynge, chairman of the Inuit
    Circumpolar Council
03 A Nuuk fisherman
04 A narwhale hangs from the ceiling of
    the Institute of Natural Resources
05 Greenland Institute of Natural
    Resources in Nuuk

questions belong to Greenland. I want a further discussion about this. When Denmark says it's a question of defence and security, I want a clearer definition of defence and security," Hammond says.

On the other side of town, in an area that's still under construction, rain has made the ground muddy. TV journalist and activist Jørgen Chemnitz sits in his office, smoking mini-cigars while waiting for the rain to stop before he leaves for the day. Chemnitz, who was born here but moved to Denmark at 13, returned to his roots 10 years ago. He seems to have brought a bit of hip Copenhagen along with him to Nuuk: while others here decorate their offices with traditional Inuit tools, statuettes and maps of Greenland, Chemnitz has surrounded himself with kilim rugs, rattan armchairs and tasteful black-and-white photographs. Today, he's planning a demonstration for the parliament's opening day, and shows us images he has made on his laptop. They liken Aleqa Hammond to a Duracell rabbit. "She's charismatic and outspoken, but she just goes on and on, never stops," he says.

According to Chemnitz, Hammond has given Greenlanders false hope – both when it comes to future profits and independence. "The new government

04

American presence

In the far northwest of the island lies Thule, a US airbase kept far away from prying eyes. Around 600 personnel are believed to be based there – a mix of American and Danish. The base hosts the 12th Space Warning Squadron, a team that operates an early warning system designed to track ballistic missiles launched against the US. Until recently, the Americans pretty much had Greenland to themselves. China's growing mining interest has not gone unnoticed, particularly given China's increased diplomatic presence elsewhere in the Arctic (*see page 062*).

created panic among the mining companies. If you're about to invest around $2bn [€1.48bn] in a project, you want political stability. But the new government wanted to raise royalties. So the companies said, let's wait and see," Chemnitz says. But while most Greenlanders welcome at least some mining, some of them would rather see all the multinational companies leave. One of them is Aqqaluk Lynge, chairman of the Inuit Circumpolar Council. Gazing towards the mountains outside his office window on the outskirts of Nuuk, he asks, "Would you want to have a uranium mine where you live?"

As he moves his hand across a map of Greenland, Alaska and Canada, he says that fishing and hunting are the Inuits' way of life – and should continue to be.

"We're fighting the climate fight and the culture fight. The fishing industry is based on our people, on our knowledge. Knowledge that's been passed on from father to son. If the oil companies arrive, we'll soon be finished. We'll be a minority in our own country. People here have a choice and I think the people should say no," he says.

Sara Olsvig, a local politician who is a member of both the Danish and the Greenlandic parliament, is another critical voice: "The planned uranium mine would be in an area where we do our only sheep herding, our only vegetable growing. And they want to dig an open uranium pit in the middle of that?"

However, she welcomes the project developed by Tanbreez on a site that contains no uranium, just rare earths, saying that Greenland has to find some kind of new income. If the country doesn't reform its welfare system and the fishery-based economy, its budget will be shrinking every year.

"I have a seven-year-old daughter. Of course I want a good school for

05

01 The Nuuk shopping
    mall and the locals'
    vehicle of choice,
    the jeep
02 Jørgen Chemnitz,
    activist and journalist
03 Julia Pars, director of
    Nuuk's culture centre,
    Katuaq
04 Nuuk architecture

01

02

her. Of course I want a good healthcare system. The key issue is that we do this in the proper manner. Democratically and responsibly towards the environment."

Anyone arriving in Greenland is struck by its beauty. The white snow, the ice that glistens in hues of blue, white and grey, the peculiar patterns in ice-free areas you see from the aeroplane, indicating that there is permafrost hidden underground. But when you read the local newspapers, it's difficult not to worry for its people. Families with small children are leaving because the school system isn't up to scratch. The amount of sexual assaults is 15 times higher than in Denmark. Average unemployment is 10 per cent. Where will Greenland be in 20 years' time?

Poul Krarup, editor of the local newspaper *Sermitsiaq* (named after Nuuk's highest mountain) is optimistic. "In 20 years, Greenland will be industrialised. I don't think we'll have oil. But I see a prosperous mining country. I hope more people will move in. I hope we'll have a higher level of education and better infrastructure. I hope we'll be more independent, and that we won't need the subsidies from Denmark any more," he says.

Krarup, who's Danish but moved to Greenland 30 years ago, says the country will be changing no matter what. Its people, while living in remote areas, are in many ways like everyone else in the Western world. "We have people living here and these people want to be part of the modern world."

To Aleqa Hammond, that scenario is exactly as it should be. "This will change us. It will change our labour market and it will change us culturally. We'll be negotiating with new countries. We'll have a new view to the outside world and to ourselves. All this will have a strong effect and we need to be prepared," she says. — (M)

Meet the Greenlanders

With a small population of just over 57,000, 16,000 of whom reside in Nuuk, you might be surprised to find Greenland has such a diverse – and potentially conflicting – group of people making a living there.

01 The fisherman

The fellow in yellow hoping his industry is going to survive. Half the economy is based on fishing with cod, halibut and salmon among the biggest earners.

02 The miner

A relatively new arrival on the island; still adjusting to the cold and not looking forward to the dark of winter. Possibly British, maybe Chinese.

03 The Inuit campaigner

Constantly worried about the possible disappearance of the Inuit way of life and environmental issues. Fishes and hunts, but is not so keen on mining.

04 The dogsled patrolman

An invasion of Greenland is unlikely, but someone has to patrol an area of 160,000 sq km. The Sirius Sledge Patrol team is made up of 12 men and many huskies.

05 The independence campaigner

Tends to think the potential influence of foreign mining companies is less paternalistic than the current influence of Denmark.

03

04

Going the distance

SERIES: 03/03

WEBSITE: GE.COM

Individual achievement is something to be celebrated but some of the best victories take teamwork. GE is working with the Sochi Olympic Winter Games to help secure world-class healthcare and facilities for the world's best athletes.

The success of any global event is only as good as the team behind it. From facilitating great sporting achievements to rolling out world-class medical infrastructure, GE Healthcare and the 2014 Sochi Olympic Winter Games are teaming up to make the most of one of the world's greatest showcases.

On the global stage there are few greater honours for a nation than hosting the Olympic Games. Next year, the iconic torch will rest in the Russian resort city of Sochi, on the eastern coast of the Black Sea. With the world watching on, 6,000 athletes from around 85 countries will test their mettle against the best in winter sports. As healthcare innovations help athletes to push the boundaries of performance, competition and recovery, the expertise and global healthcare credentials of partner GE will keep the show on the road. From imaging technology to monitoring equipment in the Olympic park, GE Healthcare is working hard to keep the Olympics moving.

PHOTOGRAPHER: GEORGE DUBENETSKY

GE imagination at work

A crucial member of the Olympic team

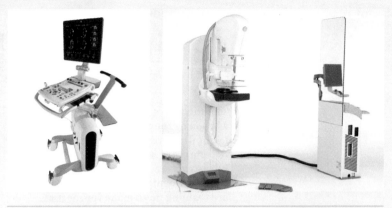

Injuries are a frustrating but inevitable risk when you're representing your country at the highest level. When the competitive margins are so fine, the difference between a day in rehab and one in training can be the difference between a medal around the neck or a head in hands.

In keeping with its global mission to improve the quality and access of healthcare, GE's suite of expert technologies will be supporting the world's most successful athletes at next February's Winter Olympics in Sochi. At the Olympic village polyclinic facility, GE's world-class range of digital-imaging equipment – including X-rays, CT scanners and ultrasound machines – will be on hand to diagnose injury and keep coaches in the know. High-speed snow sports are risky but GE's global experience means it can handle an emergency as well as knowing exactly what equipment to trust. With cardiovascular scanners and portable defibrillators on hand, athletes and onlookers can rest assured that GE's experience during previous Olympic campaigns has raised the standard of emergency healthcare.

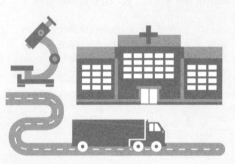

GE Healthcare has supplied advanced medical equipment to 750 hospitals in Russia

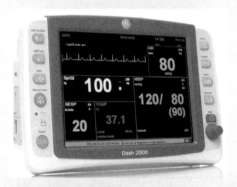

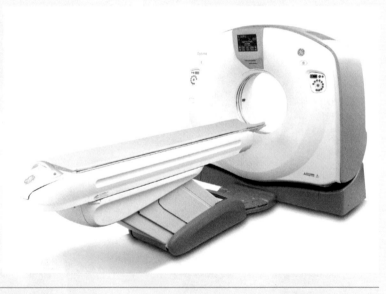

Q&A
Olivier Bosc
President & CEO,
GE Healthcare Russia

Monocle: *What is most exciting you about the collaboration?*
Olivier Bosc: The Games provide a great platform for the country to put its best foot forward and construct world-class facilities. For GE, an event of this scale provides an opportunity to showcase our capabilities and expertise.

M: *What are the benefits of improved healthcare facilities?*
OB: For athletes pushed to their limit during the Games, providing a high level of technology-based healthcare infrastructure and services means that clinicians can intervene earlier to ensure a quick return to competition.

M: *Who are your local partners?*
OB: In Russia, GE partners with the Russian national snowboard team, as well as being the official partner of the Alpine Skiing and Snowboard Federation. GE provides support and expertise for the athletes as they prepare and compete at the highest levels.

Sochi in numbers

100%
The increase in investment for large and medium-sized businesses since 2010

38%
The increase in Sochi's birth rate since 2005

0.17%
Sochi's unemployment rate, the lowest in Russia

39,000
The number of tourists that visited Sochi between 2011 and 2012, more than double compared to the previous year

1
Sochi's quality-of-life ranking among Russian cities according to Urbanika, the institute of territorial planning

€4.8bn
The investment in Sochi's economy in 2012. This accounts for almost half of investments in the entire Krasnodar region

€276m
The value of the spa and resort service in Sochi, representing a 106 per cent growth since 2011

458
The number of sport venues in the city in 2013

Universal appeal

GE's commitment to providing world-class healthcare and support for the athletes competing at next year's Winter Games is just one facet of its investment.

With buildings including permanent bases for each of its 14 sporting disciplines and 22 additional facilities aimed at keeping the Games running, next year's Winter Olympics will create a legacy felt long after the torch has changed hands. GE's services are also fuelling the local economy. The city's population has boomed by 30 per cent in the last six years and the Games have already created and supported over half a million jobs in the region – a contribution set to continue beyond 2014.

GE healthcare has been in Russia for over 20 years

GE в России

PHOTOGRAPHER: GEORGE DUBENETSKY

A winning partnership

Having collaborated with Olympic organisers since 2005 and worked in Russia for over 20 years, GE Healthcare will be a familiar face at the 2014 Sochi Olympic Winter Games next February.

Beyond the beautiful choreography of an Olympic opening ceremony and the ambitions of its medal-hungry competitors, helping to safeguard the health and welfare of athletes is the true test of organising this revered event. From Sochi 2014 to the bright lights of Tokyo in 2020, GE is helping to provide healthcare on the global stage. On top of its ambitious mission to improve medical treatment, access and availability from Australia to India and the US to Qatar, it is GE's expertise that makes it a reliable partner the world over. Being able to provide healthcare solutions on the grandest of stages is what makes GE such a valued member of the Olympic family.

GE's Healthymagination campaign will invest €4.5bn in improving access to healthcare around the world

GE has around 3,000 employees in Russia employed across a wealth of industries

HIGH SUMMIT
—*Kiruna*

Preface

The Arctic Council has a somewhat informal approach to politics, but the challenges it faces are very real. Monocle joins a meeting and asks two foreign ministers how they balance economic and environmental interests.

WRITER
Steve Bloomfield

PHOTOGRAPHER
Lina Haskel

01 Arctic Athabaskan Council members interviewed outside Kiruna town hall
02 Swedish ministers Carl Bildt (left) and Lena Ek
03 Sami delegation members greet a participant

The Statler and Waldorf of Arctic politics are trying to find a diplomatic way of describing the events of the night before. Swedish foreign minister, Carl Bildt, and his Norwegian counterpart, Espen Barth Eide, had a private dinner with their fellow Arctic ministers but the morning after there are rumours of raised voices and rather a lot of swearing. Over Swedish coffee the next morning the pair give MONOCLE a flavour of the discussion.

BILDT: *I mean, back and forth, can be said; isn't that the way of phrasing it diplomatically? Back and forth.*
EIDE: *I think frank and open…*
BILDT: *Frank and open, back and forth, lively, intense…yeah.*
EIDE: *Creative.*
BILDT: *Yeah, creative.*
EIDE: *Well, bordering on a bit destructive…*
BILDT: *But after midnight…*
EIDE: *From midnight it was creative.*

The drink-fuelled dinner and the relaxed refusal to hide the evidence of an argument says a lot about the way the Arctic Council works. The issues may be serious but the atmosphere is relaxed, typified by the knitwear Bildt and Eide have chosen to wear. The dress code for the ministerial meeting in Kiruna, the northernmost town in Sweden, is "Arctic Casual" – a

01

02

phrase that perfectly sums up the way the summit operates. Decisions are made by consensus, hence the late-night, four-letter-infused debate.

For a meeting of seven foreign ministers, including the US secretary of state John Kerry, there is a refreshingly calm approach to personal security. Hours before the summit begins, anyone can come and go from the unpretentious four-storey town hall. Cars park right outside; officials wander in and out. If there is a police presence it is well hidden.

At times, Kiruna can feel like the set of a particularly disturbing Swedish horror film. The quiet side roads, next to thick woodland, are covered in a thick layer of snow. The fog falls suddenly. The hills and the mine, visible on the other side of the road moments ago, disappear. Weak yellow lights appear in the middle distance, a car slowly navigating its way through the haze. A middle-aged woman, blonde and wrapped in Gore-Tex, emerges five feet away with a husky. This is not the sort of place one would expect to host a major political summit.

The politics may be informal but the challenges are very real. The melting of the Arctic ice caps has dramatically changed the High North. Ships can now pass through the Northern Sea Route, travelling from Asia to Europe without going through the Suez Canal. The possibility of drilling for oil and minerals has attracted investors and worried environmentalists. There is, at times, a disconnect between the indigenous groups who live in the Arctic and the politicians around the dinner table deciding

03

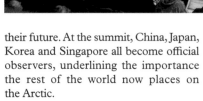

their future. At the summit, China, Japan, Korea and Singapore all become official observers, underlining the importance the rest of the world now places on the Arctic.

As the number of players grows – even if they're sat at the back of the room – the fear is that the voices of those who call the Arctic home will be even harder to hear in future. It is something that Bildt and Eide, in one of his final official visits before losing office in September's election, are determined to ensure does not happen.

Monocle: *One of the big Arctic battles seems to be between the importance of the environment and the importance of the people who live there. Is that fair?*
Carl Bildt: Well I wouldn't say battle but you have to balance these two things. I mean, look here in Kiruna. There were some fairly opposite economic interests up here. There would have been nothing had it not been for the mining. At the same time, there are some environmental considerations, there are the interests of

the reindeer-herding peoples here, and so we see the different interests that need to be balanced.

Espen Barth Eide: We have that discussion in Norway as well because the reindeer-herders need vast areas, much more than other people working in livestock because of the particular nature of what they do – and that conflicts with building more mines and things like that.

Then you have on our side questions about where to drill for oil, and typically you will see more people who live in the region that say, "Let's drill more," because it brings service industries there and more work places to the region, and then in the capital far away you'll have more principled environmental concerns.

CB: And then you go to other countries and there are further views.

EBE: Oh, yes, the farther away you get the stronger the views are.

CB: From some quarters there's a tendency to see the Arctic as a sort of museum to be preserved. And the indigenous people react quite strongly against that.

EBE: To put it mildly.

CB: Yes. And we want to contribute to the possibility of them living decent lives up here as well. Not living in a museum.

EBE: One of the many arguments for opening up the new observers is that people are not only observing the Arctic process but the political process in general. And I think it's good for some of the people who are becoming observers to be at a forum where an organisation for Inuits and Samis are actually at the table and are involved in decision making. That should be inspiring.

Monocle: *Are you at all wary of China's interest in the Arctic?*
CB: Not really. What happens in the northern polar areas sweeps down over Siberia, and does affect economic

01

02

03

01   Foreign Ministers Carl
     Bildt (left) and Espen
     Barth Eide
02   Arctic Council flags
03   Klemetti Näkkäläjärvi,
     chairman of the Sami
     parliament of Finland

conditions in China. They're investing quite a lot in research. They have the world's largest commercial icebreaker which was up at the North Pole for the first time last year and they've opened up a research station in Svalbard. Then they have some forecasts for how much shipping they think will be possible up there in the next 20 or 30 years.

Monocle: *How does the fact you operate by consensus affect decision making?*
CB: We know each other fairly well. That has to be said. This is a small gathering of people who have met before and we can be very open. Then personalities come into the picture as well…

EBE: Formally, any contributor can say "No" or "nyet" or "ne", or whatever, and block it and walk away. But you don't do that. You know, you try. And everybody is in this group in order to try and find a solution.

CB: As Espen said, at the end of the day, you find some sort of consensus that everyone, for a start, is prepared to live with, but for the most part everyone is very happy with.

The big elephant in the room is of course Russia. Russia is 40, 45 per cent of the Arctic in every single way – in terms of population, economic impact, property, and in military significance probably even larger. And they also have perhaps a slightly different political mentality than the rest of us sometimes. And an amount of tension is created by that. But all of this being said, it works.

We sit around the table and discuss as equals, whether it's small Iceland or big Russia. And that's rather unique. And that's because we focus on issues on which, at the end of the day, we have a common interest. — (M)

The L.U.C Collection
Each part is a masterpiece

This less than 13 mm winding lever and its invertor are the key to the micro-rotor automatic winding system featured in the **L.U.C XPS**. They take their cue from a three-sided cam to wind the twin barrels any time the wrist deviates at all from the horizontal plane. Like every component in the L.U.C Calibre 96.12-L, each winding lever is hand-decorated and finished by the artisans at Chopard Manufacture. The L.U.C XPS houses a movement that is chronometer-certified by the Swiss Official Chronometer Testing Institute (COSC).

L.U.C XPS

Chopard

Love trains
Czech Republic
Transport officials in Prague are keeping lonely hearts warm as the mercury dips. By the end of the year they plan to introduce train cabins that are designed for singles to meet one another.

STYLE LEADER NO.48
It's a herd life
Stefan Mikaelsson [SWEDEN]

This year the Sami Parliament of Sweden, a representative body of the Northern European indigenous people, celebrates its 20th anniversary. King Carl Gustaf may have attended the ceremonial opening but in the two decades since its inception there has been continuing conflict with the Swedish state over issues such as mining, farming and land ownership. The Sami want visibility and recognition for their community, which has its traditions rooted in reindeer-herding. This struggle to be noticed does not, however, extend to clothing.

The striking garb is not worn by all of Sweden's estimated 20,000 Sami population, nor by all 31 members of the Sami parliament, who are chosen in a general election every four years by Swedish Sami registered to vote. Yet, for Stefan Mikaelsson, who has served as president since 2009, it is so integral to his identity that it would be "impossible to attend a meeting without traditional clothing".

The Sápmi homeland is spread across Finland, Sweden, Norway and Russia's Kola Peninsula, leaving the Sami scattered over four states. Yet they retain a powerful sense of being a single people. As Mikaelsson says: "My passport says I am a Swede but my heart says I am a Sami." — ETL

Sami glam:

01 A kolt collar (*goahkka*) and bib (*gájraksliehppá*) are made from fabric and white leather and are worn on ceremonial occasions. Subtle threads of colour indicate Mikaelsson's gender and differentiate his Lule Sami origin from those of the other two groups of Sami in the Norden region – the South Sami and North Sami. Few elements of Mikaelsson's attire reflect his prominent political status.

02 The kolt (outer garment) that a male Lule Sami wears is called the *gábdde* and is not sold commercially. Instead, it is made from several tailored pieces by a female family member. They use traditional methods learned within the family home but occasionally modern materials -- in this case, brown suede. Mikaelsson's sister fashioned his *gábdde*.

03 Trousers (*sassnegálsoga*), and shoes (*tjátjega*) are made from functional bark-tanned reindeer skin, a natural material that reveals the Sami's close link with reindeer. There is limited differentiation in style on the grounds of prestige, wealth or class; this is an egalitarian society.

Gunnar Bragi Sveinsson
Foreign minister
Reykjavík

Iceland has been drawing itself further away from its earlier ambitions to join the EU. Its new foreign minister explains why.

Why have talks been halted?
It was a mistake to enter negotiations in 2009. There was no consensus in parliament or in the wider nation. Since then, entry has become even less attractive.

Why is Iceland better off outside the EU?
Iceland's recovery has come about because we can control our own resources and currency. Being tied to the euro would have prevented us from undertaking our most effective measures in achieving recovery.

Can Iceland still be in Europe without being a member of the EU?
We share European values but we disagree with the centralising ideology of the European Union, countries' loss of control over their own finances and the lack of democratic participation. — ETL

A few good men
Rome [POLITICS]

Italian politics has always been colourful. Quite aside from the travails of former prime minister Silvio Berlusconi, the country's current electoral law has been dubbed a "pigsty" even by its author. But one of its more undemocratic aspects may do the nation a few favours.

The head of state is allowed to nominate a handful of senators for life to parliament, a throwback to the politics of ancient Rome. On paper, President Giorgio Napolitano's recent picks should improve the quality of debate in the upper house.

Among his choices are an MIT-trained researcher, an orchestra conductor, a Nobel physicist and architect Renzo Piano. — IC

Large oil and natural gas fields found in Arctic Circle

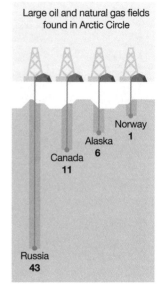

Norway
1

Alaska
6

Canada
11

Russia
43

ILLUSTRATORS: MARTIN MÖRCK, STUDIO TIPI. INFOGRAPHICS: LAMOSCA. INFOGRAPHIC SOURCE: ERNEST AND YOUNG

THE SENSE OF SPACE

AS PART OF OUR INVESTIGATION INTO HYUNDAI'S 'MODERN PREMIUM' CONCEPT, WE DISCUSS HIGH-TECH INTERIOR DESIGN AND RETAIL SPACE WITH WILHELM OEHL, HEAD OF EIGHT INC, ARCHITECT ALEXANDER BAUMGARDT AND HYUNDAI'S CHIEF MARKETING OFFICER, WONHONG CHO, AT A ROUND TABLE AT EIGHT INC'S HQ IN SAN FRANCISCO. WE THEN TAKE A LOOK AT HYUNDAI'S GDSI (GLOBAL DEALERSHIP SPACE IDENTITY) AND THEMED DEALERSHIPS – THE NEW LIFESTYLE HUBS FOR TODAY'S CONSUMERS.

THE PANEL

 WONHONG CHO
CHIEF MARKETING OFFICER, HYUNDAI MOTOR

Cho oversees Hyundai Motor's global marketing, including brand strategy and communication. The Wharton business school alumnus was previously president of the Korean office of the Monitor Group, a global management consultancy.

 WILHELM OEHL
PRINCIPAL, EIGHT INC

Oehl joined Eight Inc, a design and innovation studio spanning three continents, in 1995 and became partner in 1998. He has worked with household brands such as Gap, Apple, Nokia, Nike and JCPenney.

 ALEXANDER BAUMGARDT
ADJUNCT PROFESSOR,
CALIFORNIA COLLEGE OF THE ARTS

San Francisco-based Baumgardt brings valuable real-world experiences to his academic role: he has held leadership positions in renowned design firms including MetaDesign and Method. Outside the classroom, he consults on award-winning projects from automotive to information technology.

HYUNDAI

MONOCLE: How do you define "Modern Premium"?

WONHONG CHO: Modern premium has two aspects in terms of space communications. The first one is affordability. Modern premium is affordable premium. It's the premium value that modern consumers expect at a reasonable price. Another aspect is that modern premium is about the total consumer experience, not just the product itself. That's the big difference between modern premium and typical luxury.

One of Hyundai's dealerships features an art gallery housing a car painted with a famous Van Gogh work.

WILHELM OEHL: It goes beyond the object and space. The environment, communication and behaviour are all important. All these elements need to work in tandem and need to be addressed at the same level. You can't have a superior product and inferior communication. You can't have a fantastic brand strategy when the product is not at the same level. Only if these elements are tightly controlled under the brand umbrella are you going to have a homogenous experience that people can connect to.

M: Do you think today's consumers are able to catch up with all technology advancements and innovation brought up in interior design?

For Baumgardt, Google Glass shows how technology will develop to keep people constantly informed.

ALEXANDER BAUMGARDT: Yes, consumers are very tech savvy and they'll get even more so. But they will totally forget that it's about tech at all because for them it's just the new "normal". For me, technology is just another layer that helps create better and more immersive experiences. It's like being a sorcerer and engineer. Use your creativity with a foundation of science and understanding of what drives humans and then you can create magic experiences.

M: How relative is the tangible when designing space identities – is there a shift towards the intangible?

WC: In the automotive industry, the tangible still matters in terms of space. However, the intangible has a much greater impact on customer experience in the space. According to the modern premium perspective, as I mentioned earlier, modern consumers are expecting premium experience, from reception to farewell across the entire consumer journey within the space. For example, the car-showroom: as you're well aware, this is one of the worst experience places in many countries. The main reason is they're getting poor service at the space itself.

M: Can you give us an example of brands that have successfully combined the two?

AB: For the longest time when the internet and the digital sphere arrived, it was the traditional bricks-and-mortar companies that had to become digital. We now see a strong trend where the big digital companies are becoming basically physical. There's a big one in Europe called Zalando, which sells overstock of clothes, shoes and so on. It now create stores where people can physically come and buy their stuff.

At Citibank, Eight Inc created a streamlined space for customers to quickly see what's on offer.

WO: We worked with Citibank for a duration of three years to create a banking experience to give the customer a choice of how they would like to interact with the bank and also to look at what the offering was. So we streamlined it down. We offer the technology within the physical experience to quickly see what's offered, what the rates are and how to go about the process of opening an account. And then go on to an individual, a human being to help them as needed.

M: If we add art to the equation, do they [art, technology and design] clash or coexist?

WC: We have seen various convergences with art and technologies and I believe this will continue in the future and even more quickly. I believe there are two main drivers to this kind of convergence. One is sophisticated customer needs and the other the development of digital technologies. But given the development of recent digital technologies, we can expand the number of consumers who enjoy the art experience we provide so we are trying lots of convergence technologies, including art and technology in brand communication and space design.

M: What are the benefits of only one specific designer or company creating the entire identity or marketing strategy for a brand?

Keeping a single space designer gives a tremendous benefit when maintaining a consistent brand message across different places over time

WC: Space communication should be aligned with our brand strategy. As chief marketing officer responsible for brand building, I feel it's always difficult to interpret brand as space. So if we have multiple space designers and multiple design firms, it's going to be very difficult to share the same understanding of the brand philosophy. So the key is how we can share the brand philosophy between the client and the space designers. In my view, keeping a single space designer gives a tremendous benefit when maintaining a consistent brand message across different places over time.

M: What's the most inspiring product design that you've come across as consumers and designers?

Both Baumgardt and Oehl credit Apple's iPhone for being revolutionary and modern.

WO: The first is the Leica M series. It's a simple photography company from Germany that is going back to basics, creating a black and white digital camera, nothing superfluous. The second was when Apple launched the iPhone.

Technology is just another layer that helps create better and more immersive experiences

The environment, communication and behaviour are all important. Only if these elements are tightly controlled are you going to have a homogenous experience that people can connect to

A
The Issey Miyake store concept is almost a work of art in itself.

B
Richard Serra's Torque steel sculptures change angles as you walk between them.

At that point, Nokia and other phone companies all had their little segments and models but Apple came up with one single phone with one interface and one operating system combined with the whole eco-structure that was created with iTunes. At that point, it was revolutionary and mind-blowing and it got my heart beating faster.

05 Braun designer Dieter Rams' philosophy of simple, clear design resonates with Baumgardt.

AB: It's tough to answer that without naming Apple, right? But first for me it's Braun products. I'm a German designer at heart and Dieter Rams' design philosophy has always rung true – the products that he designs give me peace of mind. The designs reduce complexity and are very clear. Choices and features are getting more complex for most consumers. Designers need to really simmer it down to make it clear, easy and simple to do what they want to do – that's the key. So for me, when the iPhone came out it was a perfect, modern product that totally fits my little Alexander eco-system.

M: And space-wise, what's the most exciting interior and building you've even been to?

06 Richard Serra's steel sculptures immerse you in a different environment, according to Oehl.

WO: One really good example is the Chichu Art Museum in Japan, designed by Tadao Ando. It is submerged into the mountainside, so the entire experience is subterranean with openings that let natural light in. Inside, there are only three artists. There's James Turrell, Walter de Maria and Monet, and all of the artwork is only illuminated by natural light – no artificial light is illuminating the place. So you see a Monet in a completely different light with no reflections. Absolutely beautiful. And the space itself is phenomenal. If you have a chance to visit you should. Tadao Ando as an architect in general is very inspiring and he did a masterpiece over there. Another is Richard Serra's Torque steel sculptures. When you walk between these massive pieces of steel, which slowly change angles, you have to move your body because otherwise you might hit it with your shoulder. You're completely transcended

into a different environment; you're immersed in something that took two steps to get into.

AB: The spatial experience for me was the Therme Vals spa in Switzerland, which was built by Peter Zumthor. It's just amazing because it's built into the mountain, entirely of slate. There's only a certain number of people allowed to come in, so it's never crowded. It's a magical place. Maybe this is a mutual thing among designers – they like places that transcend the normal space. There's also the Issey Miyake stores, like the one in New York. I love it. It is almost art.

07 This Hyundai showroom has a kids' lounge specially designed for parents accompanying children.

PHOTOGRAPHER: NATASHA PHILLIPS

A NEW WORLD

HYUNDAI'S COMMITMENT TO 'MODERN PREMIUM' EXTENDS TO THE CAR SHOWROOM. SINCE 2011 HYUNDAI'S THEMED DEALERSHIPS HAVE BECOME LIFESTYLE HUBS FOR THE SAVVY MODERN CONSUMER; CLIENTS CAN HAVE A DRINK AT THE CAFÉ, TAKE IN SOME ART OR JUST ENJOY THE GREENERY AS THEY ADMIRE THE CARS ON DISPLAY. MOST RECENTLY, THE COMPANY'S GLOBAL DEALERSHIP SPACE IDENTITY (GDSI) CONCEPT ADDS ANOTHER LAYER TO THE MODERN PREMIUM CONCEPT BY CREATING SPACES THAT EMBRACE BOTH NATURE AND TECHNOLOGY. SO TAKE A LOOK AROUND AND BE CHARMED NOT JUST BY THE CARS BUT ALSO BY THE SPACES THAT HOUSE THEM.

HYUNDAI

GLOBAL DEALERSHIP SPACE IDENTITY

Hyundai's dealerships around the world have adopted the Global Dealership Space Identity (GDSI) concept, a statement that technology and nature are not conflicting forces. The concept of GDSI is defined simply as E Motion Park (Emotional Experience Mobility Park). This means using a mixture of creative design factors motivated by nature and emotional experiences. For example, a special pattern reflecting the sky is applied to signboards on the façade and ceilings, and interiors are nature-friendly with plants and real wood, resulting in a space that feels like a park in harmony with an artificial space.

THEMED DEALERSHIPS

Hyundai's themed dealerships span the gamut from cafés to flower shops to art galleries and even golf clinics. In Yeouido, the showroom takes its cue from European outdoor cafés. It has a lounge where customers can have coffee and snacks among the cars. Seocho's showroom, meanwhile, features a flower shop – an unusual combination of cars and plants that's a big hit with customers.

Joining the club
USA
Hawaii could join the 13 US states that recognise gay marriage. Governor Neil Abercrombie has called for a special legislative session in late October to discuss a bill to legalise same-sex marriage.

ME AND MY MOTORCADE NO.42

You can go your own way
Alaska [LISA MURKOWSKI]

It's hard to find a photo of Alaska's Republican US senator Lisa Murkowski where she isn't on the move. It makes sense, given the state she represents. It can take hours to fly across America's 49th state and the slog to her office on Capitol Hill in Washington DC takes more than seven hours in a jet. But the long-hauls don't keep her from meeting her constituents.

She surely learned a few valuable lessons from her dad – the former US senator and Alaska governor Frank Murkowski was embroiled in the controversial state purchase of a private jet that many said couldn't even land at many of Alaska's rural airports. The junior Murkowski's motorcade is decidedly more modest and on many journeys she's just hitching a ride.

On a recent trip to the remote island of Little Diomede – which literally splits the distance between the US and Russia – Murkowski flew on a US Coast Guard helicopter. She even sported a government-issued orange flight suit for the trip.

Only about 30 per cent of the state's roads are paved, which means any sort of executive car won't get you very far. "In Alaska, where we are twice the size of Texas with fewer miles of road than Rhode Island – it's far more complex. There's no such thing as 'you can't get there from here' but it may require planes, trains, automobiles, boats, ATVs, snowmachines or dogsleds," says Murkowski's communications director, Matthew Felling. Indeed, for the twice-elected senator sometimes it means taking off those patent shoes, slipping into a pair of rain boots and heading upstream in a skiff. — TMA

Alaska Airlines Boeing 737-400 Combi
Built for utility, the modified Alaska Airlines 737 is unique to a few carriers in the world. The jetliner holds cargo in the front and has space for passengers in the back.

Cessna Conquest II
This small, civilian plane is popular with air carriers across Alaska. Because the plane can climb to 35,000 feet, it can easily hop over the Alaska Range (which tops out at just about 20,000 feet).

Sikorsky HH-60 Jayhawk
Long the workhorse of US Coast Guard rescue missions, an Alaska-based fleet of these stands ready to pluck someone out of the Bering Sea's icy waters. And, of course, bring a senator along on a goodwill mission or two.

Xtratuf rain boots
If metal and tyres won't do the trick, many Alaskans simply go by foot. A mainstay in much of the state, the Xtratuf boot has been the shoe of choice for an Alaskan bride or two.

Aircraft
Boeing 737-400 Combi

Cessna Conquest II

Sikorsky HH-60 Jayhawk

Footwear
Xtratuf rain boots

Dominican order
Dominican Rep [WINE]

Visitors to the Dominican Republic are more used to sipping dark rum on the beach than locally produced wine in the mountains. However, that could be about to change.

Billed as the first wine tourism development in the Caribbean, the Dominican Republic plans to develop vineyards in the country's southern Azua region where the cooler mountain climate lends itself to wine producing.

With the help of wine growers trained in Chile, the $167m (€123m) joint US-Dominican venture hopes to lure tourists to wine-tasting tours and brand the Caribbean state as a wine destination in the region. — ANM

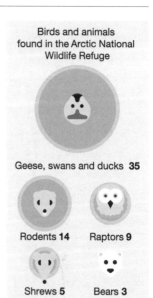

Birds and animals found in the Arctic National Wildlife Refuge

Geese, swans and ducks **35**

Rodents **14**   Raptors **9**

Shrews **5**   Bears **3**

In a bid mood
USA [WINTER OLYMPICS]

The sub-Arctic city of Anchorage is considering a bid for the 2026 Winter Olympics. Mayor Dan Sullivan and his city hall cohorts say Alaska's most populous city is an even stronger contender than it was when it lost bids for the 1992 and 1994 games. "Historically, a bid is not awarded to a city on the first try. It is often three or four attempts before it becomes host city," says a hopeful Lindsey Whitt, communications director for Sullivan.

Anchorage has grown up a bit since it last threw its name into the ring. Ted Stevens Anchorage International Airport is a first-rate gateway that is one of the busiest freight hubs in the world, so a few more ski bags and hockey sticks won't jam up the luggage carousels. And it is equidistant between Tokyo and New York, so it could be an interesting crossroads between East and West.

Other US cities Reno/Lake Tahoe and Salt Lake City are considering bids as well. One thing's for sure: it's hard to beat the view atop Mount Alyeska, home to Anchorage's giant slalom course. — TMA

For the very latest on events around the globe, tune in to Monocle 24. We regularly check in with live interviews from the US and across the Americas all throughout the day. Listen at monocle.com/radio.

A
BRIEFING
Americas

WILLIAM & SON

LONDON

To have and to gold
India
November sees India's wedding season get underway – good news for the global gold industry with prices at a three-decade low. Nuptials account for 50 per cent of India's gold consumption, worth €18bn a year.

On a power trip
Japan [ENERGY]

It may not be attracting the same attention as the country's uncharacteristically adventurous economic policies but Japan's diplomatic strategy is showing similar signs of fresh vigour. Prime Minister Shinzo Abe and his team, apparently eager to avoid the intransigence that marked Abe's first stab at power, are going all out for what is known in Japan as *shigen gaiko* – resource diplomacy.

With its own nuclear power plants all but switched off and thermal power stations now going at full pelt, the Middle East is in sharper focus than ever before. Abe has been to the region twice this year, scrupulously calling on key players in the Gulf Cooperation Council, who supply Japan with nearly three quarters of its petroleum needs and a substantial amount of its gas. This year Abe has been welcomed in Bahrain, Saudi Arabia, United Arab Emirates, Qatar and Kuwait (*pictured*).

Energy is not the only thing up for grabs either. With countries such as Kuwait and Qatar – which will host the 2022 football World Cup – planning vast infrastructure projects, Japan is keen to get its foot in the door.

Abe's excursions have proved fruitful, drumming up energy and business deals including a number of joint development projects ranging from the Doha Metro to desalination and water treatment plants. Middle East expert Professor Satoshi Ikeuchi from Tokyo University sees Abe's "extraordinary willingness" to pay court to the Gulf monarchies as part of a bigger picture.

"I don't think the Gulf is their sole destination in terms of resource diplomacy," Professor Ikeuchi says. "Of course in the short term Qatar's gas is vital and [the] Saudi capacity to stabilise the market is vital. But I think their Gulf policy is part of a comprehensive portfolio of resource and technology diversification." — FW

ELECTION WATCH
Tajikistan

Type: Presidential
Date: 6 November
Candidates: Emomali Rahmon, president since 1994, is seeking a fourth term and an extension of his mandate until 2020. Given his colossal personal wealth, unanimously supportive media and an electoral process of debatable transparency, there is no chance he won't win it but a coalition of opposition parties plans to field civil rights activist Oynihol Bobonazarova as token competition.
Issues: The poorest ex-Soviet state is also corrupt – few were surprised by WikiLeaks revelations about Rahmon's looting of the economy.
Monocle comment: Voter apathy is sad but understandable. — AM

The Mao factor
China [POLITICS]

December is the 120th anniversary of Chairman Mao's birthday. more than ¥15bn (€1.8bn) is being spent on celebratory projects in Mao's hometown. "It's a chance for the leadership to demonstrate power and pay respects to the man who founded the nation," says historian Frank Dikotter. But politically it is tricky. Bo Xilai, the disgraced politician, for instance, embraced Mao to push a more left-wing agenda and some in Beijing took it as a criticism of the recent, more liberal economic direction. — VL

ON AIR
From Tokyo to Seoul, our correspondents bring you the latest news from Asia and around the world at Monocle 24. Tune in for news, views and analysis throughout the day at monocle.com/radio or via the smartphone app.

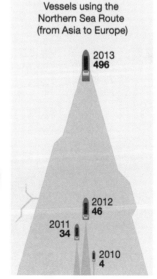

Vessels using the
Northern Sea Route
(from Asia to Europe)

2013
496

2012
46

2011
34

2010
4

Shipping forecast
Singapore [DIPLOMACY]

Singapore may seem the most unlikely of the six new nations to be granted observer status on the Arctic Council but the tropical city-state has been quietly developing an Arctic policy for years.

Singapore knows that a rival Northern Sea Route could someday threaten its pre-eminence as a global shipping hub, so it's mitigating the losses by becoming an Arctic stakeholder.

The country was the first in Asia to develop icebreakers for the Arctic and is also designing jack-up rigs and other ice-class vessels. It also believes its expertise in running major port facilities could prove invaluable should an Arctic country one day decide to build a "Singapore of the North". — JB

IMAGES: GETTY IMAGES, REUTERS, ILLUSTRATORS: TY WILKINS, STUDIO TIPI
INFOGRAPHICS: LAMOSCA, INFOGRAPHIC SOURCE: AUSTRALIAN ANTARCTIC DIVISION

STARTS WITH JAMBOX

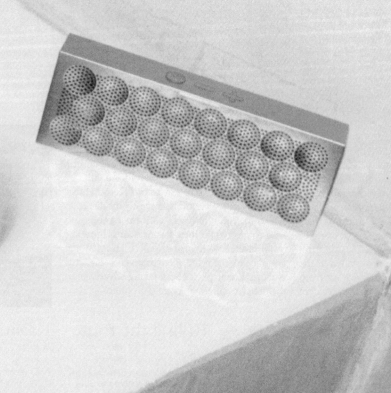

STARTS WITH JAMBOX

Getting hitched
Israel
Religious weddings are a matrimonial-must in Israel, so the non-religious are flocking to Cyprus to tie the knot. Two thirds of Jews would like the law changed but the influential Orthodox community disagrees.

FLIGHT PATH NO.10
Hunting bigger game
Kenya [KENYA AIRWAYS]

Route: Nairobi to Guangzhou
Airline: Kenya Airways
Plane: Boeing 777-300ER
Frequency: Three times a week (Mondays, Wednesdays and Fridays)

The economic ties binding China and Africa will be strengthened this month by a new direct route from Nairobi to Guangzhou, southern China's leading industrial city.

When it comes to doing business in Africa this is China's century. Bilateral trade worth €7.4bn in 2000 grew to €147.9bn by last year. A large chunk of this is accounted for by huge, state-led resources deals – such as a railway line for copper in DR Congo and loans for oil in Angola – but Chinese private businesses are increasingly seeking opportunities in Africa and vice versa.

Kenya is rightly regarded as the gateway to east Africa and has a growing population of consumers with disposable income. Traders come to sell to them and builders to construct their high-rises. Increasingly, Chinese tourists are following the businessmen and flocking to Kenya's national parks and beaches. During this year's famous wildebeest migration in the Maasai Mara there were more visitors from China than any other country. Kenyan president

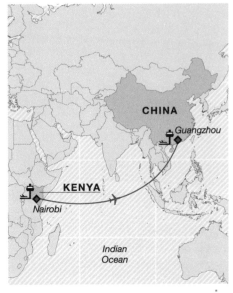

Uhuru Kenyatta hopes to attract more than a million Chinese tourists a year to his country (though after the recent mall attack in Nairobi, Kenya's tourism numbers are set for a fall).

It won't all be one-way traffic. Kenyan businessmen will seize the chance to fly direct to China in search of cheap consumer goods and well-connected business partners amid the communist state's no-holds-barred capitalism. When announcing the route, Kenya Airways CEO Titus Naikuni was explicit about taking advantage of the better business links now on offer. — TMC

ELECTION WATCH
Mauritania

Type: Parliamentary
Date: 23 November
Candidates: President Mohamed Ould Abdel Aziz's party dominates parliament and that will probably continue. The Coordination of Democratic Opposition will attempt to at least keep him honest.
Issues: The election itself has been repeatedly delayed and most recently postponed under threat of a boycott from opposition parties, who wanted it administered by someone other than President Aziz, who came to power in a coup in 2008.
Monocle comment: Mauritania needs a transparent and respected election badly. They really should get on with holding one. — AM

Inviting round the neighbours
Lebanon [TOURISM]

Lebanon's tourism industry ebbs and flows, tugged one way or the other as conflict in the region rises or falls. Just four years ago Beirut was seen as one of the best places in the world to holiday; today hoteliers say the situation is catastrophic. The war in neighbouring Syria has dissuaded westerners, Gulf Arabs and Lebanese expats from visiting. So the Lebanese Hotel Owners Association has called on the Ministry of Tourism to shift its promotional budget away from Europe towards neighbouring Arabs, for whom Lebanon still offers a modicum of peace close to home. — CC

ON AIR
From general elections to innovative business ventures, we bring you the latest news, views and analysis from across the globe at Monocle 24. Tune in for bulletins and regular shows at monocle.com/radio.

Ruling the route
Egypt [SUEZ CANAL]

While the Northern Sea Route is not yet a direct rival to the Suez Canal, Egyptian authorities are watching the route's rise with alarm. Here are three ways the Suez is trying to hold on to its business:

01 Allowing China and others to build factories nearby in the hope it becomes an export hub, not just a gateway.

02 New investment in the port to make it easier for ships to dock there on their way through.

03 Convincing the West that political instability will not affect the canal. Not an easy task. — SJB

Raising the bars
Kenya [TECHNOLOGY]

Kenyan software company Ushahidi is building its first-ever piece of hardware: the "backup generator for the internet" is a sleek black plastic box, the size of three stacked iPhones, called BRCK (pronounced "brick").

It is a globally useful solution to a very African problem: power-cuts. "We wanted to create a way for people to continue being productive and online despite the power going out. It was a response to our reality," says co-founder Juliana Rotich.

The BRCK has an eight-hour battery life, uses ethernet, wi-fi and 3G and 4G, and is rugged, dust-proof and water resistant – "the Land Rover of modems", according to Rotich. — TMC

ILLUSTRATOR: STUDIO TIPI

FOR THE NEW EMPERORS

www.dewitt.ch

DEWITT

REVOLUTIONARY BY TRADITION

POWER AND EFFICIENCY IN PERFECT BALANCE

IS 300h consumption figures: urban 64.2 mpg (4.4L/100km), extra urban 62.8 mpg (4.5L/100km), combined 65.7 mpg (4.3L/100km

An impressive combination of 223hp with just 99g/km CO_2. **lexus.eu**

The new IS

AMAZING IN MOTION

300h CO_2 emissions from 99g/km.

Passport to parenthood
Australia
Commercial surrogacy is illegal in Australia so would-be parents are looking overseas. India is popular: the number of Australian babies born there has increased by 300 per cent in the past five years.

Renovate to accumulate
Australia [URBAN RENEWAL]

An urban renewal company that has helped to transform the central business district of Newcastle, New South Wales is now taking its message to other Australian cities and building interest in the US, Canada and Europe too.

Five years ago, many of the buildings in the heart of the city, two hours' drive north of Sydney, were empty – boarded up and often vandalised. Marcus Westbury, a writer and festival director, believed that if landlords were more flexible and creative, new life could be breathed into rundown districts.

Westbury initially returned home to Newcastle to start a bar but exorbitant rents foiled his plans. "Sidetracked, I decided to find a solution to address the unaffordability of the CBD. Renew Australia is my attempt to share my experience and save others the time, trial and error I went through," he says. Renew Australia is an organisation that works with landlords to find the right tenants willing to take a risk. It provides short-term licences to local projects, at limited costs, with the hope that it will help to rejuvenate forlorn areas.

In Newcastle alone, more than 120 new enterprises have been set up in 55 buildings, including art spaces, furniture makers and even a studio designing handpainted bicycle bells.

Renew has recently spread to Melbourne, where an abandoned Dockland Spaces food

court has been transformed into an arts venue and exhibition space. Another enterprise at Dockland is The Revolution Project, which assists young people who are long-term unemployed. The project includes an online shop, retail outlet and office. — VL

Upcoming Renew Australia initiatives:

01 Newcastle: Reconfiguring the former David Jones building, one of Newcastle's iconic retail locations. Expect a number of boutiques and galleries to pop up in the next few months.

02 Leichhardt, Sydney: A project to turn a 1980s inner-city mock-Italian piazza into a home for artisans.

03 Mildura, Victoria: In a riverside town known mostly for its grape production and wines, Mildura is one of many smaller local communities supported by Renew Australia. The first empty shop became a gallery in September.

Soldiering on
Australia [GOVERNMENT]

An early task awaiting new prime minister Tony Abbott will be to choose Australia's governor-general, the local representative of the British Crown. Favourite to succeed incumbent Quentin Bryce in March is former Australian Defence Force chief General Peter Cosgrove (*pictured*), a popular figure who won the Military Cross in Vietnam. A former soldier would be appropriate: 2015 will mark the centenary of Anzac Day and the Gallipoli campaign, Australia's most cherished foundation myth. — AM

Lame plane
Tonga [TOURISM]

Tonga's tourism industry – the country's second largest source of hard currency – is in trouble, thanks to a faulty Chinese-made plane. The MA-60 aircraft was a gift to Tonga from China but concerns over its safety have led New Zealand to suspend tourism aid of around €6m. The plane is one of just three in the fleet belonging to Real Tonga, a new airline that launched in March. — SJB

Annual voyages to the Antarctic carried out by the Australian Antarctic Division

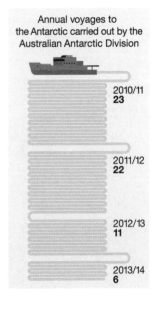

2010/11 **23**

2011/12 **22**

2012/13 **11**

2013/14 **6**

IMAGE: GETTY IMAGES, ILLUSTRATORS: SAM ISLAND, STUDIO TIPI INFOGRAPHICS: LAMOSCA

For the third year in a row, we are chosen the best airline in Europe.

Every year, Skytrax, the world's largest airline passenger satisfaction survey asks millions of passengers around the world to choose their favourite European airline.

For the past three years, the answer has always been the same.

Turkish Airlines remains the best airline in Europe.
We would like to thank you and congratulate our employees for making this possible.

Globally Yours | **TURKISH AIRLINES**

Voted Europe's Best Airline at the 2013
Skytrax Passengers Choice Awards

turkishairlines.com

A STAR ALLIANCE MEMBER

FROSTY RELATIONS
—*Arctic*

Preface
As parts of the Arctic become increasingly ice-free and its role as a valuable commodity is realised, questions of ownership are spurring a bigger military presence in the region. But the 'Arctic Five' insist any competition will be amicable.

WRITER
Trefor Moss

ILLUSTRATOR
Tokuma

The Arctic melt is uncovering more than just resources and trade routes – it is also opening up a whole new theatre of military operations.

Of all the world's territorial disputes, the ones in the Arctic – and there are plenty – used to matter the least: the only prize at stake was frozen ocean, and most of the time it was too cold for military forces to operate there anyway. National boundaries were left to blur among the floes.

Suddenly those vague Arctic territories matter. The region is increasingly ice-free and the open ocean means rich fishing, undersea mineral and energy resources and new sea lanes. The Arctic, in other words, has become a valuable commodity.

Best placed to assert ownership are the "Arctic Five", littoral Arctic Ocean states with well-established territorial claims and regional bases. "Russia and Norway are the two states most active and deliberate in raising their capacity for operating in the Arctic," says Ernie Regehr, senior fellow in Arctic security at the Simons Foundation – a Canadian think-tank. Canada, Regehr says, made some "dramatic announcements regarding enhanced military capacity in the north", but these have since run up against financial realities, while the US has been too preoccupied

elsewhere to devote much energy to revamping its Arctic presence.

Russia is arguably doing the most: its North Sea Fleet is being restocked and is due to receive a new Mistral-class amphibious assault ship from France; six new $1.1bn (€816m) icebreakers, which, at 170 metres in length, will be the world's biggest; and later new aircraft carriers. The Norwegians, meanwhile, have procured a new fleet of five Fridtjof Nansen-class frigates, which, together with its six Ula-class submarines, have significantly boosted its naval clout.

Yet it would be misleading to suggest that an Arctic arms race is underway. Bases are being upgraded, ice-breaking fleets expanded and modernised, and Arctic battalions retrained and up-armed. But the sheer remoteness of the Arctic makes conflict almost unthinkable, says Regehr.

"Military preparedness in the Arctic is really only meaningful if it enhances a capacity to contribute effectively to search and rescue, emergency response and support for public safety," he says, citing a "universal insistence" among the Arctic Five that any competition will remain amicable.

New interest in the Arctic threatens to make it a crowded place, however. The Arctic Council – which already includes Finland, Iceland and Sweden in addition to the Five – voted in May to admit several new observer members, including China, India and Japan. Of these, China has taken the keenest interest: in 2012 its sole icebreaker, *Xuelong*, completed the first transarctic voyage by a Chinese vessel and a new $200m (€150m) icebreaker is due for delivery in 2014, with additional ships planned, as Beijing seeks to open up the High North as a conduit for Chinese trade.

Regehr is optimistic that these new players can be peacefully accommodated. "The risks are not China or India specifically," he says. The concern is that more and more ships will be operating in waters which will remain dangerous even as they become navigable. "Human and commercial activity are in a sharply ascending arch; so too are the risks." — (M)

Five Arctic flashpoints
Territorial disputes

The Barents Sea

Cold War rivals Norway and Russia settled their decades-old Barents Sea border dispute in 2010. However, the subsequent discovery of huge oil and gas deposits on Norway's side of the line has left some Russians questioning whether they're getting their full share.

The Bering Strait

China plans to start using the Arctic as a key trade route to cut long-distance transit times. But ships must access the region via the Bering Strait – a narrow chokepoint between Russia and Alaska. A blockade of this chokepoint would be an obvious play should conflict arise between China and another power.

Greenland

The retreat of the icecap covering Greenland – an autonomous territory that is part of Denmark – is attracting foreign firms keen to exploit the island's resources. But commercial pressures are making it a contentious place to operate, while over-exploitation of its fragile environment could stir up trouble between local Inuit people, foreign business and the Danish government (*see page 39*).

The North Pole

Ever since a Russian submarine planted a national flag on the seabed at the Pole in 2007, ownership of the High North has been a contentious issue. The Pole itself matters much less than the vast hydrocarbon resources thought to lie beneath it. Canada, Denmark, Russia and the US all have overlapping claims based on their conflicting interpretations of the maritime borders.

The Northwest Passage

Melting sea ice has opened up the fabled Northwest Passage, which runs along northern Canada and links the Atlantic and Pacific oceans. But while Canada claims sovereignty over the route, citing its proximity to the Canadian coast, other Arctic claimants – plus China – say the Passage is in international waters. As more ships ply the route, Canada must choose whether to enforce its claim or bow to pressure.

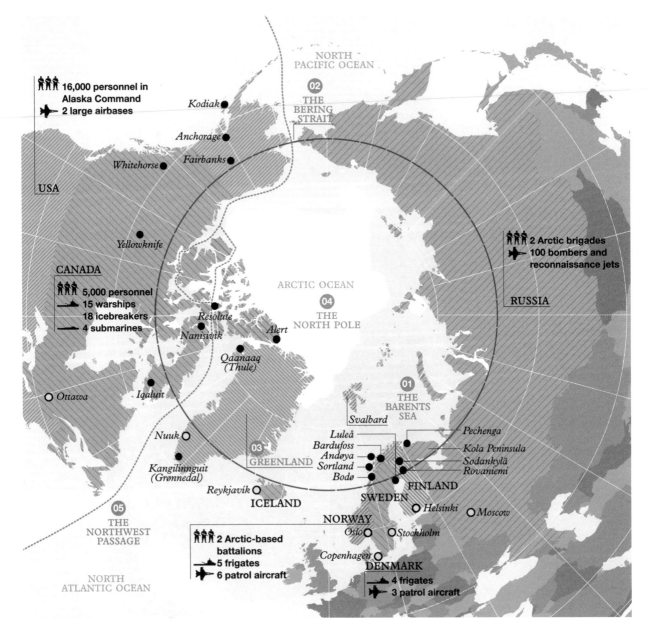

††† 16,000 personnel in
Alaska Command
✈ 2 large airbases

Kodiak

Anchorage

Whitehorse · *Fairbanks*

USA

Yellowknife

CANADA
††† 5,000 personnel
⚓ 15 warships
🚢 18 icebreakers
➤ 4 submarines

NORTH
PACIFIC OCEAN

02
THE
BERING
STRAIT

††† 2 Arctic brigades
✈ 100 bombers and
reconnaissance jets

RUSSIA

ARCTIC OCEAN

04
THE
NORTH POLE

Resolute

Nanisivik · *Alert*

Qaanaaq
(Thule)

THE
BARENTS
SEA

01

Svalbard

Pechenga

Luleå
Bardufoss
Andøya
Sortland
Bodø

Kola Peninsula
Sodankylä
Rovaniemi

FINLAND

○ *Ottawa*

Iqaluit

Nuuk ○

Kangilinnguit
(Grønnedal)

03
GREENLAND

SWEDEN

○ *Helsinki* ○ *Moscow*

Reykjavík ○
ICELAND

NORWAY

Oslo ○ ○ *Stockholm*

05
THE
NORTHWEST
PASSAGE

††† 2 Arctic-based
battalions
⚓ 5 frigates
✈ 6 patrol aircraft

Copenhagen ○
DENMARK

NORTH
ATLANTIC OCEAN

⚓ 4 frigates
✈ 3 patrol aircraft

Capabilities of the Arctic nations
Military operations in place

01
Canada

Several military bases are currently being upgraded on Canada's Arctic coast. A €2.25bn programme for the construction of a new fleet of Arctic offshore patrol ships is underway.

02
Denmark

The Danish military launched an Arctic Command in 2012 as part of its Arctic defence strategy, with a special-ops force that patrols northeast Greenland by sled.

03
Finland

The Finnish army's Jaeger Brigade, based in Sodankylä, specialises in polar warfare. The air force's Lapland Air Command operates from its base at Rovaniemi. Also home to strategically important Santa's village.

04
Iceland

With no military forces of its own, Iceland relies on security provided by its Nato allies. Nato conducts air patrols in Icelandic airspace.

05
Norway

In 2012, the Norwegian army's 2nd Battalion started converting into a new highly mobile Arctic Battalion. The navy's latest frigates and submarines patrol the Arctic. Svalbard, Norway's most northerly territory, is a demilitarised zone.

06
Russia

The army's first Arctic special forces brigade was recently set up in Pechenga in Murmansk Oblast. The navy's Northern Fleet has Russia's only aircraft carrier. Long-range Tupolev Tu-22 bombers patrol the polar region and six nuclear-powered icebreakers are in the pipeline.

07
Sweden

The Swedish military has an Armed Forces Winter Unit, which specialises in Arctic operations, while the air force operates Gripen fighters from its Arctic air base at Luleå.

08
USA

The US military's Alaskan Command operates two major airbases, as well as the US military's premier fighter jet, the F-22 Raptor. Washington is spending €750m on expanding its Alaskan missile defence. Aircraft carrier battle groups exercise annually in Arctic waters, but the US Navy only has one polar research vessel.

Knoll

Marking the territory
Canada
Canada's northernmost provinces are pride of place in the country's latest passport. Depicting some of the routes explorer Joseph-Elzéar Bernier took, it asserts Canadian control of these Arctic trade routes.

AMBASSADOR NO.22

UN phased

New York [ZAHIR TANIN]

Zahir Tanin, Afghanistan's permanent representative to the United Nations, is recalling the moment he returned home after living in exile for two decades. "Everything was familiar: the faces, the mountains, the trees, the stones. It was always with me," he says. The visit was to cover the inauguration of the new Afghan government for the BBC in December 2001. Five years later, Hamid Karzai told Tanin it was time for him to cross to the other side.

Tanin is intimately linked with his country's struggles. The People's Democratic Party of Afghanistan – a communist regime that led a bloody coup against Afghanistan's first president in 1978 – imprisoned and tortured Tanin, who was a politically active, left-leaning medical student. "Many people were killed. It was only luck that I survived," he says.

After his release by the Soviets, he abandoned medicine to practise journalism. But his political stance made him enemies, and in the early 1990s Tanin and his family fled to France as political refugees. He moved to the UK in 1994 to work as a research fellow at the London School of Economics, followed by an 11-year stint as a journalist for the BBC World

Service. In 2006, President Hamid Karzai asked Tanin to join the Afghan government; Tanin chose his current post. During his tenure he has served as vice-president of the General Assembly and has led delegations at Least Developed Countries conferences.

He also chairs the group that calls for Security Council reform. "Can we have a Security Council that's more representative, more efficient, more legitimate?" asks Tanin, who has presided over eight rounds of discussions.

Tanin is acutely aware of the fine balance he must employ as an envoy for a nation as mired in conflict as his own. "Smaller countries are not equal in resources and capacities but their [success at the UN] depends on the quality of their representatives and how they relate to the reality there." — SK

Permanent Mission of Afghanistan to the United Nations in New York

01 The mission: The mission has been housed in a Midtown Manhattan skyscraper, located a few blocks west of the United Nations, since 2009. In Tanin's office, gold brocade chairs, multicoloured rugs and black-and-white photographs of famed Afghan monuments speak to the rich cultural history of Afghanistan.

02 The staff: The mission's 18 staff members include 10 delegates in addition to a deputy permanent representative and Tanin.

03 The challenges: Afghans will go to the polls in April 2014. Maintaining a peaceful transfer of power will be an important test of the government's claim of a strategy of self-sufficiency. The fair distribution of international aid for development programmes will also be watched closely.

Friends in hot places

Latin America [UK DIPLOMACY]

A new wave of British diplomacy is targeting Latin America and the Caribbean to reverse the retreat of UK influence in the region and tap into emerging markets. The UK is said to trade two-and-a-half times more goods with Belgium than it does with the whole of Latin America, even though Belgium's economy is half the size of the state of São Paulo's. The UK closed seven diplomatic posts in Latin America from 1997 to 2010. But in recent months a new chargé d'affaires has arrived in Haiti, embassies have been opened in El Salvador and Paraguay and a consulate has opened in Recife, Brazil. — ANM

Monocle 24's correspondents are on the ground to bring you the latest news, views and analysis around the clock. Tune in for live debate, regular shows and events as they happen at monocle.com/radio.

Bore games

Santiago [FINNISH TIES]

Finland's prime minister Jyrki Katainen dropped in on Chilean president Sebastián Piñera this year after a Europe-Latin America summit in Santiago. One result was a bilateral commission to bring Finland's energy-efficient mining technology to the world's biggest copper producer.

Purchases of mining and forestry gear have raised Chile to second place behind Brazil among Finland's Latin American markets, says Ilkka Heiskanen, Finland's emissary to Chile. But Finland has more than machinery on offer. It gives Chile tips on education reform and indigenous rights and a Finnish firm is designing the residence at a radio telescope in the Chilean desert. — SEB

PHOTOGRAPHER: DUSDIN CONDREN, ILLUSTRATOR: TY WILKINS, STUDIO TIPI. INFOGRAPHICS: LAMOSCA

INTRODUCING

Discovered

AT JCREW.COM

J.CREW

dis·cov·ery
—noun
\dis-'kə-v(ə-)rē\

An uncommon item found elsewhere,
or designed in-house.

Over the years, from word of mouth, trips across the
world and our own archives, we've come across items
that have changed the way we think about design.
Items with a story that really caught our attention—
and even inspired a few expletives. Items that deserved
their own destination. So we created a home for them
at jcrew.com and on these next few pages.

We found them, you collect them.

jcrew.com/discovered

PRIVATE WHITE V.C.

WHAT
Impeccable outerwear from one of Britain's coolest brands.

OUR TAKE
Founded by a WWI hero—"V.C." stands for Victoria Cross, Britain's highest award
for valor—and now helmed by his great-grandson, the label cleverly reinvents classic
English styles (we handpicked our favorites for you). "We stumbled across Private
White's storefront while scouting locations in London for our new men's shop,"
explains Frank, our men's designer. "Turns out, we're going to be neighbors."

PRIVATE WHITE V.C.™ WOOL FLIGHT JACKET

A MADE-IN-THE-USA BAG

WHAT
The field bag that will last a lifetime.

OUR TAKE
Filson's motto is "Might as well have the best," and since 1897, the people at this Seattle-based brand have been proving that when it comes to hard-wearing, handsome bags and outerwear, theirs are. Take the rugged twill field bag: It's crafted in the USA of industrial-weight cotton twill and bridle leather straps. And it's exclusively ours.

FILSON® RUGGED TWILL FIELD BAG

A FAIR ISLE SWEATER

The distinct pattern is named for the tiny island off the coast of northern Scotland (population: around 70), whose artisans first started knitting it in the 16th century.

MCCALLUM FAIR ISLE SWEATER

SUNGLASSES FROM AN EYEWEAR HEIR

Garrett Leight fuses design history and family expertise— the Southern California native grew up in a household of eyewear professionals—into his shades, which are built from Italian and Japanese materials but crafted in the U.S.

GARRETT LEIGHT™ SUNGLASSES IN KINNEY BLOND

A GUIDEBOOK TO A GENTLEMANLY LIFE

Legendary writer, style icon, member of Andy Warhol's Factory... Glenn O'Brien has lived quite the life, which gives him the authority to dole out witticisms on everything from how to dress to how to fight.

HOW TO BE A MAN BY GLENN O'BRIEN

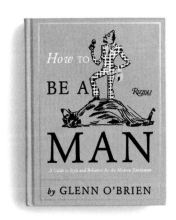

CANTON JAPANESE SELVEDGE DENIM

The denim experts at Tokyo, Japan's Canton (est. 1963) made this unique pair of selvedge jeans (woven on vintage looms, selvedge denim has a self-finished, colored edge you can see when cuffed).

CANTON™ FOR J.CREW SLIM UNSANFORIZED DARK WASH JEAN

DRAKE'S LONDON

Handmade ties and pocket squares from London with a healthy dose of whimsy, since 1977.

DRAKE'S® ANTIQUE SKIER TIE

INVESTMENT-WORTHY FOOTWEAR

The double monk strap shoe from Rushden, Northamptonshire's Alfred Sargent.

ALFRED SARGENT™ FOR J.CREW DOUBLE MONK STRAP SHOES

A TRAVEL KIT TO SHOW OFF

Billykirk brothers Chris and Kirk Bray use in-house artisans and Amish craftsmen to create their built-to-last, made-in-the-USA bags.

BILLYKIRK® TRAVEL KIT

SOCKS STRAIGHT FROM THE ENGLISH COUNTRYSIDE

Hand-knit socks in traditional patterns from Britain's Scott-Nichol, which has been producing them for over 70 years using natural, moisture-wicking wools.

SCOTT-NICHOL™ WOOLSTHORPE SOCKS

THE LUDLOW SUIT IN
BARBERIS FLANNEL

WHAT
An iconic suiting style.

OUR TAKE
A softer, warmer fabric than your typical worsted wool, flannel traces its roots back
to 16th-century Wales. For our signature Ludlow suit, we turned to Biella, Italy's
Vitale Barberis Canonico, which has been weaving fine woolen fabrics for 15
generations. We then tailored it into an updated version of the mid-century classic
(think Gregory Peck's dapper turn in *The Man in the Gray Flannel Suit*).

LUDLOW SUIT IN ITALIAN WOOL FLANNEL

"I WEAR A SUIT NOT
OUT OF NECESSITY,
BUT BECAUSE I WANT
TO, AND THE LUDLOW
MAKES IT EASY. AND
I LOVE THAT YOU CAN
MONOGRAM THEM SO
NO ONE STEALS YOUR
JACKET AT THE PARTY."

ALEJANDRO RHETT
MEN'S MERCHANT
Wearing the Ludlow suit in English wool.

Photograph by Bryan Derballa.

INSIDE STORY

THE LUDLOW

WE ASKED THREE OF OUR VERY OWN GENTS FOR
THEIR THOUGHTS ON THE SHARPEST ITEM IN ANY
GUY'S CLOSET—THE LUDLOW SUIT.

"FOR ME, WEARING A THREE-PIECE SUIT IS JUST AS COMFORTABLE AS JEANS AND A TEE."

MARCO MADEIRA
LONDON STORE DIRECTOR
Wearing the Ludlow suit in Italian wool.

Photograph by Justin Chung.

"I'VE GOTTEN LOTS OF FRIENDS INTO THE LUDLOW, A FEW THAT DIDN'T EVEN KNOW WHAT SIZE THEY WEAR, AND IT'S AMAZING TO SEE HOW THEY RESPOND THE FIRST TIME THEY SEE THEMSELVES IN THE MIRROR."

MIKE HEANEY
MEN'S MERCHANT
Wearing the Ludlow suit in Italian wool flannel.

Photograph by Bryan Derballa.

Collect all our discoveries at

JCREW.COM/DISCOVERED

Share them

#DISCOVERED

01 Rama takes the floor of
    Albania's parliament as
    prime minister
02 Rama visiting Kosovo's
    parliament

THE EAGLE REBRANDED
—*Tirana*

Preface
Albania's new prime minister has a daunting job on his hands. With unemployment levels at 12.8 per cent and corruption rife, the nation is ready for change – and the somewhat eccentric Edi Rama is ready to step up.

WRITER
Andrew Mueller

PHOTOGRAPHER
Heiko Prigge

Edi Rama is taking the floor of Albania's parliament as prime minister for the first time. His task is the formality of introducing his new government's programme. It doesn't go altogether smoothly. In his opening remarks Rama pledges to respect his political adversaries but observes that they haven't always extended him the same courtesy when they were in charge. This elicits hissing, harrumphing and unparliamentary language before the opposition bloc stands, en masse, and leaves the building.

"I understand it," Rama tells MONOCLE later. "It was just too much for them, after years of saying bluntly that me becoming prime minister would never happen. But it's a pity."

Rama, 49, has not yet moved in to the prime minister's office. Since he led the Socialist Party and its accompanying alliance to victory in June's elections, he has operated from the party's purple-carpeted headquarters behind Skanderbeg Square in central Tirana. When I met Rama 10 years ago, the artist and former basketballer was Tirana's mayor and had decorated his office with the same eccentric exuberance he had brought to the job – most memorably expressed in a campaign to paint Tirana a rainbow of lurid colours.

Rama's current digs do not disappoint. More arresting features include

a model of his campaign bus, a Franz Kafka mouse mat, dozens of small sculptures, the hundreds of pens and crayons with which he doodles on diary pages during meetings – a book of these spontaneous abstracts has been published by Swiss art imprint JRP Ringier – and a pair of surprisingly lively turtles, named Fatos and Sali, after Rama's immediate predecessors as prime minister, Fatos Nano and Sali Berisha.

"A friend of mine told me turtles would be good for my allergic asthma," he explains. "I don't know why. But I have felt a change. Since I was a kid, I wanted to believe in miracles."

As mayor, Rama became famous for his apparent whimsy but his caprices were always underpinned by a deep, faintly fretful seriousness about the possibilities of government. Which of those competing instincts triumphs when you're put in charge of the country?

"I expected to feel more joyful," he says. "But it was too big, too burdening, and it humbled me in my soul and my body. I didn't feel bigger; I felt smaller. For a week after the result, I felt empty, asking myself if I was really the person on whom all this should be placed."

It's a daunting prospect. Albania has a lower GDP per capita than Turkmenistan. Unemployment is 12.8 per cent – and nearly three times that among young people. Electricity and running water cannot be taken for granted. The corruption is proverbial. Where do you even start?

"We have to be bold," says Rama, "or as bold as we can be with little money. We'll move against illegal gambling and illegal weapons. There will be a national clean-up – there's an epidemic of illegal building, especially on the seaside. And we need to address corruption. People don't corrupt systems; systems corrupt people. So we change the systems."

Rama and his ministers have set themselves the challenge of making a difference in their first 100 days. They have little experience of national government. Aside from Rama, who was minister of culture in the late 1990s, none has held cabinet rank before. This

01

02   03

is by design: Rama wants a break from how things have been done in the past. His cabinet tends towards youth but they are not idealists. Like many youngish Eastern Europeans who recall life under communism, they are uninterested in dogma, and focused instead on practicalities.

It is telling that Tony Blair's New Labour is frequently cited as an inspiration (and that Blair staffers Alastair Campbell and Jonathan Powell have been advising the new government).

What will be the very first instruction he gives as leader of his country's government? "I'm going to take down the fences around the prime minister's office," he says, as Fatos – or possibly Sali – meanders around his red-laced sneakers. "They're horrible."

"The prime minister," says incoming foreign minister Ditmir Bushati, "is a unique character, with an unusual career behind him. So he's an asset in terms of rebranding but Albania is a higher hurdle than Tirana." Bushati, who is 36, is preparing to spend the

01 Rama's colourful desk
02 Model of Rama's
    campaign bus
03 Rama's shoes, with
    either Fatos or Sali
04 Socialist party HQ
05 Downtown Tirana
06 Erion Veliaj (left) on
    Klan TV show 'Opinion'
07 Reporter outside
    government building
08 Ditmir Bushati
09 Staff oversee moving-in
    process in PM's office

04 05

06

07 08

09

Monocle fixes

Nowhere else in Europe can you see a helmet-free motorcyclist steering with one hand while dangling a baby on the petrol tank with the other. Albania's chronically idiotic motoring needs urgent and ruthless correcting

---

The colourful civic paint jobs that were a signature of Edi Rama's mayoralty are fading. They were a terrific quirky selling point for Albania's capital and should be touched up

---

There is still nothing much being done with the dowdy villa once occupied by loopy dictator Enver Hoxha. Its prime location amid the bars and cafés of Tirana's Blloku district would make it an ideal gallery and/or museum

---

On which subject, Hoxha's deranged pyramid mausoleum has fallen into grim, graffiti-slathered disrepair. It had a certain ironic cachet back when it was repurposed as a disco and event space, but now it just needs bulldozing

---

Tirana needs more small, cool and competently run hotels. The exemplary Hotel Boutique Kotoni, where Monocle stayed, should be giving lessons

majority of his first week in the job out of the country – in Pristina, Brussels and New York.

"Albania is peculiar," he says, "in that a third of the nation lives abroad. And those people are not involved enough in branding Albania. I know we have a bad image but there are talented Albanians in the diaspora we could be proud of, and we want to involve them. We need to go beyond classic diplomacy."

Bushati speaks of cultivating relationships with Albanian communities just outside Albania's borders – in Kosovo, Macedonia, Montenegro and Serbia's Preševo Valley. He acknowledges that this has to be done without inflaming paranoia among Albania's neighbours.

"We are very sober in that respect," says Bushati, shaking his head emphatically. "Our future is the EU. There will be no discussion of Greater Albania. But we want to be more positive in the region."

Bushati notes that it's easier to fly from Tirana to Vienna than to Belgrade, Skopje, Zagreb or Sarajevo – which raises the risk of missed connections for a foreign minister who will be largely relying on scheduled flights, given the lack of official aircraft at his disposal.

"Geography," says Bushati, "is not an option. But if France and Germany can get along, so can Albanians and Serbs. I'm aware of the realities of the Balkans. I know we produce more history than we can consume."

For this and other reasons, Albania's defence portfolio is a sensitive one. "Part of the army," says the new defence

01   Rama's first foreign visit
      as PM in Pristina
02   Statue of Skanderbeg, a
      15th-century nobleman
03   Rama meets the press
      in Pristina
04   Defence minister,
      Mimi Kodheli

minister, Mimi Kodheli, "has worked against the opposition – against the law."

On 21 January 2011, Albanian soldiers fired on a demonstration in Tirana – one of many protests that followed the 2009 election, lost by Edi Rama's Socialists and widely believed to have been rigged. Four people were killed.

"I'll never forget what I saw that day," says Kodheli, 49. "I was quite close to one of the people shot dead."

A cornerstone of functional democracy is the willingness of the military to accept civilian command. Kodheli, it seems safe to assume, will be taking charge of at least some soldiers who don't care much for her or what she represents.

"I am wondering how the first day will go," she says with a smile. "Some media call me the 'Iron Lady', which I'm not. But I'm tough. And maybe it's not the military's fault. The Berisha government cut people into two categories – those with them, or against them. People lost their careers for liking Edi Rama. The military served the party, not the people."

Albania's incoming cabinet talk about tackling corruption, and so they should – Transparency International's Corruption Perceptions Index rates Albania alongside Ethiopia and Niger, which is a stretch from where an EU aspirant wants to be. But defence departments in the most honest nations are prone to skullduggery, encouraged by a combination of fabulous spending and secrecy. At a lower level, Kodheli says she has heard of officers buying rank, or troops paying for postings to Afghanistan, for the extra wages.

"On my first day," she says, "I'll meet the commanders – aviation, marine, army. I need to present the military budget by the end of this month and I don't know if they've prepared anything."

Like all her cabinet colleagues, Kodheli has requested handover meetings with her predecessor – and, like all her cabinet colleagues, has been ignored.

Rama's first foreign visit as prime minister is next door to Kosovo. His motorcade leaves Tirana early and weaves through the mountains of northern Albania as dawn crawls across the peaks. Over the border, saluting Kosovar policemen punctuate the highway. In Pristina, Rama is greeted by a Kosovo army band and his prime ministerial counterpart, former Kosovo Liberation Army commander Hashim Thaçi. Despite their radically different backgrounds, the painter and the guerilla get on well.

"It's true," says Rama. "One of us comes from war, and one from art, but we both entered politics for freedom. And in terms of political skill, he is the best adviser."

Back in Tirana, Rama spends two long days in a marathon sitting of parliament, followed by the eventual ceremonial recognition of his new government. In the early evening, to a fanfare of Queen's "One Vision", his cabinet gathers on the steps of the prime minister's office and Rama makes a brief speech to a few thousand enthusiasts.

"It's still too humbling," he says afterwards. "And in the next 100 days we'll see if we're too optimistic." — (M)

WHERE EMPERORS ROAM.

Drum Tower, Beijing

ROSEWOOD

A SENSE *of* PLACE™

A TRUE JOURNEY NEVER ENDS. *rosewoodhotels.com*

AMERICAS | ASIA | EUROPE | MIDDLE EAST | *Soon* LONDON BEIJING

PRESENT COMPANY —*Lapland*

Preface
For someone who's soon going to be delivering billions of presents, travelling more than 175 million miles and eating around two billion mince pies – all in one night – Santa Claus looks in great shape when Monocle meets him at his home.

WRITER
Steve Bloomfield

PHOTOGRAPHER
Juho Kuva

Rovaniemi, Lapland, northern Finland. Santa Claus shuffles out from the fire exit of his grotto, walks towards MONOCLE's small Skoda hire car and squeezes himself – beard, belly and boots – into the passenger seat.

"This is a little strange," I say.

"I get that a lot," Santa replies.

Let us, for a moment, just for this one page, suspend our disbelief. It will make things easier, I promise. This Santa, it should be pointed out, is the real Santa. Swedes, Norwegians and Danes may disagree – actually, they *will* disagree, vociferously – but Santa is associated with nowhere as much as Lapland.

There is very little in Rovaniemi that does not appear to be connected with Santa and the season of goodwill. His image is plastered across the airport, where posters proclaim it to be the "official airport of Santa Claus". Hotels and restaurants are named after him. There is even Santa Hair & Beauty, although it is unclear whether it does a special deal for beards. The only venue in Rovaniemi that does not appear to be Santa-themed is the Kitty-Cat, the lap-dancing club. Having said that, MONOCLE did not enter the lap-dancing club so who knows?

We drive to the reindeer farm, a few kilometres farther north. A Skoda isn't Santa's normal ride but given the mild weather it is a bit more practical. "When it comes to winter and deep snow, nothing beats reindeer," he says as we walk down the hill towards the forest. A group of seven reindeer gallop towards us out of the trees, called by Santa banging a bucket of food against the fence.

None of them has a red nose, I note. "Well it's not Christmas Eve yet, is it?" Santa replies. As Santa feeds the reindeer we skirt around the difficult conversation about what Santa himself eats. This is, after all, a town where everyone appears to eat his preferred mode of transport.

While Santa is happy to show off his reindeer he is a little more coy about where he keeps all the presents. "I can't show you all Santa's secrets now, can I?" Nor, despite persistent questioning, is he willing to reveal whether certain individuals are on the naughty or nice list. He will take us to the post office though. If a letter is addressed to "Santa Claus, North Pole", this is where it ends up. Piles of opened envelopes are stacked in boxes – MONOCLE's favourite is one from Singapore with the address "1 Reindeer Lane" scrawled in red crayon. The post office also does a lively business in postcards sent *from* the "North Pole". Thousands are sent every week, each with a special Santa-themed postmark, while it's also possible to send postcards that won't arrive until Christmas. A female worker at the post office – she giggles when asked if she's an elf – says they expect to send 500,000 this Christmas.

The actual elves are nowhere to be seen. They work "somewhere else", Santa says, treading a fine line between mystery and vagueness. At Santa's House – it's not a grotto, apparently – the two blonde 20-something women in cartoonish Christmas outfits greeting us at the door are probably best described as Santa's Little Helpers. They shepherd families into the living room where Santa sits on his big chair next to the flickering (electric) log fire. Once the child's five minutes is up, the Helpers guide them out again. Along the way they show them the picture they've just taken and gently try the hard sell – €25 for one large picture, €49 for a special Santa USB.

> This is a very international place. One day I counted 44 different nationalities. The youngest was three weeks old

This is, be in no doubt, a proper, thriving business. Santa Park was little more than a couple of huts 20 years ago; now there's a post office, a series of cafés, gift shops, a bakery, a gallery, a bar and Santa's House.

Santa may be very old – he is a bit vague about his exact date of birth too – but in the past two decades it is fair to say he has become a little more entrepreneurial. "There are always more people coming, so we needed more room," he says. His house has been rebuilt and extended more than half a dozen times as the tourist numbers have increased. Santa may be Nordic by birth but he is truly global. In the post office the letters are placed into pigeon holes depending on the nation they were sent from – the ones for Kyrgyzstan and Yemen both look fairly full.

"This is a very international place," he says. "One day this summer I counted 44 different nationalities. The youngest one was three weeks old, and the oldest was 97."

Today the youngest is four-year-old Igor from Murmansk. His family have driven the 580km for a week-long holiday, of which the visit to see Santa is the centrepiece. Igor is shy of strangers, turning his face into his mother's legs at the sight of anyone he doesn't know. Santa isn't a stranger though. Igor's face lights up, he jumps onto Santa's lap with glee and the smile is still stuck on his face 10 minutes later after his parents have politely declined the sales pitch from the Helpers and they are walking back to the car park. And why not? He's just met Santa. It's impossible not to smile, whatever your age. — (M)

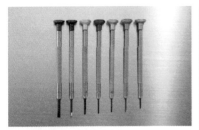

SOMEDAY THEY'LL CALL GENEVA THE DETROIT OF SWITZERLAND.

THE RUNWELL FEATURING A BLACK DIAL WITH REMOTE SWEEP SECOND IN A STAINLESS STEEL CASE AND DETROIT-BUILT ARGONITE 1069 MOVEMENT.

SHINOLA
DETROIT

Where American is made.

01

01 A scale model ice-
breaking cargo ship
is tested in the Aker
Arctic facility
02 Finnish Environment
Institute (SYKE) re-
search vessel 'Aranda'

02

FINN BLUE LINE
—*Helsinki*

Preface
Icebreaking is in the DNA
of Finns, whose shipping
heritage and expertise put
it in good stead to face the
changes ahead, from foreign
competition to climate
change and a race for the
Arctic's resources.

WRITER
Ben Williams

PHOTOGRAPHER
Johannes Romppanen

There's a reason the *Urho* and *Voima* –
two huge icebreakers bunkered in the
docks at Katajanokka – are popular with
Helsinkians. It's not just because their
towering hulls make a good picture for
tourists to snap. The Gulf of Finland
freezes every year and exposure to the
harshest winter conditions has bred a
deep understanding of ice among Finns.

These two vast ships were built to
secure the waterways so vital to the country's economy – more than 80 per cent of
Finnish foreign trade travels by sea – and
form a part of what Captain Jarkko Toivola, head of the Winter Navigation Unit
at the Finnish Transport Agency (FTA),
calls his country's "mature ice system".
"In a hard winter, there are about 5,000
icebreaker assistances," he says, from his
Helsinki offices, where a scale model of
the *Voima* sits proudly in the foyer. "This
is a totally different scale of operation
from anywhere else in the world."

As the Arctic ice melts, this deep-
seated knowledge is becoming increasingly marketable. The region is subject
to a new and intense phase of development and corporations and governments
are jockeying for position. Thirteen per
cent of the world's remaining oil and 30
per cent of its gas is thought to exist in
the Arctic.

Aker Arctic, Finland's largest icebreaker engineering company, is

01   02

03   04·

Going nuclear

responsible for 60 per cent of the world's icebreakers. Which is why its managing director, Mikko Niini, can count the governments of Canada, China and Russia among his clients, as well as a host of corporate names with a distinctly Russian flavour – including Norilsk Nickel, Gazprom and Rosneft. Niini clearly knows his market. "Today we are concentrating on Arctic issues only," he says as he shows MONOCLE around Aker's Helsinki facility, which overlooks the container port at Vuosaari on the eastern flank of the city. "We are not doing anything else."

Vuosaari is home to Aker's ice model basin and some 1,300 tonnes of freezing water, which is key to its global success. Here, extreme ice conditions are recreated on a miniature scale to test some of the world's toughest ships prior to real-world production. "We build the boats on a 1/30 scale, so we need to build the ice on a 1/30 scale also," he says.

Niini is happy juggling geopolitics but he is also the sort of executive who moves nimbly around the minus 20C ice-modelling facility wearing a good suit while everyone else is dressed in thick winter jackets. The facility is a hybrid of hi-tech and craft, somewhere between a workshop and a colossal walk-in freezer. Small, hand-modelled ships wait to enter the vast water tank; soon the space will be filled with a fine mist of water droplets, settling on the surface to simulate snow.

Testing here shows how Aker-designed icebreakers, ice-going vessels and structures for Arctic oil and gas field operations will cope in different extreme conditions. They can experiment with the manoeuvrability of a ship and tweak the design of a hull or power thruster accordingly. For example, Aker discovered that when using multi-directional azimuth thrusters (propellers that power the ship but also act as rudders), certain cargo vessels performed better stern-first, smashing into the ice backwards. "Developing new concepts for new operations is our bread and butter," says Niini. "We use model testing to verify the novel ideas we develop."

Aker's clientele is global but one of its concepts is in production not far away at the huge Arctech Helsinki Shipyard in the centre of the city, where employees traverse the site by bicycle. Here, Arctech's managing director Esko Mustamäki shows MONOCLE a €76 million icebreaker ship it is building for the Russian Ministry of Transport. He allows himself a smile at the unusual, asymmetric design of the ship – an angle that will allow it to be piloted sideways into the ice, cutting a wide channel. "Some people think it's a radical design," he confides. "This is at the very least an innovative vessel."

The Russian icebreaker is the latest of more than 400 ships built during a 150-year history at these yards, which have changed ownership and name several times. The current rebranding as Arctech reflects a refocusing of efforts back to the Arctic and a return to what the Finns do best. A glance down the list of ships built here over time shows Arctech has been busy making cruise vessels too and retro-fitting existing ships with everything from oil-recovery equipment to pizza restaurants. But the boom in cruise vessel and ferry manufacturing that powered the global shipping industry since the 1980s is over, according to Mustamäki. "Even the Chinese are now suffering the same problems as the European yards," he says. "Simply put, since 2008 there are not enough orders."

Arctech's future may well be secured by the thawing north. Ironically, less ice in the Arctic means more icebreaking ships will be required as companies become ever braver in pushing their resource operations into the frozen ocean. Ships have already started to cross the Northern Sea Route and scientists from the US

01 Building an icebreaking vessel for the
Russian Ministry of Transport

National Snow and Ice Data Center predict that the North Pole itself could be
ice-free in summer by 2030.

In a tough but growing international
market, Finnish yards now compete for
icebreaker contracts with big players
from the broader global shipping industry, and must fight to protect their niche.
Success for companies such as Aker
Arctic doesn't necessarily translate into
success for Finnish manufacturers: ships
currently in the design phase at Aker will
go on to be built in Canada and China.
The new €125m FTA icebreaker, commissioned this year by the Finnish government, will also go out to mandatory EU
open tender. Captain Toivola is secretive
about who is competing. Will it be frustrating if the build goes outside of Finland? "I can't give a view," he says. "It's a
sensitive matter. But the design of it also
went to open tender – and was won in
competition by Aker Arctic."

Meanwhile, the surge in interest in the
High North is ushering in a new era of
international co-operation – both in geopolitics and manufacturing – and Aker
is clear about the importance of being
in on the act. Back in his office, Niini
gives an example of a recent infrastructure project: three 70,000 tonne-capacity
ice-worthy oil tankers to serve the new
Russian Arctic port of Varandey on the
Barents Sea, designed by Aker, built in
South Korea and with Russian money
– to serve world markets. In part, this is
down to Russian pragmatism.

"They simply don't have the technology or money to develop the Arctic
alone," adds Niini, who goes on to
explain the importance of the port to the
future of oil exports. "Varandey has now
been in successful operation for more
than five years and other oil companies
such as Total are joining for these export
systems, so that Arctic traffic is increasing and more of these tankers will be
needed in the future."

That the Finns have much to offer
internationally is recognised – albeit
from a different perspective – by envi-
ronmentalist Juha Flinkman, from his
offices at the Finnish Environment Institute (SYKE). "We have a lot of know-how

01

Smash hit

Icebreakers are designed to smash their way around frozen waters, creating channels that more ordinary vessels can follow. The archetypal icebreaker is powerful for its size – and heavy – and can generate a lot of force at low speed. It has a rounded, reinforced bow, which pushes brittle sea ice aside away from its more delicate propellers. The bow can also be ridden up onto very thick ice, or used to ram it repeatedly, so the heavy weight of the vessel fractures the ice and carves out a clear passage for other ships. Oil and gas companies have recently demanded a more flexible type of ship for use around their new refineries in the thawing Arctic, able to operate in open water as well as ice. From this the double-acting ship (DAS) was born, which operates bow first in open water and stern first in lighter-ice conditions. The DAS model uses powerful multi-directional thrusters, which "mill" the ice and flush it away from the ship.

01 Model of icebreaking multipurpose
   emergency and rescue vessel
02 'Aranda' research vessel

01

02

here and Finland should be even more active," he says. "In the future we should be even more involved."

In typical Finnish style, even Flinkman loves a big ship, and part of his research role at SYKE involves working on an icebreaker for months at a time. But as a scientist unbeholden to the imperatives of commerce and trade, he is clear about more global challenges ahead. In fact, he's off to Brussels to address a meeting of the European Defence Agency about navigation and military affairs in the Arctic environment.

"I'm going to say that if the polar ice cap melts, it's going to change commercial navigation, military operations – everything," he says. "And that the worst threat to world security is what happens when ocean currents change."

It's clear that this changing climate will have an effect on the icebreaking industry. Yet in the harsh and increasingly competitive environment of the High North, Finnish nautical expertise – with its icebreaking heritage – looks well placed to tackle the challenges ahead. — (M)

FRONTIER MAN —*London*

Preface
Monocle meets Koji Sekimizu, the man responsible for maritime safety and security in the Arctic. It's a huge task but thanks to his Polar Code, Sekimizu is confident he can deliver.

WRITER
Ben Williams

PHOTOGRAPHER
Benjamin McMahon

Koji Sekimizu is tasked with bringing order to the development of the Arctic high seas. As secretary-general of the International Maritime Organisation (IMO), the UN organisation concerned with the safety of shipping and cleaner oceans, he is the driving force behind a new draft Polar Code that will regulate the activities of oil and mining-industry ships as they rush to extend their operations into the Arctic.

With 36 years of working on maritime issues at the Japanese Ministry of Transport and the IMO, starting as a ship inspector in 1977, Sekimizu brings considerable experience to his role. We meet him in his London offices overlooking the Thames on his return from a week aboard the Russian state nuclear icebreaker, the *50 Let Pobedy*.

M: *How was your trip? What is it like to be on an Arctic icebreaker on the Northern Sea Route [NSR]?*
KS: There was a lot of sound, noise and vibration continuously. When our vessel encountered a huge mass of ice even an icebreaker as powerful as ours was forced to change course. It was really dynamic. We met the convoy of another icebreaker leading an LNG [gas] tanker and they were struggling to get through. Our icebreaker had to help them out.

M: *What is the traffic like up there?*
KS: This year I was informed there have been more than 400 requests made and Russian authorities have already endorsed more than 350

passages. This has been a dramatic increase over the past four to five years [there were 46 passages in 2012 and only 10 in 2010] and they are expecting more dramatic increases in the coming years.

M: *Do you foresee an increase in trade because of this?*
KS: That belongs to the future. But the fact is the ice is melting and I'm sure that route will attract interest from shipping – particularly the industry carrying oil and gas from Russia or Norway to Asian countries. The total length of passage is around 6,000 [nautical] miles if you go through NSR; if you choose the Suez Canal route the total length would be doubled to 12,000 miles. If you go round the African continent it's tripled.

M: *How can you ensure that the Russian Arctic infrastructure is capable of supporting an increase in traffic?*
KS: There are similar elements when it comes to regulating any support system. First and foremost we need to establish international regulations. This means a robust new Polar Code in 2015, to be implemented in 2017.

M: *And this code is mandatory for everybody, including Russia?*
KS: This is compulsory. This will cover ship design, structure, equipment, qualifications for seafarers, environmental regulations, communication. Those are fundamental conditions when it comes to the future of this passage.

M: *What happens if there is an accident in these sensitive environmental regions?*
KS: We need to be prepared for any incident, not only in the Arctic but all over the world. Maritime rescue and coordination centres need to be established [in the Arctic], and supported. The Russian government has already established a centre in Dixon, to be supported by two subcentres. When it comes to the search and rescue operations they need to provide actual resources – boats and other equipment – for operation in what is a very difficult environment. — (M)

TOMORROW

LAND

SINCE 1978
www.tomorrowland.co.jp

how to spend it.com

- Content of 100+ issues
- Exclusive columns
- Daily posts
- 1,000+ gift ideas

From the FT's award-winning luxury lifestyle magazine

01

OPEN SEASON
—*Burma*

Preface
Monocle meets the foreign investors and returning natives making the most of a budding business market in Yangon, Asia's new rising trade magnet.

WRITERS
Francis Wade
& Gwen Robinson
PHOTOGRAPHERS
Alessandro Costa
& Cattleya Jaruthavee

02

01 View of Shwedagon Pagoda in Yangon from Vista Bar terrace
02 Fresh from the oven at Yangon Bakehouse
03 Trainee chefs learn the ropes at Shwe Sa Bwe restaurant

03

Tucked away down a leafy side street on the northern shore of Yangon's Inya Lake, two Michelin star-winning French chefs show young Burmese how to slice truffles for a rich *forestiere* sauce. Shwe Sa Bwe recently celebrated its first birthday and its bookings list reflects a city in flux: tourists, embassy staff and wealthy businessmen.

It's one of a number of recent arrivals to join the city's restaurant scene that is driven by new money and a hunger for high-end cuisine. Yangon is a city playing catch-up. The trainees here are drawn from a network of monasteries and orphanages across the country, and schooled in the art of French cooking. Its owner, François Stoupan, doesn't expect to turn a profit until the end of next year but has a wider goal to train nearly 50 young locals who will disperse to kitchens around the city. "We take in underprivileged, but not destitute, children and train them to a high standard of cheffing," he tells MONOCLE.

Setting up business in Burma is riddled with obstacles. But as the country emerges from decades of stultifying junta-led rule, bold investors are streaming in. "I felt there was a gaping hole in the hospitality industry," says Nico Elliott, who left a London career in finance and moved to Yangon earlier this year to set up the chic riverside Union

01 02

03

❝

We want to set up a variety of places here: to stay, to eat, to drink. After all, this is the time

❞

Bar and Grill with his partner, Camilla Stopford Sackville, and local investors.

Business has exceeded expectations but the Union is "just the start", says Elliott. The couple are working on their next projects – a contemporary "chickenery", or yakitori and sake bar, as well as a boutique hotel and a speakeasy-cum-nightclub. "We want to set up a variety of places here: to stay, to eat, to drink. After all, this is the time," he adds.

Burma's quickly changing former capital presents an exciting prospect to entrepreneurs such as Elliott. But some argue that years of political oppression have left the Burmese at a disadvantage to foreign investors. Myo Min, who runs the PS Business School in Yangon, fears that the changes are happening too quickly. "We used to understand the market here," he says. "Now we don't know what will happen next and how to compete with the new giants. There are very few financial resources if we want to [start] our own business. [The government] is deregulating the market but there are lots of things that need reforming."

Despite this, a crop of homespun businesses is emerging. Many of them are Burmese natives who have returned to their estranged homeland bursting with ideas. Such an example can be found in the fifth-floor apartment of a nondescript Yangon block – the last place you'd expect to find a New York-style fashion operation. Here, designer Mo Hom and several assistants cut and sew swathes of silks next to racks of creations for her first Asian boutique, opening in Singapore later this year.

It's a long way from the world Mo Hom built when she left Burma a decade ago to study fashion design in New York. She worked for various fashion houses before opening her own boutique Lotus Hom in Soho in 2011.

Even as the business was taking off, Burma's rapid opening in 2012 appeared to be the "perfect moment" to re-engage with her home country. "I wanted to be part of it and to contribute to Burma's development," she says.

Not long after, she closed up in New York and returned to launch an entirely new range of "Made in Myanmar" creations in Yangon's first professional fashion show in early 2013. Mo Hom's clothes include high-end silks and fine linens from Shan state, with minimalist, clean lines, sold at Yangon's exclusive Governor's Residence hotel and in the new Singapore boutique. She is also branching out into food and has launched a range of packaged, organic homemade dishes based on her Shan traditions, which sell through Citymart, the country's leading supermarket chain.

04

01 Shwe Sa Bwe chefs
02 François Stoupan, owner of Shwe Sa Bwe
03 Union Bar and Grill
04 Nico Elliott, founder of Union Bar and Grill
05 Pote Lee and Tun Hlaing, founders of Water Library, Yangon
06 Water Library
07 Bar at Water Library
08 Water Library entrance
09 Coffee Club, Yangon
10 Fashion designer Mo Hom
11 Shwedagon Pagoda

05 06

07 08

09

The new wave

The arrival of Water Library, a gourmet restaurant and cocktail bar in a sprawling colonial mansion in an affluent part of central Yangon, is a discreet yet powerful symbol of Burma's international emergence. Diners can easily pay $150 (€110) a head for dinner and drinks here. With training from chefs who have worked at Copenhagen's acclaimed Noma restaurant, it has already made a mark with distinctive, elaborate cuisine and cocktails created by Italian bartender Mirko Gardelliano.

It is also an important symbol for Pote Lee, a Burma-born publishing tycoon, who is re-engaging with his country after decades away – not just with high-end restaurants but also a range of philanthropic programmes including supplying educational resources to schools and institutions. "I want to give back to this country. I left in my late teens but it gave me so much," he says. Lee left Burma for Bangkok and landed a scholarship to study engineering. He specialised in water systems but soon realised that books were his passion.

After setting up a textbook publishing company with his Thai wife Yoon, he turned to his other great love – fine food and wine. It seemed a logical fit to call his first restaurant Water Library. "It brings together all the things I love," he says. He is now rapidly expanding the Thailand restaurant empire, even as he moves into Burma.

Is Yangon ready for Water Library? "Most definitely," he says. "There is money here and discerning people who want the best of everything when they dine out – and I want to be the best of the best."
mywaterlibrary.com

Foreign interest

Corporate giants have been piling into Burma since sanctions were lifted in 2012. Japan lent $3.2bn (€2.36bn) to build a special economic zone and deep-sea port in Dawei. Nissan plans to build a car assembly plant. US giants Cisco, PepsiCo and Visa have set up shop and Coca-Cola opened a Yangon factory in June. Yet a new report says that Chinese investment has plummeted. Two Chinese projects – the Myitsone dam and the Letpadaung copper mine – were suspended after local protests. But Chinese firms have built a $2.5bn (€1.84bn) oil and gas pipeline to supply China's Yunnan province.

10 11

01

02   03

One untold story of the democratisation process in Burma has been the return of the Burmese who fled abroad during the era of military rule. Of those who cut their teeth in businesses overseas, many have returned to invest in their homeland as the government loosens its grip on the economy and liberalisation gains pace. They are also a part of the changing face of Yangon and seek the same indulgences as the newly arrived Westerners.

Sébastien Rabeux, store manager for The Warehouse, a French-owned wine distributor that sells only imported produce and that last year moved into a property on Bogyoke Aung San Road, says he recently made a $3,200 (€2,390) sale to a Burmese businessman. "Burma is the best place in Asia to start a business, but you have to get here now," he says. "At the moment the market is young; by next year the competition will have grown and it may be too late."

There's no doubt that entrepreneurs in Burma are still finding their feet as investors flood in. Yet the food scene in Yangon has become both a barometer and agent of change. At one outfit, the Yangon Bakehouse, former female prisoners and factory employees are trained as cooks and readied for employment in the city's kitchens. Co-founder Heatherly Bucher says the women of the Bakehouse are part of "a lost generation" whose livelihoods were curbed by a junta that failed to provide the most basic social protections. Bucher says, "For the first time Burma sees that there can be benefits from entrepreneurship. The environment encourages creative thinking and this didn't exist before." — (M)

Click return

It has been a long road for Thaung Su Nyein, a rising media and IT executive and one of Burma's most successful young entrepreneurs. In the 1990s, Thaung Su Nyein left New York in his final year of computer science studies to catch a new opening back home. He arrived back in Yangon 13 years ago with just $5,000 (€3,697) to invest and a dream to start the country's first internet café. "When I arrived I discovered internet cafés were illegal, so the best way to proceed seemed to be to set up magazines about the internet and technology."

That enterprise, which began on a shoestring with just seven employees, has grown into an empire of nearly 450 staff and a multi-million dollar turnover. Along the way were tragedies, including the death of his father, a former foreign minister, who was imprisoned under dictator Than Shwe and died in jail in 2009.

Even so, Thaung Su Nyein has built a business that spans Seven Media, with publications including a daily and weekly newspaper, magazines and Information Matrix, which is involved in the telecoms and software businesses. The next phase is to capitalise on what he calls the "new connected era" as Burma upgrades its internet. "This is creating a whole new market for digital plays," he says.

04   05

06

01   Yangon Bakehouse
02   Bakehouse staff including Kelly Macdonald (third from right)
03   Lunch hour at Yangon Bakehouse
04   Sébastien Rabeux, store manager of The Warehouse
05   The Warehouse
06   Thaung Su Nyein, managing director and founder of Information Matrix
07   Su Yi Lwiz, journalist at Information Matrix

07

BMW i3

Launched in July, the BMW i3 is the definitive statement on what urban cars should be: sharply designed, intelligent and fully electric. Every detail has been optimised for its purpose, from the distinctive kidney grille front to the BMW i Connected-Drive Services navigation system.

BMW i8

The BMW i8 has revolutionised the world of sports cars by packing cutting-edge BMW EfficientDynamics technology within a sleek design with dynamic proportions. Its hybrid concept allows for a thrilling driving experience while managing the emissions values of a compact vehicle.

VISION AND DRIVE

BMW i.

LOOKING THE PART

The BMW i3 may not be the first fully electric car on the market but it has set itself apart by keeping an eye on clean aesthetics and intelligent technologies.

ELECTRIC DREAM
eDRIVE

The BMW i3's eDrive is the latest development as part of the BMW EfficientDynamics technology; emissions free, it offers a near-silent driving experience. The BMW i3's agile electric motor is fuelled by the lithium-ion high-voltage battery and, intelligently managed, offers maximum efficiency: a fully charged car covers up to 160km.

READY TO GO
CHARGING

Powering up the BMW i3 is fuss free thanks to the option of using either a standard electrical socket or a BMW Wallbox. By installing the Wallbox Pure home-charging system, the i3 takes three to six hours to reach 80 per cent capacity. On the road, the navigation system helps drivers locate an official charging station.

THE WAY FORWARD
CONNECTIVITY

Stay in control with the BMW i3's navigation system and smartphone app: BMW i ConnectedDrive Services. Its range assistant and dynamic-range map charts out the most efficient route to your destination, factoring in battery charge, traffic and topographical conditions. It also shows you the nearest parking space.

BMW i3

Sustainable design makes the BMW i3 ideal for urban environments. Its long wheelbase hints at the roominess of the passenger compartment, accessible through opposing doors.

BMW i
×
MONOCLE

PERFECT SYNERGY

The BMW i8 is proof that performance and sustainability are not opposing forces – its hybrid engine system makes it one of the most innovative sports cars on the market.

COMBINED POWER PERFORMANCE

The BMW i8's superb driving experience boils down to its state-of-the-art hybrid system. The BMW's petrol engine is enhanced by the electrical boost from the motor, which saves on fuel consumption and translates to a system output of 266kW and acceleration of 0-100km/h in 4.2 seconds.

LAP OF LUXURY INTERIOR

Inside the BMW i8, all the elements are impressively light and dynamically positioned. Seats are designed for comfort and support – even on those abrupt turns – and drivers can choose naturally tanned leather interiors, proving that sustainability doesn't have to mean a dearth of premium products.

BUILT TO LAST LIFEDRIVE

The BMW i8, like the BMW i3, benefits from the LifeDrive architecture that epitomises weight-optimised construction. It has an aluminium chassis and its ultra-light passenger cell is made from high-strength carbon fibre, resulting in reduced weight, a higher level of safety and a vastly improved driving performance.

BMW i8

Unmistakably sporty, the BMW i8's surfaces and lines layer to create a sense of agility. Its scissor doors swing upwards, accentuating the car's aerodynamic body shell.

BMW i.

BMW i3

The BMW i3 signifies a turning point in the evolution of electric cars. Made with the urban dweller in mind, the vehicle reduces noise and air pollution, helps drivers plan the most efficient routes around the city, has ample range to accomplish all of the day's errands and guarantees driving pleasure.

BMW i8

Embodying premium mobility from its aesthetics to its range of driving options, the BMW i8 has upped the ante in the world of sports cars. It is a truly versatile vehicle that, thanks to its sporty nature, is equally comfortable in the city or heading off to the country in style to escape the daily grind.

Two cars so different in appearance yet fulfilling the same goal: electrifying driving pleasure combined with maximum efficiency.

BMW i.

If the hat fits
Tibet
Tibet has become the biggest importer of the Akubra, an Australian-made hat commonly worn by outback stockmen. The recent popularity has been attributed to the Dalai Lama wearing one during a trip to Adelaide.

Radar waves
Canada [SHIPPING]

The icy sea lanes of northern Canada will always be treacherous but a new type of radar technology is helping icebreakers, exploration companies and coastguards to find a clear path. The Sigma S6 Ice Navigator developed by Rutter, a Newfoundland company, sifts through the noise of traditional radar returns. It picks out the small variant sizes of iceberg – growlers, bergy bits and other rogue chunks – that can wreak havoc on unsuspecting vessels, causing costly and dangerous setbacks.

"When we look at ice, it's not just a matter of whether you're seeing it," says Rutter's CEO Fraser Edison. "You're trying to figure out its characteristics, its age and its thickness. There's a whole calamity of different things that all these companies are going to need to know as they go into the Arctic."

The technology is used by Newfoundland's offshore-oil industry and both the Canadian Coast Guard and the Royal Navy in the UK. The latter recently used a Sigma-equipped vessel to guide a stricken cruise ship in Antarctic waters to safety.

As nations increasingly try to protect their sovereignty in the North and seismic survey vessels continue the hunt for the Arctic's vast oil reserves, Edison hopes that Rutter's technology will help with both exploration and environmental protection. The next generation of Sigma technology may be sophisticated enough to detect oil within ice. "That's the new frontier for us," says Edison. "Get in and clean up spills as quickly as possible to minimise damage to the environment." — PTP

Buying power
Hong Kong [RETAIL]

Help is on the way for the small retailers of Hong Kong. With rents high and mall culture dominating the scene, the advertising firm Ogilvy has launched a service that allows shoppers to scan the barcodes of products they like and find information about similar, independently designed items to complement them. *Shop Elsewhere* allows designers to recommend their peers while the app provides street directions. David Paysant, managing director of OgilvyAction in Hong Kong, believes it will draw focus offline and out of malls. "Hong Kong has many small shops tucked away in local neighbourhoods with a lot to offer," he says. — VL

Ed Kean
Iceberg hunter
Canada

Ed Kean, a fifth-generation sea captain, lassoes icebergs bobbing towards St John's, Newfoundland. His haul – iceberg water – is highly sought after for its crisp, untainted taste.

How did you start harvesting icebergs?
We worked in fisheries before and used icebergs to pack fish. In the 1980s the government came up with new regulations requiring that all the water in the ice be checked. We discovered that iceberg water is the purest. Then in 1997 the Canadian Iceberg Vodka Corporation came to us with the idea of making vodka from icebergs.

Is iceberg water just a fad?
Our initial harvest was 200 tonnes and everybody figured it would be a fad but sales just keep climbing. Our clients include Auk Island Winery and Quidi Vidi Brewing Company, which makes iceberg beer just outside St John's. My crew now provides 1.5 million litres of iceberg water a year.

Will you be exporting it?
The market is growing but there's a lot of red tape when going into different countries. — JZL

Clear vision
Austria [OPTICALS]

Austrian family-owned business Swarovski Optik has been making high-precision specialist kit for hunters, military types and ornithologists since 1949. Its binoculars, telescopes, rifle-scopes and night-vision instruments are all made in a small factory in the village of Absam in the Tyrolean Mountains.

Now the company is seeking to move into the luxury leisure market by teaming up with high-end travel companies to promote its products as a sightseeing tool. Its new "Pocket journal" website encourages users to pack a pair of pocket binoculars on trips to the likes of Paris, Madrid or the tennis in the hope of snagging new customers not usually found twitching in the wilds. — DEP

Clean slate
Timor-Leste [COMMUNITY]

Nearly 15 years after Timor-Leste gained independence from Indonesia, poverty and a weak economy continue to affect growth. In response to this, the Hummingfish Foundation set up by Daniel Groshong, a veteran war journalist, has set out to nurture local eco-friendly businesses.

"Not only do we aim to alleviate poverty, a core belief for us is to create opportunities with nature conservation in mind," says Groshong. In 2010, the Hummingfish Foundation set up a small workshop in Timor-Leste to support a group of young women who call themselves Ai-Funan (*pictured above right*), which means "flower" in Tetun, to establish a soap-making business. The hands-on enterprise

not only empowers women in a country where gender equality is not prevalent but has also created an opportunity for sustainable economic development. Groshong hopes Ai-Funan can serve as a model for other developing countries. — VL

Turning the table
Belgium
Saluc, the Belgian company that makes 80 per cent of the world's billiard balls, is trying to snooker its competition with a new line of innovative pool tables. The so-called Fusiontables come in sleek, minimalist designs and double as dining surfaces.

High flyers
Arctic [AVIATION]

Aviation in the far north can be extreme. A lack of suitable Tarmac in much of the Arctic means helicopters are essential for jumping from taiga to tundra and all points between. It's no surprise, then, that many chopper operators have popped up above the 60th parallel and there are a few we've determined to be masters of their domain.

Whether you're based in Alaska, northern Canada, Greenland or far-northern Europe, these four brands cover a significant portion of the Arctic – and their pilots have the stories to prove it. "I once landed a happy couple at the highest fell in Finland where they were married," says Heliflite pilot Pekka Tuononen, "I actually got to witness a wedding."

Heliflite, like its industry peers, can safely plant a whirlybird on just about any tract of tundra, and for any purpose – nuptial or not. And the economic model of catering for both business and pleasure keeps these birds flying all-year round. — TMA

Arctic chopper charters:

01 Heliflite, Sodankylä, Finland: Whether you're a film crew looking for an icy backdrop or a holidaymaker, Heliflite have the gear (and the guts) to put you down above the Arctic Circle.

02 Era Helicopters, Anchorage, Alaska: These birds give sight-seeing tours over Alaska but also assist in mineral exploration trips.

03 Air Greenland, Nuuk, Greenland: The Danish territory's flag carrier also runs a fleet of red helicopters (*pictured above*) for regular service and the occasional search-and-rescue mission.

04 Great Slave Helicopters, Yellowknife, Northwest Territories, Canada: Helping keep remote communities connected and providing vital industrial transport, Great Slave has the whole of Arctic Canada covered.

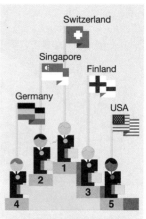

Since 2004 the World Economic Forum has ranked nations by how easy it is to do business. This year's rankings are as shown above.

Sweet success
China [FOOD]

When New Zealand cookie company Mrs Higgins developed an offshoot brand for China it didn't expect its product line-up to change so dramatically. "Chinese customers prefer less sweet varieties," says Greg Harvey, licensee of Mrs Higgins' Chinese arm – Kiwi Cookies, which now has three Shanghai shops. "We worked with Mrs Higgins to alter our product mix to suit; ending some chocolate lines, introducing low-sugar cookies and developing savoury options such as Parmesan and oregano," says Harvey.

Tailoring flavours hasn't been the only challenge during the launch. "There are numerous regulatory hurdles in China," says Harvey. "None of these are insurmountable, though a high degree of patience is required."

But perhaps the biggest challenge was securing the right Shanghai locations. "We are a small, non-famous brand competing against big global names for the right spots," says Harvey. After months on the ground, Kiwi Cookies has secured sought-after shop fronts in Jinqiao, Lujiazui, and Gubei districts. — LS

For more news, business insight and profiles of unlikely ventures and exciting new start-ups, tune in to our weekly show, *The Entrepreneurs*, on Monocle 24. Visit monocle.com for a full schedule.

Positive growth
Canada [FARMING]

In a bid to reverse escalating food prices in the remote town of Norman Wells, 145km south of the Arctic Circle in Canada, local grower Doug Whiteman decided to grow his own potatoes to cut import costs. His mixture of silt, sand, clay and acidic topsoil has been slowly reaping returns in the unforgiving environment, yielding 13,600kg of potatoes in 2012. By eliminating shipping costs, his products are half the price of imports. "As local interest and government support increase, the future of Arctic farming is very bright," he says. — JZL

Carving a niche
UK [FURNITURE]

Furniture producer Olivier Geoffroy's East London-based company, Unto This Last, is bringing small, affordable industry back to the historic manufacturing areas of town. "Our philosophy is all about how a localised economy makes sense, how technology can enable the artisan to come back to the city," he says.

Customers can choose from over 2,000 products and the latest 3D-modelling software allows all orders to be carved on-site in the atelier's back room – a "mini-factory" where customers can see their order being made. Efficiency in pricing arises from the logistics — there's no packaging, storage or transport costs and deliveries are made by electric van. — AVF

STILL LIFE: DAVID SYKES, ILLUSTRATORS: SARAH VANBELLE, STUDIO TIPI. INFOGRAPHICS: LAMOSCA

**Kvadrat
by Camper.
Why upholster
a shoe?
Why not?**

alicante
PUERTO DE SALIDA
VUELTA AL MUNDO A VELA

PLANTING THE SEEDS
—*Copenhagen*

01

02

Preface

Royal Copenhagen is one of the world's oldest companies and Flora Danica porcelain is its flagship product. Handpainting the delicate dinner set is an art that takes years of intensive training. We meet the master and her apprentice.

WRITER
Michael Booth

PHOTOGRAPHER
Jan Søndergaard

03

"I've never been good with computers or books but I've always been able to draw," says 28-year-old Royal Copenhagen Flora Danica apprentice, Jacqueline Tranemose Fredericia. "I saw an advert in my technical college newspaper inviting people to apply to study porcelain painting [a course in partnership with Royal Copenhagen] and I thought it sounded exciting. Actually, I thought, 'Yes, that's what I want to do for the rest of my life.'"

Flora Danica is the flagship product of Royal Copenhagen porcelain, a hand-made dinner service with a tradition dating back more than two centuries. Jacqueline must learn to paint more than 3,000 indigenous plants during an initial, intensively supervised training period of four years – she is in her third year – followed by 10 years' on-the-job training.

In 2008, Royal Copenhagen moved virtually all production of its trademark "blue fluted" porcelain to Thailand but the 12 Flora Danica artisans remained in Denmark. One casts the white porcelain pieces and 11 do the painting.

"I just don't think they will ever be able to make Flora Danica anywhere else," says Jacqueline's "master", Judith Sørensen. "You have to have the Danish light when you paint, you have to be surrounded by the Danish plants, to get them inside you. You must always be thinking, 'How would this flower be in

nature? How would its curves be; how would it be in this light?'"

"Yes, and you have to express your feelings," adds Jacqueline. After two years working together at close quarters, master and apprentice often finish each other's sentences. "Each day is different: the light and your mood are reflected in how you paint on any given day. And I always hear Judith's voice in my head when I am working."

The mutual respect and affection between the two women is clear: Judith acknowledges the compliment with a shy nod. "It's like handwriting, it's so individual," says the older woman. "It's your soul, you could say. I can always tell who has painted a piece."

Out of 10 students accepted for the course, Jacqueline is the only one who became an apprentice at Royal Copenhagen's base in the Copenhagen suburb of Glostrup. It is time and labour-intensive work. Painters copy original prints from the 18th-century Danish botanical guide *Flora Danica*, inspired by the work of Carl Linnaeus in Sweden. The first

04

A royal history

Royal Copenhagen porcelain was founded in Copenhagen in 1775, its trademark blue and white designs inspired by Chinese glazed porcelain. Under royal patronage from the start, Royal Copenhagen introduced its flagship Flora Danica range in 1790. The first set of 1,802 pieces took 12 years to complete and was delivered to Crown Prince Frederik as a gift for Catherine the Great. The 1,503 surviving pieces are on display at Rosenborg Castle, Copenhagen (apprentice Jacqueline visits it at least once a year), and are still used for state dinners.

Master
Judith Sørensen

1947 Born in Copenhagen
1964 Painter at Royal
Copenhagen
1976 Mother/music teacher
1982 Over-glaze painter at
Royal Copenhagen

Apprentice
*Jacqueline Trane-
mose Fredericia*

1985 Born in Frederiksberg
2010 Graduates Gladsaxe
Technical School, be-
comes 'Blue painter'
at Royal Copenhagen
2011 Becomes Flora
Danica apprentice

Judith Sørensen
Master
43 years at Royal Copenhagen

Jacqueline Tranemose Fredericia
Apprentice
3 years at Royal Copenhagen

05 06 07

01 Royal Copenhagen headquarters
02 'Flora Danica' botanical guide volumes
03 Apprentice watches the master at work
04 Page from 'Flora Danica'
05 Handpainting a dinner plate
06 The plant name is added to the back
07 Flora Danica serving plate
08 Artist's workstation

08

stage, the drawing, has been the greatest challenge for Jacqueline. "You do the first drawing with pen and ink and it has to be so accurate. You copy from the original prints but you have to scale it by eye to fit the piece you are working on.

The artists use old-fashioned pen and ink before filling in using water-based colours and brushes made from soft cow and reindeer hair. They begin with a first layer of the lightest paints, then a second darker, and a third darker still, before adding the gilding. They must fire the piece after each stage and, at the end, all the painters gather to quality check one another's work. "A bit frightening, that bit," says Jacqueline. A plate can take between one and two days, a tureen up to a week. Prices range from around €700 for a plate to the most expensive piece, the Ice Bell, at €30,000, although the sky is the limit for bespoke orders.

When Judith trained in the 1960s her instructors were all men but that changed during the 1980s and, today, all the Flora Danica painters are women. When she began working for Royal Copenhagen, its main markets were the US, UK and Scandinavia. Today, the Far East (predominantly China, Taiwan and Japan) is a growing market, along with the Middle East and Russia. They have not made a full dinner service for a few years but sales are on the up and, fittingly given the company's royal roots, each year they supply the Danish queen with around 50 Christmas gift plates.

When Judith says she plans to retire in a couple of years, panic flashes across her apprentice's face. "Oh, no, I can't work on my own yet. I've only done two years of painting flowers and six months of gilding. I will probably spend the rest of my life doing this. It has become a second home, a second family for me. Judith and I are different but we enjoy each other's company." When asked whether she can foresee a point in the future where she might introduce her own innovations, Jacqueline shakes her head vigorously: "No, no. My work shows my personality, but for me, it will always be about honouring what Judith has taught me." — (M)

PRIVATE V.C. WHITE
FOR THE BRAVE

19 17

MANCHESTER 27 JUNE 1917 ENGLAND

ICONIC BRITISH MADE
Clothing

OFFICIAL WORKWEAR SUPPLIER OF GOODWOOD REVIVAL

THE PRIVATE WHITE V.C. RACING TEAM
SIR CHRIS HOY

MANCHESTER	LONDON	TOKYO
—	—	—
1 Cottenham Lane	*55 Lambs Conduit St*	*5-14-1 Minami_*
Salford	*London*	*Aoyama Minato-Ku*
M3 7LJ	*WC1N 3NB*	*Tokyo, Japan*

www.privatewhitevc.com

01 View of Yellowknife
from Pilot's Monument
in Old Town
02 CBC North's
headquarters
03 Reporter Kate Kyle

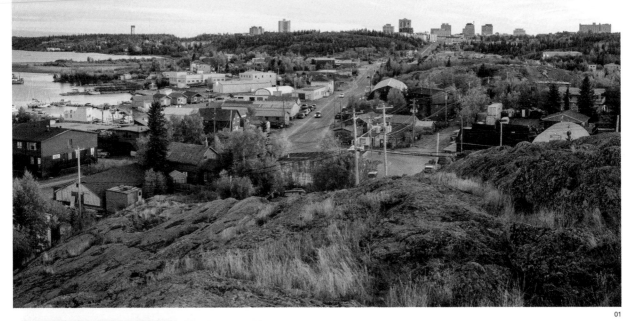

01

02

THE NORTH LIVES HERE
—*Canada*

Preface
The intrepid team at Canadian radio and TV service CBC North report on everything from whale hunting to minus 40C weather conditions. Monocle braves the harsh terrain to meet them at their headquarters in Yellowknife.

WRITER
Nelly Gocheva

PHOTOGRAPHER
Grant Harder

As the plane descends over the sun-glossed surface of Great Slave Lake in September, the scenery of spruces, endless water and rock stretches out for as far as your eyes can see. "Welcome to beautiful Yellowknife!" an overexcited air hostess announces in the midst of the "oohs!" and "ahhs!" of passengers. Less than a month from now and we would have been welcomed by snow and ice.

Set amid Canadian wilderness, 400km below the Arctic circle, Yellowknife is the largest city in the far north of the country. Here winters are harsh, summers alluring yet brief. The 20,000-strong capital of the Northwest Territories (NWT) is mostly made up of miners and government workers. It is also home to the CBC North services.

"Wintertime you can't drive much further north from Yellowknife," says Janice Stein, our host and CBC North managing director, upon our arrival at the station's headquarters on the outskirts of the town. "We only fly up north from here – that's the only way to commute when temperatures fall below minus 40C." She's quick to kill our romanticised expectations of journalists getting around on a husky sledge. "And we don't live in igloos," she adds.

CBC North has been in Yellowknife since the late 1950s. Today it covers the area of the three northern territories of Yukon, Northwest Territories and

03

ALASKA

Iqaluit •

Yellowknife

Whitehorse •   ◆

CANADA

NORTH PACIFIC OCEAN

Vancouver

UNITED
STATES

01

02   03

04

05

Nunavut and caters to just over 100,000 viewers. CBC North carries daily TV and radio programming in English, French and eight aboriginal languages. Besides the primary production centre in Yellowknife there are additional offices in Yukon's Whitehorse and Nunavut's Iqaluit.

The 1970s purpose-built Yellowknife headquarters are now home to one TV and two radio studios, accommodating a total of 60 full-time staff. On the day of MONOCLE's visit, reporters and producers are working on the editorial floor under colourful Inuit-inspired banners that hang from the ceiling, clearly indicating specific departments: Current Affairs, News, Television.

"The north is a hot spot for career advancement. The advantages of going to a smaller station are that you get to do everything – reporting on breaking stories, writing your own script, producing news bulletins. In the end you get a broad range of experience and expertise," says Stein of her young staff. "Sometimes we receive 50 to 60 applications for one opening – ranging from college graduates to more experienced staff within CBC. Usually these are two to three yearlong placements, then reporters either move on or fall in love with the North and stay," adds Stein, who moved to the city in 2011 after spending six years as a managing editor of the CBC office in Newfoundland and Labrador.

"When you come up here there is an opportunity to travel, to explore places you never thought you'd go to," says radio presenter Loren McGinnis, who hails from North Vancouver. "I always wanted to live up north and Yellowknife is still quite accessible." McGinnis's show *The Trailbreaker* airs every weekday from 06.00 to 08.00 and has covered everything from cultural appropriation to pollution from Alberta's oilsands. "Working here is a bit like being a foreign correspondent: you travel a lot and you work in a multicultural society, both story and language-wise."

On the TV side, as a part of the larger CBC Television network, CBC North essentially airs the same programming as the main broadcaster with some noteworthy exceptions: the hour-long evening news programme *CBC News Northbeat* with anchor Randy Henderson and the preceding 30-minute daily newscast in Inuktitut, *Igalaaq*, presented by Rassi Nashalik. Launched in 1995, they remain the key TV programmes of the northern service. Nashalik herself is considered Yellowknife's broadcasting star – every night she simultaneously side-translates the English script in her mother tongue, Inuktitut.

"The programme comes out more naturally this way and reaches way more aboriginal viewers," says the Ottawa-trained interpreter, who moved to Yellowknife in 1979 to work as a translator for the NWT government. "*Igalaaq* covers a lot of Inuit stories. Working with the communities is tricky; it takes time

01	CBC North's HQ	06	Hilary Bird, producer
02	Janice Stein, managing director	07	Randy Henderson and Rassi Nashalik
03	Inuit-inspired banner	08	CBC North dishes
04	Senior radio producer Peter Skinner	09	NWT licence plate
05	Upstairs at CBC North	10	Robyn Burns and Mitch Wiles ready for action

08

09

CBC North
High North headlines

01 'Yukon buys giant scissors': The Yukon government has purchased a pair of oversized golden scissors for use in ribbon-cutting ceremonies.

02 'Arctic ice level rebounds from record 2012 low': The amount of ice in the Arctic Ocean shrank this summer to the sixth lowest level.

03 'First commercial hauler travels Northwest Passage': Danish ship carrying coal entered western end of the Northwest Passage.

04 'Yukon minister Currie Dixon to visit Fort McMurray': Economic development minister to attend forum in Alberta's oil patch.

10

to win them over – make them trust you and share things with you."

Quick to prove her point is TV producer Hilary Bird. The Torontonian moved to Yellowknife drawn by the charms of working with the First Nations. "There is a special way of approaching aboriginal communities. You have to meet the chiefs and get their blessing first." In the harsh realities of the Arctic, knowing the traditions and playing by the rules can often save your life, as Bird found out last winter when working on a story about a small community farther north. "We had set up a camp for the night. Halfway through my interview, I could suddenly hear people screaming 'bear, bear!' Women, kids and the elderly gathered in the middle of the camp, while the men grabbed their guns and formed a protective circle around us," Bird recalls, minutes before the start of *Igalaaq*.

Lights are up, mics are on. Nashalik takes her spot in front of the cameras for yet another live instalment of *Igalaaq*. In the next 30 minutes the grid of screens in the studio becomes a rollercoaster of

01

02

> The weather can become the leading story. Sometimes we get so much snow that even the snowmobiles won't work

changing backgrounds and scenarios. Images of whale hunting or icebreakers stuck in the Northwest Passage alternate with political discussions about Canada's Arctic sovereignty claims, or a report on the art troves in Yellowknife's Gallery of the Midnight Sun.

Undoubtedly, the office takes its tagline "The North lives here" (an adopted version of CBC's "Canada lives here") very seriously. Journalists here cover all things local – from polar-bear attacks to aboriginal elections. Stories about an elder chasing a moose on snowshoes, a burned-down post office in Fort Good Hope or imminent severe blizzard conditions would all make it into the news segment.

"We have to report for and about the North – this is our main purpose. We

01 Robyn Burns and Mitch Wiles report from Gallery of the Midnight Sun
02 Technical director Allan Gofenko at the controls with a gridwall of screens
03 Meteorologist Christy Climenhaga gets ready for the weather forecast
04 Loren McGinnis, host of weekday morning show 'The Trailbreaker' on CBC North Radio
05 Fingers at the ready in

the radio control room
06 CBC North reporter/ editor Sonja Koenig gives a news update
07 Things are looking windy for Yellowknife

03

Yellowknife media

"We don't have a daily newspaper here," says CBC North's TV producer Hilary Bird. "CBC strives to somehow fulfil this gap with its daily news bulletin." However, given its small size and remoteness, Yellowknife comes packed with media outlets. Besides CBC North, also covering the city and the region are CKLB radio station, owned by the Native Communications Society of the Northwest Territories; CJCD radio, the only licensed commercial station in Yellowknife, run by Vista Broadcast Group; and the weekly *Northwest Territories News/North* newspaper. On the magazine side there is *Up Here*. Published eight times a year, it covers curious stories from the Northern areas, while its monthly spin-off *Up Here Business* magazine is dedicated to more entrepreneurial-spirited readers.

Yellowknife is also home to two of History Channel's reality TV hits: *Ice Pilots* and *Ice Road Truckers*. Now in its fifth season, *Ice Pilots* portrays family-run airline Buffalo Airways, while *Ice Road Truckers*, in its seventh season, follows truck drivers on seasonal routes across the frozen lakes and rivers in Alaska and Canada's Arctic territories. Rumours persist of a big-screen version.

04

05

06

deliver not just breaking news but also vital information to the local communities," Bird says. "Wintertime, when temperatures fall to minus 40C, the weather becomes the leading story. Sometimes we get so much snow here that even the snowmobiles won't work. But we have to make it to the office, especially in tough weather conditions; this is when locals need to know what's going on out there the most. In this sense, we see ourselves as community service TV."

Reporting on stories that are thousands of miles away remains a main challenge for the office. Until recently, CBC North operated smaller bureaux and rebroadcasters in the Canadian Arctic, which ensured coverage to a vast majority of communities. Following major budget cuts mandated by CBC last year most of them shut down.

"This could impact our programming. For us, it means adjustments in how we deliver service and in the territory that our journalists can cover," Stein explains. "The changes present a major challenge and we have to adapt

07

01 Juanita Taylor doing a live check-in
02 Poster at CBC North
03 What to pack when heading north, including satellite phone, hand warmers and pencils (pen ink would freeze)
04 Arctic-proven parkas and boots are a must

02

03

in order not to lose presence in those communities."

One of them is Cambridge Bay on Victoria Island in Nunavut. To make up for the closure of the local service, journalist Kate Kyle is now being sent there once a month to follow up on developing stories or gather breaking news. Kyle is among the few reporters here who have also trained as videographers.

With return trips to remote northern communities costing as much as CA$4,000 (€2,900), flying north is clearly CBC North's main expense. Depending on the urgency of the story the reporters usually use commercial flights. However, breaking news requires chartered services, typically provided by local Air Tindi and one of its seven-seater float planes. "We are usually allowed to carry five pieces of luggage at no extra charge including all our shooting gear and personal items," Kyle explains.

Astute packing skills are crucial. Kyle learned it the hard way. "I was on my way to Cambridge Bay on a commercial flight. The thing is that often these double up as cargo flights - carrying food and medical supplies to the communities. So the moment they reach capacity, they'd just leave the remaining bags behind. This particular time it happened to be all my clothing," recalls the ex-CBC

Newfoundland and Labrador reporter. "From then on, I'd always pack a warm sweater, a pair of gloves and underwear in my camera bag that I carry on board with me, and some mascara; after all I'm getting in front of the camera," she adds with a smile.

A multi-day survival course and risk assessment is always in place before tough reporting trips. Stein outlines the ground rules: "When you send your reporters out there in severe blizzard conditions and snowfall warnings you have to make sure they have all the right gear; do they know how to drive a snowmobile, or set up a tent?"

Another working week in Yellowknife is gone when we leave the office on Friday evening. The few remaining staff are wrapping up before joining the rest of the team in The Black Knight Pub, a local watering hole in the city's centre.

"It's the community spirit – this is the amazing thing about Yellowknife," says Bird on her way out. "Things might get tough in the wintertime but we are all in it together." — (M)

04

Executive decisions

Today's Victorinox suits all types. For the business traveller it's as much about style as it is amenity: from the Swiss made (and Swiss quality) timepiece and a smart jacket to luggage that is durable, light and stylish.

THE NEW EXPLORERS

In the late 19th century, when Swiss soldiers needed a tool to help them in the field, Carl Elsener, a Swiss cutler, came up with the Officer's Knife. Patented in 1897, it is the original Swiss Army Knife. The brand's range has since grown to include travel and fashion but its core values of quality and innovation remain.

Q&A
Carl Elsener IV
CEO, Victorinox

Elsener has been CEO of Victorinox since 2007. In 2008, the firm won the Company Prize from the Swiss Environmental Trust for its "Green Shield" ecology programme. It has an annual turnover of over €400m.

Monocle: *What does the VX brand represent?*
Carl Elsener: As the founder's great-grandson, to me the Victorinox brand is a wonderful and precious legacy, one that arises in the interplay of tradition and innovation.

M: *How have you maintained the integrity of the brand and how do you balance stability with dynamism?*
CE: Hasty, ill-considered expansion can put a brand at risk. This is something we wish to avoid. We try to bring the energy of the market into the company and take from it that which is sustainable, reflects our culture and contributes to our brand values.

M: *How would you describe your management style?*
CE: Everything that I expect from my employees and teams is first and foremost something I have to expect of myself. That's why I believe setting a good example is the most important part of successfully managing people. When I look back at our company history, the people in the key leadership positions have always been strong role models. But I like to delegate authority to my employees; my leadership style embodies the highly developed Swiss sense of democracy.

01 Victorinox Airboss Mechanical Chronograph Titanium Timepiece Aviator-inspired precision.

02 Travel Blazer Lightweight poly blazer is just as good for long-haul as it is for the boardroom.

03 Hybri-Lite Travel Gear Hard-working luggage that won't weigh you down – or let you down.

HOW THE STORY BEGAN

Karl Elsener opened his cutlery workshop in Ibach-Schwyz, with the support of his mother Victoria, in 1884. Seven years later, Elsener began delivering knives for the Swiss Army. However, it wasn't until 1921 that the brand name was truly born: Victorinox combines the name of his mother with "-inox", derived from the French word "inoxydable", meaning stainless.

The city slicker

In the city, functionality and fashion are in balance. From Raeburn's forward-looking PROTECT range paying homage to the company's heritage (with a stylised camouflage) to the more classic and elegant.

Q&A
Christopher Raeburn
Artistic director, fashion

Independent British designer Raeburn started collaborating with Victorinox in 2010 and this year was appointed artistic director for fashion.

Monocle: *What does the Victorinox brand represent for you?*
Christopher Raeburn: The appeal is the fact that it's family owned and has such integrity. You only have to visit the factory and headquarters in Ibach to understand what Victorinox is all about. Full of character and characters, it's a big part of what makes the firm unique.
M: *What are you hoping to accomplish as artistic director of Victorinox fashion?*
CR: Victorinox fashion is already well respected so the mission is about evolution, not revolution. For me it's about bringing more authenticity into the products; focusing our attention on detail, fabric quality and construction will be important but I also see great opportunities to push more innovative approaches with the look books, moving image and online.

Q&A
François Nunez
Product director, timepieces

Nunez has been with Victorinox Swiss Army since 2010, after working for Rado and Georg Jensen.

Monocle: *How do you translate the brand into its watch design?*
François Nunez: The idea is not about directly transferring the features of an Army Knife to a watch. Rather, the idea is to try to capture the essence of the brand. We try to incorporate not only the values of the firm but also the legitimacy provided by the Swiss watchmaking tradition.
M: *What distinguishes Victorinox's timepieces from the rest of the brand?*
FN: It's a very young brand: while the Swiss Army Knife has been around for over a century, the watches will be produced for only 25 years from next year. There is a different responsibility, which doesn't have to do with heritage but with aligning the brand to what today's customers want, the way they experience the world. And it's important the watches are resistant; they have to last a long time and have a design that won't date.

01 Ulm Turtleneck Sweater
Slimline, warm and versatile, for nights out and evenings in.

02 Women's Officer Coat
There's military precision in the details with this bonded wool coat.

03 Small Slimline Laptop Carrier
This padded case will keep your computer perfectly protected.

INNOVATION IN MANUFACTURING

At Victorinox HQ in Ibach-Schwyz, the company uses the heat generated in its production plant to help boost the thermostat of 120 apartments in the village and nearly its entire facility through a heating distribution network. Victorinox also reuses around 600 tonnes of metal-shavings sludge from its own production.

The nomad

It's the raison-d'être of the brand: portable, useful tools for even the lightest packer. From the iconic Swiss Army Knife to mountaineering tools, Victorinox meets a range of challenges faced by the ardent adventurer.

01 PROTECT Insulated Parka
Both tough and clever, this doubles as a hard-wearing bag.
02 SwissChamp Army Knife
Your constant companion.

The master chef

The Victorinox knife isn't just for outdoor escapades. The company was founded with a range of household and professional kitchen knives, such as the Chef's Knife – ideal for perfecting your rösti-making skills.

01 The Cutler Hoodie
Reversible zip jacket for two looks in one.
02 8" Chef's Knife
The sharpest blades and beautiful, ergonomic handles.

ESSENTIAL KIT

01 Travel Blazer
Wool blend with full-bodied quilted lining in recycled fabrics.
02 AirBoss Mechanical Chronograph Titanium
Stainless-steel case, triple-coated anti-reflective sapphire crystal, water-resistant to 100 metres.
03 Swiss Unlimited Energy Eau de Cologne
Notes of cedar, amber and musk in a bottle made of unbreakable recycled material.
04 SwissChamp Army Knife
Combines 33 high-quality tools.
05 Santoku Knives
High-carbon stainless steel blades with Swiss ceramic ergonomic handles.

VAST RANGE

There are over 360 models in the Victorinox range of Swiss Army Knives but the cutlery range is even more impressive, with 540 different pieces. The Victorinox Ilbach factory sends out 120,000 products a day, split between household and professional knives, Swiss Army Knives and other multitools.

VICTORINOX.COM

A GLOBAL VOYAGE

Both in terms of product range and commercial presence, Victorinox is a dynamic and forward-moving company. It has adapted itself to a global market, with storefronts the world over and growing markets across four continents. But one thing remains: the quality is definitely Swiss.

KEY MARKETS
—

Anchored by flagship stores in London and Geneva, Europe remains central to the Victorinox brand. Switzerland and Germany have remained the biggest markets for Swiss Army Knives for years. But across the Atlantic, Victorinox timepieces and travel gear have made their mark in North America: the US and Canada now account for 25 per cent of the company's turnover. *Up next: Victorinox is continuing with bricks-and-mortar retail, planning to expand its retail presence in key locations in the US.*

EMERGING MARKETS

With its Brazilian subsidiary tripling its turnover in three years, a strong presence in Mexico's leading department stores and a flow of mainland Chinese picking up its goods in Hong Kong, it's clear Victorinox is making serious gains beyond its strongholds. It's a key brand name in Japan – the quality, innovation, functionality and design connects with consumers there. *Victorinox is represented by subsidiaries in nine countries: Brazil, Chile, Hong Kong, India, Japan, Mexico, Poland, the US and Canada.*

Q&A
Veronika Elsener
Global Brand Management, Victorinox

Monocle: *Why is Victorinox a force in newer markets?*
Veronika Elsener: To be successful in new markets we have to offer products that mean something to the consumer, as well as compelling services. We're also taking our products into the digital age. That's what defines our era: young people have grown up with it.
M: *How has the market for Victorinox changed?*
VE: At one time pocket knives were for everyman. Now we have bespoke versions designed to the highest standard for specific life circumstances, situations and occupational environments (such as a USB stick).
M: *What is key to establishing the brand with new consumers and markets?*
VE: The Swiss Army Knife has always been the beacon and the gateway to discovering our brand. It is the symbol of Swiss quality and reliability and remains an object of desire.

USA
Victorinox launched its fashion line in the US in 2001, the same year it opened its shop in SoHo

Norway
Victorinox sells more kitchen knives in Norway than anywhere else in the world (6 percent of global sales)

Switzerland
Victorinox has a flagship store in Geneva and its first airside-travel shop in Zürich airport

Japan
Victorinox has 37 brand stores in Japan. The first subsidiary was opened in the country in 1992

Panama
Fragrance is a top-seller here, contributing 5 per cent to global turnover

Brazil
Brazil is home to the brand's biggest social-media fan base

Hong Kong
The company has 138 staff in Hong Kong and China, the largest of its emerging markets

- Flagship stores
- Key markets
- Emerging markets

CANADA · USA · NEW YORK · MEXICO · PANAMA · BRAZIL · NORWAY · SWEDEN · DENMARK · London, UK · FRANCE · Düsseldorf, GERMANY · Köln · Zürich · Geneva, SWITZERLAND · UAE · MALAYSIA · SINGAPORE · INDONESIA · S.KOREA · CHINA · HONG KONG · Tokyo, JAPAN

01 Birgir Jón 'Biggi' Birgisson at work mastering recordings
02 Sundlaugin studio by the water's edge

01

02

HIGH ART —*Global*

Preface
From music to radio dramas to art exhibitions, the nations of the North are exploring their own cultural identities while making the world sit up and take notice. Monocle takes a look at what some of them have to offer.

01
Sundlaugin
Reykjavík

Of the eight High North nations, Iceland is something of a plucky pop overachiever when it comes to music. Its identity on the world stage – one whose successes range from the inquisitive and probing melodic explorations of Björk, to the recent global chart-bothering sounds of Of Monsters and Men, to the epic, critically acclaimed soundscapes of Sigur Rós – is an accessible blend of playful experimentation. And you feel those sounds, produced by a national population the size of a middling Canadian town, would get made whether the world was listening or not.

"I think it's just the Icelandic method of how we make music," says Birgir Jón 'Biggi' Birgisson, engineer and co-owner of Sundlaugin recording studio in Mosfellsbær on the northern outskirts of Reykjavík. "There's no restriction. Everything is allowed." Biggi is trying to sum up the local sound and also what it is that draws musicians from around the world to his boxy concrete studio straddling a geothermal stream in a suburb of the city. The studio was built as an indoor swimming pool in the 1930s for workers at a nearby wool company. After being drained in the 1960s it was used as storage, then a gallery, but fell into disrepair. The space was bought by Sigur Rós in

01

A sound system

02 03

04

US musician Julianna Barwick's recent album *Nepenthe* – all ethereal, swirling noise and hushed emotive harmonies – was partly recorded at Sundlaugin.

"Sundlaugin is also known as the Swimming Pool studio. You have to walk down the steps into the recording space – the pool – and the mixing console is above upstairs. It's just a beautiful building, a really well-crafted space with lots of light and natural reverb. We recorded a young choir there but it was nothing formal, they're just friends of Biggi and [US artist and musician] Alex Somers, who produced the record. The experience stuck with me and Iceland itself is stunning too – full of colours I'd never even seen before. There's no way you can't be swept up in that." — TH

the early 2000s and is still co-owned by the band's former keyboardist, Kjartan Sveinsson, along with Biggi.

Today, Icelandic musicians Jónas Sigurdsson and Ómar Gudjónsson stop by to complete mastering on a new recording. It means a lot of sitting hunched over the controls of the 1979 Neve production console – a warm-sounding mixing desk imported from a French radio station that was dropped into Sundlaugin through the roof when its new owners realised it wouldn't fit through the front door. The console looks out over the "pool" area below, now empty of water and filled instead with instruments such as Wurlitzer keyboards, Hohner pianos, a dulcitone (a compact, piano-like instrument) and vintage guitars from long-disappeared US producers such as Silvertone and Kay.

"I've got way too many of course," says Sveinsson. "I've stopped doing it now but I used to go to flea markets and simply buy shit guitars," he says, laughing. "Everyone has a Fender or a Gibson and you can presume how they'll sound. But we want something different."

The homely charm found at Sundlaugin is grown from an Icelandic music scene that is still small enough for everyone to know one another. "For me it all sounds really different," says Biggi. "I think that's its strength. Bands aren't mimicking others' sounds. There's no room for that. You might end up meeting them in a bar and it'd just be awkward."

05

And you never know when you might need friends. When the studio was flooded last year due to a burst mains, artists and carpenters from the surrounding community rallied around. The influence of Swiss artist Dieter Roth, a one-time resident of Mosfellsbær and whose former assistant Gunnar Helgason oversaw the reconstruction, can be felt throughout.

"It's not sterile. It can be a little bit shabby sometimes but that's alright," says Sveinsson of the end result. "It's about feeling good when you're trying to be creative." — TH

01 Musician Julianna Barwick
02 A tape recorder that artist Dieter Roth once owned and a stack of his work
03 Vintage electric and acoustic guitars with amps
04 Studio vestibule
05 Biggi (Birgir Jón Birgisson), co-owner and engineer at the studio

01 02

03 04

05 06

01 Main writer Christian
   Gamst Miller-Harris
02 Actors Christopher
   Læssø, Thomas W
   Gabrielsson and direc-
   tor Lasse Lindsteen
   going through a scene
03 The director and actors
   recording in the studio
04 The production plan
05 The studio mixing desk
06 Sound engineer Helga
   Prip with actress
   Sanne Broberg
07 DR Byen seen from
   the outside

07

02

DR Radio
Copenhagen

The history of Denmark and its former territory, the now self-governing state, Greenland, is not without its controversies and residual bitterness. Denmark's national broadcaster, DR (Danmarks Radio), however, is addressing a more positive episode from this particular colonial relationship in its latest radio drama, *Menneskenes Land* (Land of Men): the ultimately ill-fated expedition of the Danish missionary, Hans Egede, to the Arctic island's east coast in 1721.

"It is an incredibly dramatic story," says the six-part drama's English-born writer Christian Gamst Miller-Harris. "Egede comes across as a complete drama queen in his memoir. He is strong willed and overpoweringly devout but also melodramatic, so we had to tone him down to make him believable."

Norwegian-born Egede – the "Apostle of Greenland" – was sent by the Danish king to colonise Greenland and persuade the indigenous population of the virtues of Christianity. This he did with fire-and-brimstone teaching and a level of compassion that was unusual for missionaries of the time. He also founded Nuuk, Greenland's capital.

"This is a story of colonisation," admits Miller-Harris. "That's never really positive but Egede did it in a Danish way, with no soldiers or massacres. It would have been worse if the Dutch, who were hunting whales up there at the time, had got there first. For me the story of Denmark and Greenland is neither 100 per cent horror, nor 100 per cent glory."

01

02

01 Thomas W Gabrielsson
     reading his lines
02 Sound engineer Helga
     Prip, director Lasse
     Lindsteen and producer
     Dorthe Riis at work in
     the studio

Miller-Harris and his co-writer, Lasse Lindsteen (whose idea the drama was), chose to avoid overt reflections on the current state of affairs between Denmark and Greenland but they were sensitive to the historical issues. "Though one of the Greenlanders in the cast was concerned we were depicting Egede as too benevolent at the start, they have found it quite balanced," says Miller-Harris.

"It was also a challenge to evoke the landscape of Greenland on radio," continues Miller-Harris, "but we tell the story from the viewpoint of Egede looking back on that period in his life in retirement in the Danish countryside and he described it vividly."

For the cast, DR is drawing on its – understandably limited – repertory company, so you'll hear voices from its global television hit *Forbrydelsen* (The Killing): Thomas W Gabrielsson, in the title role, and Henrik Birch, as the captain of the ship that bore Egede to Greenland.

Menneskenes Land airs from 23 October on P1 and will be available as a podcast on dr.dk/radiodrama. — MB

03
Louisiana Museum of Modern Art
Copenhagen

Preface: *Poul Erik Tøjner, director of the Louisiana Museum of Modern Art, talks us through its new exhibition, ARCTIC, which runs until 2 February 2014.*

The Arctic's not just about endeavour, triumph and failure against the elements. Artists have always been intrigued, too – eager to track and investigate the motives of solo explorers, resource-hungry nations and, sometimes, just to stare into the wilderness.

In contemporary artist John Bock's video work "Skipholt", we follow an explorer who struggles across a rugged landscape wearing a monstrous, poorly mounted backpack. The film recalls the finest images of noble, heroic men of great stamina, for it is based on one of our basic stories: "Man Against Nature". But it delivers these icons up to parody.

We find another wanderer in Darren Almond's video work "Arctic Pull", in which parody has now been replaced by a monomaniac struggling through a blizzard in the dark, where everything is an indistinguishable mass around the protagonist who pulls a sledge across what can barely be called a landscape.

Finally we find a third wayfarer in Guido van der Werve's video "Nummer Acht, Everything is going to be alright" (Number Eight, Everything…). Here we meet a man who is walking across the ice towards us, closely followed by an ultra-modern icebreaker that ploughs up a channel where the man has just passed.

Three men in a landscape, all images of "Man in the Wilderness" – and above all images with antecedents in a history that is itself full of images. Louisiana's major ARCTIC show presents this historical background as a foundational narrative of our culture and its use of images and ideas, myths and stagings.

For that, more than anything else, is what the story of the conquest of the Arctic and the race to the North Pole was: a major cultural project that called upon the greatest and most reckless heroes, including some who should have been wiser than they were. Heroes who were also nourished and supported by a culture that for 150 years, from the late 1700s on, hungered for a meeting with the unknown, and staged its own desire afterwards in the great images and stories and ideas that came to define the magical North – often before they had even been there.

ARCTIC encompasses a basic narrative of our culture and its use of images and constructs, myths and mise en scènes. Louisiana's exhibition unfolds the dream of the far North as image, cultural ideal and scientific field. From the Romantic Age to present-day contemporary art, the Arctic plays a role as a place where everything terminates in endless whiteness and something new can begin. An untouched landscape, terrifying and dangerous. Once a territory to be conquered, the Arctic today could well mark the perimeter of human power. — (M)

THE WORLD'S
FIRST LUXURY COMPACT
DIGITAL CAMERA

The New Stellar from Hasselblad
Everything else is history.

HASSELBLAD

Join the Guardians of The Glenlivet to select a new whisky

The Glenlivet is the original distiller of single malt scotch whisky, a spirit of distinction marked by its production at a single distillery. Its reputation has been nurtured since George Smith first created it in 1824 in the remote Livet Valley. From its roots as the first licensed distillery in the parish of Glenlivet, this is the "single malt that started it all". The fundamental components of natural spring water, copper stills, oak casks and a dedication to flawless craftsmanship have remained the same ever since.

The Glenlivet's master distiller Alan Winchester (*right*) oversees the making of every drop of this refined whisky. With decades of experience he has honed his craft – now he presents three distinctive new whiskies for your enjoyment. They have been created with the distillery's exceptional cask collection – renowned for its unparalleled smoothness – and will set sail on a tasting tour across the globe this autumn, offering the chance for whisky enthusiasts to help determine the future of The Glenlivet by selecting which will become its next limited-edition single malt.

It's the latest offering in a rich heritage dating back almost two centuries to the very heart of Speyside, Scotland's foremost whisky-making region – and the choice will be made by The Guardians of The Glenlivet.

A global community
The creation of a new single malt whisky.

The Guardians of The Glenlivet are a collection of individuals who are deeply passionate about craft and connoisseurship. They know their favourite cities and brands, for example, and are confident in their cultivated sense of personal style. They are, essentially, very much guardians of good taste.

Now, in recognition of those discerning tastes, The Glenlivet is offering the opportunity for its members to take responsibility for defining a new expression in single malt whisky – they aren't called the Guardians for nothing.

New experiences

Discover your common passions.

Register to become a Guardian on The Glenlivet website and your selection from the tastes created by master distiller Alan Winchester will play a huge part in defining the next phase of the famous brand's journey.

Each of the three flavours created by The Glenlivet for the global tour has a unique taste. Will your choice be the timeless and enduring craft of a Classic, a regard for the past renewed with a contemporary twist of Revival or the invigorating, enigmatic depth of the Exotic? (Take a look at the panel on the right to further whet your appetite.)

Tasting events offered around the world by The Glenlivet over the coming months will allow Guardians to come together to celebrate their common passions and pursuits. They will also be able to unite their good taste to write the next chapter of The Glenlivet's legacy.

All the votes will be tallied and a range of opinions shared on *theglenlivet.com*. This will offer a rare meeting of minds and a place for Guardians to share their views and offer their opinions on interests including culture, art, design and style.

Three exceptional tastes

01 *Classic:* Two centuries of craft are concentrated in a taste bursting with soft, sweet caramel and toffee notes yet tempered by the smooth, cultured, runny honeyed tones of experience. For those who trust traditions passed down through generations to produce flavours imbued with the richness of history.

02 *Revival:* Relish for modern life is flavoured with a hint of nostalgia, a value for the history of craft and a regard for the style of the past. So the nose of this whisky adds a dash of fruitiness to a rich vanilla and runny honey. When opposites collide, such as in a Scottish highland castle revived with modern luxuries, it's then that Revival is born.

03 *Exotic:* Appealing to curious minds always seeking out the local cuisine, savouring unusual flavours and looking for new experiences. Tastes of enigmatic depth – plump juicy raisins seasoned with the subtle warmth of spice – hint at seasonal winds of far-off lands and distant climes.

 24 *Tune in: Aperitivo*

Aperitivo premieres weekdays at 17.00 London time with an hour of relaxed conversation, news and opinion to complement a refined single malt such as The Glenlivet. Monocle's editors, contributors and correspondents share their views with agenda-setters from the realms of business, design, culture and fashion. It is this blend of eclectic tastes and social settings that makes us proud of the association between The Glenlivet and *Aperitivo*. monocle.com/radio

Books

Graphic novels
The Encyclopedia of Early Earth
Isabel Greenberg

There's much myth and magic in the pages of this colossal work of illustrated fiction that riffs on the style of the epic: Norse legend, Greek mythology, the Bible, Steinbeck. Taking stories that appear familiar and then giving God the head of a bird might sound like too much Pharaoh-fancying, but Greenberg's words and pictures sparkle with so much arched-eyebrowed wit, we're dissolving the monasteries as we write. — RB

Fiction
Hello Mr Bones/ Goodbye Mr Rat
Patrick McCabe

McCabe is pretty bloody horrible. Here he is, pulling out the nasty stops for a vaguely Halloween-ish double-biller chiller about a thoroughly contemporary couple who unleash absolute evil, and a tale told from the point of view of a deceased IRA bomber watching over his American ex-lover as she travels to Ireland to scatter his ashes. Take a deep breath, go without lunch; enjoy. — RB

Travel
An Armenian Sketchbook
Vasily Grossman

Written two years before his death, Jewish-Russian novelist Grossman's last book is a travel memoir as he journeys through Armenia to edit Rachiya Kochar's war novel. Spontaneous and candid in tone, *An Armenian Sketchbook* is as much about the host country as it is a self-portrait of a man well aware of his own mortality. — JZL

Culture
The View from the Train
Patrick Keiller

Keiller is best known for his *Robinson* films – those psychogeographic tours with the unseen urban wanderer. This book is a collection of essays from which much of Keiller's creation gets his wonderful shtick on cityscape, politics, architecture and the art of the perambulatory fugue. "The View" marks everyday spaces as worthy of moment and monument beautifully; I just wish Keiller, the world's most lively urban thinker, did more. — RB

Restaurants
Eating at Hotel Il Pellicano
Juergen Teller/ Will Self

That old joint's plumped its pillows, ironed its napkins and lent two arch chroniclers of wasted glamour keys to its best suites and seats at its groaningest table. Of course it's hagiography, in Self's hungry prologue and Teller's technicolor-porno food snaps, but such a lush treatment of lushness also makes sense: why be ironic all the time? I'd like to see more heiresses slurping negronis poolside but these actual dolcis stay sweet all the same. — RB

ON RECORD
Sounds from around the world

CATE LE BON's newest and dearest, named MUG MUSEUM for its hominess vibe, is the essence of the season in which it is released: the mellow fruitfulness of autumn is in abundance (despite being cut in ever-summer LA). There's a bittersweetness and an addictive accessibility to these 10 tracks that put you in mind of Karen Dalton or Sandy Denny. This is a classic in waiting.

BACK TO LAND is just what this percussive, rootsy yet psychedelic slice of magpie-eyed wonder from WOODEN SHJIPS sounds like – if, that is, that ground is strewn with lost jewels, lucky-dime guitar picks and exotic tail feathers. Feedback, ancient echo and a lazy Hammond make for a brooding, beautiful, be-fuzzed soundtrack to some sort of late, great American road movie.

I love it when a plan comes together: Matthew Caws (of Nada Surf) and Juliana Hatfield (of, well, Juliana Hatfield) – two of the quieter heroes of indie Americana – have high-fived for long enough to make a wonderful thing. As MINOR ALPS, GET THERE is a guitar-driven, hook-laden, his 'n' her's harmony-drenched stormer that's that perfect kind of American record: where plaid meets biker jacket. Bliss.

When is a MIDLAKE not a Midlake? When the former singer and lead songwriter quits. And yet ANTIPHON, new from the Texan four-piece, is a lovely piece of work that lacks a little of the gauzy-prog influence and madrigal magic of the earlier records but gains a rockier edge that might just propel them into, if not the mainstream then the um, midstream. — RB

Q&A

Sebastian Junger
Film director
London

War photographer Tim Hetherington died covering the Libyan conflict in 2011. In *Which Way Is the Frontline From Here?*, Sebastian Junger – who co-directed the documentary *Restrepo* with Hetherington in 2010 – draws an intimate portrait of the man, the artist and the friend behind the camera.

When and why did you decide to make this film?
I wanted to answer my own questions about why and how Tim died. More importantly, I realised he was no longer around to affect the world in his incredible way and that the next best thing would be for someone to make a film about him so at least that could continue affecting the world in his place. Tim was much more of an artist than he was a hard-news reporter. So I also wanted to give people a glimpse into his working process.

Is making a documentary about a close friend who has died much harder than treating any other topic?
The grieving process has its own pace and I don't think you can slow it down or hurry it. As a

war reporter, I'm used to treating very upsetting topics and that means shutting off your emotions completely when needed. So I was able to toggle back and forth between my very real feelings of grief and my professional mindset.

It seems like you also wanted to tell the story of your friendship in the film.
His death got me out of war and, theoretically at least, might have saved my life. I wanted to acknowledge that. Tim never made the decision to stop reporting wars. I think he hoped that at some point in his life he would be able to stop. I was supposed to go on assignment with him in Libya but I had to pull out for personal reasons. Moments after finding out about his death there, I decided that I would not go back at all. — DD

STILL LIFE: DAVID SYKES

PIQUADRO

TECH INSIDE

ENGINEERED
FOR BUSINESS

BLUE SQUARE, functional and soft arrangement for your documents. The best Italian leather will cherish your emotions.
Convertible to backpack. Take elegance and style to the office with you.

www.piquadro.it

MILAN, ROME, BARCELONA, HONG KONG, MOSCOW, SHANGHAI, TAIPEI, PARIS, BEIJING

PERFECT TASTE

Tapas are a quintessential element of Spanish culture and the standard is especially high in the capital. We sit back and enjoy a glass of wine with the chefs and restaurants that are pushing the boundaries.
ESMADRID.COM

SERIES 06 / 07

THE INGREDIENTS
1 MAKE IT FRESH

Recent restoration and modernisation of some of the oldest covered markets in the city have turned the likes of the *Mercado de San Miguel* and the *Mercado de San Antón* into top tapas destinations. Their central locations (San Miguel is just off Plaza Mayor and San Antón hidden behind the main shopping street of Gran Vía) make the markets a convenient stop day or evening.

THE ESTABLISHED INDIVIDUAL
IN THE BLOOD

Childhood friends *Hussi Istambuli* and brothers *Nino* and *Santi Redruello* are the trio behind La Gabinoteca, a tapas restaurant revered for its unique approach to traditional dishes. "One day we all sat at Nino and Santi's kitchen table where we used to dine as children and talked about opening a restaurant," says Istambuli. Creations include "El Potito" (egg with potato and truffle cooked and served in a jar) and an equally inventive dessert menu.

3

THE INNOVATIVE
MODERN MASTERS

Since its opening in 2009, *Arzábal* has been quick to gain attention in the culinary scene prompting the team, led by Álvaro Castellanos and Iván Morales, to open a second joint nearby a year later to meet popular demand. With its modern twist on classic dishes and 260 wines, the tavern is a perfect meeting spot for a light lunch or evenings after a stroll at the nearby Retiro Park.

4

THE ACCESSIBLE
LOCAL FAVOURITE

Having opened in November 2010, *La Cesta de Recoletos* sources only the best products, which arrive at the restaurant every day from markets and small producers around Spain. With fish from the Asturias and an extensive selection of wines by the glass, La Cesta has locals clamouring for its seasonal, affordable menu that includes classic dishes of tortilla and *croquetas de jamón* fried to perfection.

THE EVENT
THE ART OF FOOD

Madrid's *Gastrofestival* is the culinary event of the year and the next edition takes place 24 January to 9 February 2014. Restaurants, bars, cooking schools and art galleries dish out a range of food-related activities for everyone.

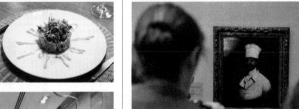

¡MADRID!

WELL HUNG
Installation nation
Auckland [GALLERY]

Hopkinson Mossman occupies two crisp white rooms in a 1960s warehouse in Auckland's Arch Hill suburb. Co-director Sarah Hopkinson (*pictured above left*) opened the gallery just three years ago. Since then the space has come to define a young, shifting group of contemporary New Zealand artists with an interest in installations – including Peter Robinson (*whose "Acktion" sculpture is shown above right*) and Andrew Barber who, as of 18 October, has painted the floor of the gallery in a sort of seascape, accompanied by semaphore flags.

"The timing just felt right for some of the artists that I wanted to work with," says Hopkinson. Key to that is a determinedly international outlook. "There's a way for a New Zealand dealer to be international in a way that hasn't really been done before," she adds.

Hopkinson and the gallery's co-director Danae Mossman – who joined last year after many years at London's White Cube – work in an intensive, collaborative way with a small stable of artists. "We try to help the artists make the work they want to make," says Mossman. "Everything else fits around that." Hopkinson adds, "It's more like an agent relationship. We're involved in every part of their career."

After Andrew Barber, an exhibition of digital prints by Dane Mitchell will be on display at Hopkinson Mossman from 22 November to 21 December. — SFG
hopkinsonmossman.com

The art of war
Stockholm [AUCTION]

Stockholms Auktionsverk
12 November
Founded in 1674 by the governor of Stockholm, Baron Claes Rålamb, Stockholms Auktionsverk predates more recognisable names such as Christie's and Sotheby's. On 12 November, the auction house holds its seventh contemporary auction with almost 600 post-Second World War art and design works from around the world.

"The interest in contemporary art has grown these past years," says Sofie Sedvall, Stockholms Auktionsverk's curator of modern art and photography. Last season saw American photographer and director Cindy Sherman's "Untitled Film Still #24", in which she photographs herself personifying the image of the modern city girl, sold for SEK640,000 (€74,111).

Helping draw in art connoisseurs to this month's auction is Italian avant-garde painter Lucio Fontana's "Concetto Spaziale, Attese". Sedvall expects it to fetch up to SEK10m (€1.16m). — JZL
auktionsverket.com

The highlights
"Nelson Mandela" (*top*)
Hans Gedda, 1990
Gelatin silver photography
Estimate: SEK300,000 (€34,750) to SEK350,000 (€40,535)

"Concetto Spaziale, Attese" (*bottom*)
Lucio Fontana, 1968
Waterpaint on canvas
Estimate: SEK8m (€930,000) to SEK10m (€1.16m)

Q&A

Nicoletta Fiorucci
Fiorucci
Art Trust
London

Nicoletta Fiorucci, an Italian collector now based in London, is founder of the Fiorucci Art Trust, which promotes contemporary art in locations ranging from the UK to the island of Stromboli, north of Sicily.

What's the role of the Fiorucci Art Trust?
I've been a collector for many years and I could buy, buy, buy but it's not a complete relationship with art. The trust organises a summer of events – *Volcano Extravaganza* – in Stromboli and supports organisations in London such as Gasworks, Studio Voltaire, Chisenhale Gallery and Serpentine Gallery. This year in Stromboli, Lucy McKenzie curated the summer with Milovan Farronato. The year before it was Nick Mauss. We offer the artist space, travel expenses and food, and don't ask anything in return. All the events are free and open to the public.

Is collecting all about business?
No. I don't think of it as business. I think it's quite an illusion to think the value of a work will increase in the future because someone had a show here or there. These stories around pieces are interesting but they're not reliable. For me, collecting is a way of life and my personality evolves with it – it's my identity.

What inspires that approach?
It's the same as for objects in daily life. We are about to enter into a period where we cannot consume so much because the planet's resources are limited. We have to learn more from experience than physicality. For artists, performance art is becoming more and more popular as it creates emotional experiences and provokes strong reactions in viewers. If you talk to artists such as Tino Sehgal, who won the Golden Lion at the Venice Biennale, they don't want to merely produce objects. We either listen to their ideas or art just becomes decoration. —— TH
fiorucciartrust.com

THE LIBERATION OF ART

Hand signed, limited editions. From over 160 recognized artists. At affordable prices.

DAVID BURTON | TRUNK ARCHIVE
Italian Wedding

$710

23.6 x 36.6 inch

limited & hand signed
56/150

TRN96

SUBSCRIBE TODAY

10 ISSUES
+ TWO NEWSPAPERS (MEDITERRANEO + ALPINO)
+ CANVAS TOTE = £90

To order now or for more information on subscribing visit monocle.com/subscribe or email subscriptions@monocle.com

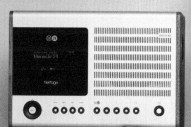

1

Monocle magazine: Your briefing on Affairs, Business, Culture and Design. Ten issues a year delivered to your doc

Website: Films, magazine archives and more, plus access to Monocle 24 radio on monocle.com

2

Monocle newspapers: Our special editions, Mediterraneo and Alpino, are published twice a year – for days on the sun-lounger and cosy fireside reading

3

Canvas tote: Created by the Monocle design team and available only for subscribers. Join the club and swing our olive Rootote

THE BENEFITS

Monocle designed and branded tote.

10 per cent discount at Monocle shops (not applicable to Japan or online).

Full online access to the latest issue and magazine archive on desktop, tablet and mobile.

Temporary suspension available – ideal for holidays, long foreign assignments or when moving cities.

Shipping costs included regardless of location.

01

02

03

CROWNING GLORY
—New York

Preface
Reopening this month
after a lengthy renovation
project, the Queens Museum
of Art will feature its boldest
and riskiest line-up since
the 1990s. Plus some table
tennis tournaments.

WRITER
Pauline Eiferman

PHOTOGRAPHER
Aaron Wojack

Walk into the Queens Museum of Art
and you are likely to come across a
middle-aged man playing table tennis.
Far from being a conceptual performer,
this man will be the museum director,
Tom Finkelpearl. "The idea is not to
play against the public but to play with
the public," he explains with a large grin.
"I'm going to warm people up and try to
really understand why they're here."

Table tennis is only a small part of
the complete overhaul taking place at
the Queens Museum, set to reopen in
November. It's been eight years since
plans for the renovation were announced
and construction is on its final stretch.

A $68m (€50m) project, led by Grim-
shaw Architects, doubles the museum's
footprint to 9,750 sq m by extending into
a former ice rink (the building's idiosyn-
crasies have always defined it). An atrium
sits at the centre under a bright skylight
enhanced by a hanging glass structure.

In the suite of the new square-shaped
galleries, the founder of the Bread and
Puppet Theater, Peter Schumann, and
his team are busy. The cult artist is
enjoying the rough environment. It's
hard to tell his team apart from the construction workers – they wear the same
hard hats. As Schumann brushes past
in his paint-stained denim overalls, he
whispers, "There's going to be a sailboat
here. It'll take you anywhere you want."

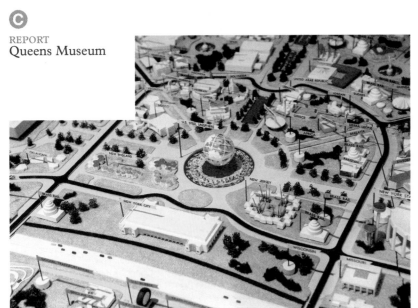

The Queens Museum:
a quick guide

Site history
1937 New York City Building designed by
Aymar Embury II
1939 Housed the New York City Pavilion
for the World's Fair
1946-1950 Home of the UN
1952 Building converted to skating rinks
1964 Hosted New York City Pavilion and
Ice Theatre for the World's Fair
1972 Queens Museum of Art created in
northern half of building

Reopening line-up
01 'The People's UN (pUN)' by Mexican
artist Pedro Reyes
02 'Queens International 2013' by artists
from around the world who live or work
in the borough
03 'The Shatterer' by Bread and Puppet
Theater founder Peter Schumann

01

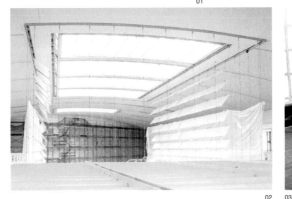

02 03

Seconds later, he's on a bucket perched on a ladder, drawing on the virgin white walls with a permanent marker.

The museum is an hour's subway ride from New York's Chelsea galleries, bordered by a highway in the middle of a park. But the renovation will address these obstacles. With five or six major exhibitions at any given time, as well as a café, a bookshop and a gift shop, Finkelpearl wants his museum to be a day-trip destination. A 60 metre-long exhibition wall facing the Grand Central Parkway will serve as a giant advertisement for the 244,000 motorists that drive by every day.

Designed to host the New York City Pavilion for the 1939 World's Fair, the building welcomed the General Assembly of the newly formed UN soon after. Almost every world leader spent time within these four walls, negotiating the partition of Palestine and creating Unicef. The World's Fair came back to the city in 1964, for which iconic steel globe the Unisphere and the Panorama – a detailed model of the city built by Robert Moses – were constructed.

By then, an ice rink occupied the southern half of the building. The Queens Museum was established in 1972 and had to make use of the rest of the space, which includes the large room that houses the Panorama. "When I arrived it was a very quirky space with idiosyncratic galleries that were 12 metres high, had multiple levels and curved walls but no light," says curator Larissa Harris, who started working here in 2009. "Having punctured the ceiling and the walls, it's just going to feel like an entirely different psychological space. A space where you can really breathe."

Queens is the most ethnically diverse urban area in the world but it is mostly ignored by the art world. True, it's home to the renowned MoMA PS1 based in Long Island City but that museum is essentially an extension of the Manhattan original. "It's in Queens, it's not of Queens," says Finkelpearl. His museum's east-facing park-side entrance, now restored to its original grandeur, includes an extended yard that provides a transitional space for those out enjoying the park.

A decade ago, Finkelpearl created "Queens International", a biennial celebration of artists who live or work in the borough – it's one of the exhibitions with which the museum is reopening. The other main shows tap into the institution's history and its attachment to social practice. It's a risky yet reflective line-up, which embodies the ethos here.

"I love art but I'm not crazy about museums," explains Finkelpearl. "I feel art deserves something better than what museums have been doing to it." — (M)
queensmuseum.org

04

Previous page
01 Peter Schumann works
on his first museum show
02 Director Tom Finkelpearl
03 The restored original
front entrance

This page
01 Model of the site during
the 1964 World's Fair
02 Skylight is enhanced
by a structure made
of sheets of glass
03 Curator Larissa Harris
04 Plaster cast of
Michaelangelo's 'Pieta'

Good look

Sunglass Hut
USA

A brand with 40 years' experience of being a leading light in a competitive market, Sunglass Hut has raised the bar yet again with the opening of a brand new store in New York's Times Square. Take a look inside…

01

Eye-catching retail
New York

There's nowhere like New York for a shopping spree and Sunglass Hut's newly opened Times Square flagship is a one-stop shop for eyewear. Offering an unrivalled range of cutting-edge frames, the space opened to a star-studded audience at this year's New York fashion week. When it comes to offering second-to-none customer service and an enviable selection of brands and styles, Persol has always taken a lead role.

02

Long view
The story so far

From its humble beginnings, Sunglass Hut has become one of the biggest specialist sunglasses retailers and now boasts some 3,000 stores around the world. Back in 1971, it would have been hard to predict that the brand's influence would grow from its small kiosk in Miami to spaces in over 20 countries around the world. Its well-appointed new retail space shows that the brand's eye for detail and commitment to good design are strong hallmarks of the company's ongoing success.

03

Well stocked
Brands and styles

As well as launching a new range of pocket-ready folding frames, Sunglass Hut's recently opened New York digs offer a stunning range of eyewear. With the shop stocking brands including Ray-Ban, Persol, Oakley, Vogue-Eyewear, Prada, Dolce & Gabbana, Ralph Lauren, Giorgio Armani and Burberry, you'll find everything from wraparounds to wayfarers. The ideal stop-off for anyone with an eye for shades, the beautifully designed shop is a spectacle in itself.

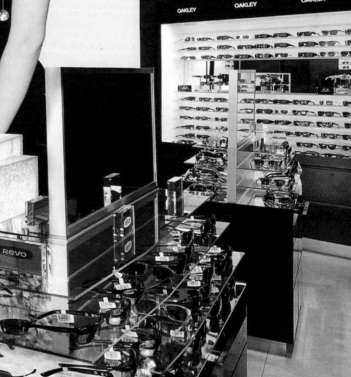

All things Arctic
Nuuk [DIGITAL]

Want to be up to date on all things Arctic but speak no Greenlandic or Danish? *Sermitsiaq* – one of Greenland's two national newspapers and leading media companies – is launching an English-language online news service, *Arctic Journal*. Its tagline is "Regional news, global perspective" with news, features, analysis and opinion pieces from across the entire Arctic region. It reports on everything from the hunt for oil and minerals to local politics, the latest research on climate change and bringing broadband to some of the most remote areas in the world.

By launching the journal, *Sermitsiaq* – which also publishes the country's other national newspaper *Atuagagdliutit* – wants to make sure it's capitalising on the growing interest in the region.

Some of the content is exclusive for the journal, penned by one of its three journalists, while other articles are translations of pieces from *Sermitsiaq* and *Atuagagdliutit.* The project is also a way of trying to find new business areas that could ultimately help finance Greenlandic news journalism. — ENA
arcticjournal.com

Winter sounds
Global [AUDIO]

A great compact speaker system arriving this winter to make any cosy igloo sound more like the cavernous interior of a corrugated tin-roofed research station – ie, a bit bigger – is the Wren V5BT. The beautifully designed speaker from the US is available in natural bamboo or rosewood and comes Bluetooth-enabled. — TH
wrensound.com

Nordic star
Karasjok [TV]

Johan Ante Utsi
Presenter, 'Oddasat'
Norway

Johan Ante Utsi is the presenter of *Oddasat*, the Nordic countries' Sami-language news programme – a joint production between Nordic public service broadcasters NRK, YLE and SVT.

On air five days a week, it reaches the Sami population in Norway, Finland and Sweden; the potential audience is almost 20 million people.

According to Utsi, "It's important to tell the Sami people about democracy, about their options in society and let them know what the different political parties in the Sami parliament offer.

"It's also important to discuss the Sami culture and the issues that affect people living in the Sami areas." What else? "Reindeer herding is central and it's also where much of our language is rooted." We're glued. — ENA

Q & A

David Castenfors
Editor in chief, Artlover
Sweden

Artlover is a Stockholm-based quarterly magazine founded by David Castenfors and Teresa Holmberg that takes a playful and unpretentious look at Swedish contemporary art. Monocle talks to the editor in chief.

How did the magazine begin?
Myself and co-founder Teresa Holmberg began the magazine in 2009. We wanted to create an art magazine that was accessible without being superficial. Art can sometimes be a little bit snobby so I wanted to open up that door and meet the people behind it.

We try to go and meet every artist in their studio or in their office and rarely use called-in press images. You don't find many installation shots from galleries in *Artlover*. It's more, "Who's doing the art and why?"

Do you only focus on the Swedish art scene?
We write mostly about the Swedish contemporary-art scene as we're based in Stockholm but we carefully select the art we find most interesting and present it to our readers in an accessible way. There are international interviews too though, and we travel as much as we can to the art fairs such as Art Basel, the Armory show in New York and Frieze. At the moment you can find *Artlover* in the main Swedish cities in galleries, museums and art centres as well as through fashion brands and designer shops.

What do you have planned for the magazine?
In April 2014, we're launching the magazine in English. We've been making the magazine for four-and-a-half years so we have a great network of museums and galleries around the world to start distributing through. — TH
artlovermagazine.com

Top title
Rovaniemi [DIGITAL]

Running the world's most northerly seven-day newspaper is not without its challenges. Covering an area the size of Belgium and the Netherlands put together, issues of *Lapin Kansa* don't get to some Lapland subscribers until dinner time. But the bright side is that there's no shortage of local issues to report on.

"Being this far up north brings its very own special questions and topics of discussion," says Antti Kokkonen, editor in chief. "Logging versus forest protection, mining and predator protection versus reindeer herding, and limitations on popular pastimes such as fishing and hunting are some of them."

The paper is headquartered in Rovaniemi in the Arctic Circle, and owned by Finnish media giant Alma Media.

"We have content in Sami, for which we receive a small subsidy from the state. We want to do our part in keeping the language vital," says Kokkonen. With the circulation of *Lapin*

Kansa slowly declining, the company is constantly trying to cut costs, distribution being a major one. Last year it carried out a trial where some of the most far-flung readers were given tablets to read the paper digitally instead. "The feedback was positive," says Kokkonen. "I myself have a holiday cabin 400km from Rovaniemi and even there the internet coverage is excellent. We save money on distribution and the readers get the magazine in the morning like everyone else." — ENA
lapinkansa.fi

SPAIN NOW!
17 October — 17 November 2013

Annual season of contemporary arts and culture from Spain in London

LONDON: A CAPITAL OF SPANISH CULTURE

From painting to dance, video art, literature and gastronomy, some serious talent is emerging from the Spanish contemporary-art scene and Spain NOW! is bringing a taste of its latest creative talent to London. In its fifth year, this exciting events season applies a special focus to the presence of art on the streets.

It will run for a month from 17 October to 17 November, in which time venues across the city will light up with exhibitions and performances; prepare for Spanish tastes to transform the city into a vibrant creative hub.

Supported by the Spanish Tourist Office in London.

OUT AND ABOUT: This season, visitors will come across art outdoors as well as indoors. A large-scale light installation by anonymous art collective Luz Interruptus will be unveiled in front of Regent's Park, while the outdoor spaces on the South Bank will be taken over by a series of flash interventions, with choreographer and performer Ana Luján Sánchez leading the finale. Visitors will also be able to view a major exhibition by Berlin-based artist Eli Cortiñas, as well as the fantastic work of 15 London-based Spanish artists that will be showcased during an open-studios weekend in November.

SO MUCH TO SEE: Other highlights will include contemporary writers Javier Montes and José Ovejero presenting their latest works and chef José Pizarro serving up culinary delights. A multiplatform art project initiated by Spain NOW!, visual artist Tracey Moberly and Dr Dacia Viejo-Rose of the University of Cambridge will also be taking place.

MULTIPLE SETTINGS: The Gallery Soho, The Hospital Club, Thirst and various artists' studios will be among the many other venues to check out.

spain-now.org.uk

Innovation. Motivation.

The new Cross Personal takes total body training to new levels of performance and style. The flowing, elliptical movement, sleek aesthetics and VISIOWEB multimedia 15.6" touch-screen offer a premium interactive experience to all users of all abilities.

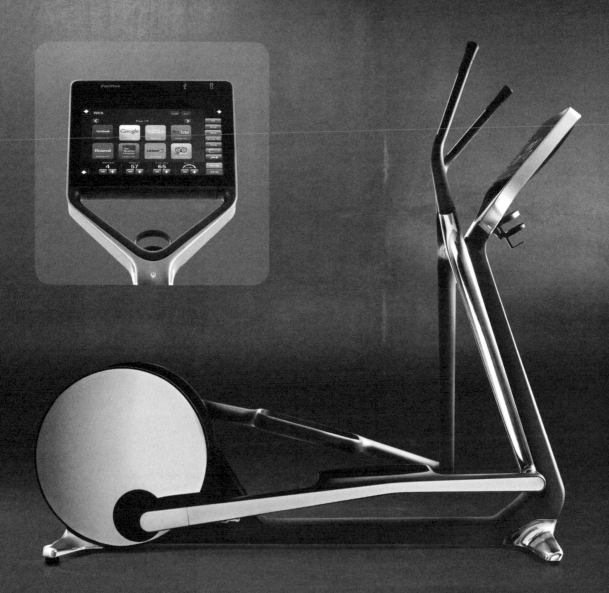

Designed by Antonio Citterio

01

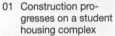

01 Construction pro-
    gresses on a student
    housing complex
02 Longyearbyen, the
    largest settlement
    in Svalbard

D
COLD FEAT
—*Svalbard*

Preface
Building in an environment
where temperatures drop to
minus 30C is no easy thing.
But in Svalbard, where the
unique developments vary from
the tent-like science centre to
the charming multicoloured
'spisshus' houses, architects
embrace the challenge.

WRITER
Tom Morris

PHOTOGRAPHER
Thomas Ekström

It's forbidden to be buried in Svalbard
– your corpse would freeze instead of de-
caying. It's also illegal to leave its biggest
settlement of Longyearbyen without a
rifle (that's the polar bears). These factors
indicate that this isn't the most sensible
place to live. Yet a mix of 2,700 residents,
science researchers and tourism workers
populate this chilly place, located almost
two hours beyond the mainland of northern Norway. In the winter, temperatures
plummet to minus 30C and the sun dis-
appears for four months. In the summer,
the sun shines all night. Life goes on
though and a canny troupe of architects
and engineers have become experts in
designing civic buildings and homes that
are braced for these challenges.

"I'm quite fascinated by the extreme
factors of the place. It gives you architectural possibilities," says Håkon Vigsnæs, a founding partner of Oslo-based
practice Jarmund/Vigsnæs (JVA). "The
resistance of the place gives you new
possibilities of making relevant architecture with a new look that's related to
the ground," he says.

02

JVA was responsible for two of the larger civic buildings in Longyearbyen – and certainly the dinky town's most impressive. The first was built in 1998 – an angled glass and zinc building for the governor of Svalbard's administration – and a second commission soon followed for an extension to the University Centre in Svalbard. The practice, established in 1996, has long been known for its emotive architectural responses to nature. For this one, the unique natural surroundings demanded a unique design approach.

"The 'tent' is the best construction because of the constant danger of very fine snow getting in," says Vigsnæs, who designed the copper-wrapped science centre so that its exterior walls and roof merge into one protective whole. "It's better to wrap it all up – like a tent."

The shape of the imposing building, close to the Longyearbyen waterfront, encourages snow to gust around it rather than collect in one area or sit on the roof for six months at a time; the weight of snow in deep winter is equal to two layers of parked cars sitting on top of a building.

"We had to be sure that the snow wouldn't pile up anywhere. If it did, we would make envelopes of closed air next to the ground, which would heat it up," says Vigsnæs, who used special digital programmes to predict where snow would settle.

Keeping the ground ice-cold is the name of the game in these parts. The layer of permafrost – frozen soil essentially – goes as deep as approximately 400 metres below ground. If the permafrost thaws, foundations get wobbly and buildings are inclined to collapse. And there are plenty of people keen on making sure that doesn't happen.

Multiconsult is a Norwegian engineering company with a small outpost in Longyearbyen. Petter Skattum heads up the office and is an expert on permafrost. "This is just frozen ground, until it gets deep enough to feel the heat of the centre [of the Earth]," he says. "Every year, the top layer thaws and makes it complicated. The climate change will increase the depth [of thawed permafrost]. That will be interesting," he says.

01

02   03

A brief history

Svalbard is an archipelago situated between 74 and 81 degrees north. Nearer to the North Pole than it is to Oslo, Svalbard covers approximately 61,000 sq km (that's almost 18,000 sq km larger than Denmark). The unforgiving terrain was essentially common ground until coal was found there in the early 20th century and the Svalbard Treaty was established giving sovereignty to Norway in 1920.

There are four settlements on Svalbard: Longyearbyen is the largest, located on the relatively temperate west coast of Spitsbergen, Svalbard's largest island. Once the home of polar bears and the odd trapper, more and more people are attracted to Svalbard for mining, science research and tourism. But polar bears still outnumber humans: around 3,000 roam the islands.

04

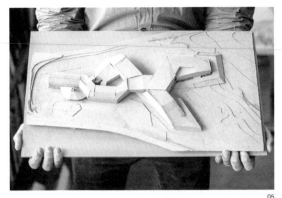

05 06

07 08

09

01 The science centre
02 Internal windows help create the feeling of an indoor campus
03 Warm wood interior
04 Science centre hallway
05 JVA's model
06 Håkon Vigsnæs
07 The governor's building
08 Inside the governor's building
09 Huset, Longyearbyen's oldest building
10 Alex H-Winge, Huset's bar and events manager

10

So that they don't warm up the permafrost underneath, almost all buildings in Longyearbyen are raised roughly 1.5 metres off the ground by stilts that extend underground up to 12 metres deep. They're traditionally made of wood; steel would act as a corridor beaming chill from the frozen ground right into the building. Stilts are also used to support the pipes that carry the heated water from the power plant into radiators across town.

Choosing building materials is an expert's game in the Arctic. JVA used zinc for the exterior of its first project in Longyearbyen, which proved tricky to keep malleable in the cold weather. Tents would be erected for builders to work in, kept warm for the zinc's benefit. "And they blew away all the time," recalls Vigsnæs. For JVA's second commission, the architects tried a different tact. "Copper is strange in the way that the material itself gets softer the colder it is, so we could extend the building season by months."

The copper science centre hugs the landscape, creating a cosy space for the 500 or so students based there, studying everything from marine biology to geophysics (science is the third biggest industry in Svalbard, after coal and tourism). Obviously, open-air Ivy League-style quads and cloisters are a no-no in Svalbard so JVA used clever tactics to create an indoor campus, with internal windows and open space between laboratories and hallways. In fact, there are more windows on the inside than the outside. "In winter, it doesn't really help you to have a large window and in summer there is too much light because the sun shines all night," says Vigsnæs. Wood panelling creates a warm, intimate environment inside the centre, while JVA was inspired by corridors in the local coal mines for the science centre's irregularly angled walls.

Of course, it's a miracle buildings in Svalbard are built at all. The construction calendar is so limited. When MONOCLE visits, two contractors from local building firm Sandmo & Svenkerud are tinkering away with hammers and nails in the bitter easterly wind that's blowing down the fjord. They're working on foundations for new student housing next to the shore, though not for much longer; construction will soon halt for the winter (the science centre was constructed over the course of almost three years). The lack of resources

01 02

up here, paired with the climate, adds further complications.

"Even in the late 1990s it was still a bit Wild West up there," Vigsnæs says. "We had one shipload of insulation that got lost for weeks and no one knew where it was. In the end we found out that the whole crew were drunk in Ireland and had harboured there for a couple of weeks."

It's clear why prefab housing is so popular. The history of quick-fix building solutions here stretches back to Longyearbyen's position as a coal-mining town. For years, local mining company Store Norske ran the show here, managing the whole community including the hospital, school and shops. The company housed most of its workers in buildings shipped in from the mainland. One of its current tenants is Store Norske property manager Per Christian Frøislie. He has lived in Longyearbyen for 11 years in a red *spisshus* (the pitched roofed houses the town is known for) with his wife and son. His house was put up in the 1970s, fabricated on the mainland by construction company Moelven Bruk.

"Even though they're not in a very good condition anymore, I love them," says Frøislie. Like all residences in Longyearbyen, wooden interiors are standard, as is a fairly extensive storage area next to the front door. It's here where obligatory full-body snowsuits and substantial boots are stowed.

These *spisshus* houses have helped create a visual identity for the Longyearbyen town centre thanks to Grete Smedal, a professor of art and design in Bergen. In the early 1980s she worked with Store Norske, helping implement a colour plan that would unify the increasing number of buildings. Smedal took her design cue from the colours found naturally in the landscape. It's admittedly rather bleak in Longyearbyen but the closer you look the more kaleidoscopic the natural elements appear. "For work like that you think, shall I hide the built things or shall I emphasise them? Do you try and mimic nature in some way or go and do it in a real contrast?"

Smedal plumped for the latter. To this day, the 38 *spisshus* houses are divvied up

03

01 Per Christian Frøislie
   outside his red home
02 Tin foil is used to block
   out the midnight sun
   during the summer
03 Panoramic view of
   Longyearbyen's ter-
   raced houses, painted
   according to Grete
   Smedal's colour plan

Home comforts

Windows
The best windows for keeping a house warm have a
split frame and three layers
of isolated glass.

Insulation
Rockwool or other types of
mineral wool are most commonly used.

Pipes
The oldest solution is to
build wooden structures
lifted from the ground and
put pipes in them, covered
with insulation so the heat
from the pipes won't melt
the ground underneath.

Exteriors
The climate in the Arctic
is dry and cold. Wood is
usually used for exteriors,
which won't rot if the house
is lifted up off the ground.

Design
Pretty gables or overhangs
are best avoided up here.
The wind is strong and
comes in all directions,
meaning your roof could
blow off. Covered porches
or wardrobes for snow suits
and skis are essential.

Orientation
If your bedroom faces
north, sleeping won't be
much fun during summer
when the sun shines on
your pillow all night.
Many residents like having
outside space facing
north-west to enjoy the
midnight sun.

01 LPO Arkitekter's Arvid Rønsen Ruud
   and Ingvild Sæbu Vatn
02 Ample storage space is a necessity
   outside Svalbard homes
03 A Longyearbyen home
04 Grete Smedal
05 The imposing Global Seed Vault

01   02

into seven colours ranging from pepper-mint green to maple-leaf red.

The charm of the multicoloured terraces in Longyearbyen belies the large-scale construction that Svalbard looks set to face as it becomes a crucial strategic point in the warming Arctic. Earlier this year, €26.7m was set aside by the Norwegian government for the development of a new harbour in Longyearbyen, as the town vies to become a search-and-rescue centre as trade routes open up. Store Norske is building a 2km road over a glacier to reach coal that's inconveniently located on the other side of it. And then of course there is the eerie and grand Global Seed Vault *(see box)*.

Svalbard's big developments have prompted a real sense of change up here and plenty of people are waiting in the wings for when that happens. The Oslo architecture practice LPO Arkitekter opened a studio in Longyearbyen three years ago and they have become experts in how to build in the cold. Run by Arvid Rønsen Ruud and Ingvild Sæbu Vatn, the studio has grand plans for Svalbard.

"The Norwegian government has a focus on the area and we want to be there when it happens," says Ruud, in the LPO studio near the shore. What's 'it'? "We don't know yet, but people here think this could be a logistics hub for gas plants, ship traffic, minerals," Vatn says. During MONOCLE'S visit, they are working on a planning project for 100 new homes in the east of Longyearbyen and a new brewery/bakery.

"As the ice pulls back, there are new areas to exploit. We are the only architecture firm, but there are many big consultant firms who have people waiting here," says Vatn. LPO, hand in hand with the other experts now located in Svalbard, is ready to turn this once-unfriendly outpost into a liveable civilisation. "It's an explored area, but not exploited." — (M)

03   04

Ready for doomsday

Although Svalbard's climate is unwelcoming to most things (trees, for example), the Global Seed Vault was positioned here precisely because of the chill and the minimal threat of tectonic activity. The so-called Doomsday Vault was built under a mountain a few minutes from Longyearbyen in 2008, designed to store around 3 million types of seed in case the world goes up in smoke.

Fashioned to last as long as possible, it's a huge, subterranean warehouse with metre-thick reinforced concrete walls. And yet, with characteristically Norwegian modesty, this gargantuan project is marked quite subtly by its entrance – a cantilevered concrete porch crowned with a light installation. Inside, a 125-metre tunnel leads to three store rooms.

05

museumtheoriginal.com

Original Outdoor Garment

MUSEUM

SINCE 1986

01 Gander's escalator,
   allegedly the first one
   in Newfoundland
02 Mezzanine level over-
   looking the mural by
   Kenneth Lochhead

LONDON

MONTREAL
NEW YORK

MOSCOW

D

ARCTIC SPECIAL
Gander airport

20·32 →

01

02

FLY IN STYLE
—*Gander*

Preface
Gander International Airport
in Canada was once the
largest and most stylish
airport in the world, where
locals mingled with celebri-
ties. Today it faces a battle
to hold on to its glamorous
reputation – and its
passenger numbers.

WRITER
Nelly Gocheva

PHOTOGRAPHER
Alex Fradkin

"She might be running a bit late today,"
says Jerry Cramm, eyeing the runway
outside from the vantage point of Gander
International Airport's striking terminal. The "she" in question is a tiny 18-
seater BEH twin-turboprop plane that Air
Canada uses for its daily domestic flights
between Gander and St John's, a town-
ship about 350km southeast. During his
25 years at Gander, Cramm has seen
umpteen BEHs and their more powerful
transatlantic peers land and take off at
the two runways currently in operation
at the airport. And he has a story or two
to share about the terminal's glamorous
past and, indeed, its quieter present.

Perched on the island of Newfoundland, the airport opened in 1938. It took
about three years and a 900-person team
to finish the project which, with its four
paved runways and a combined area of
2.6 sq km, became the largest airport in
the world. Less than two decades later,
the airport was already known as the
Crossroads of the World. All transatlantic
flights would land here to refuel, allowing
passengers en route from New York and

02

01

03

London to stretch their legs. "The island was picked due to its location," explains Cramm, now a chief commissionaire in charge of a six-strong security staff. "It is the easternmost part of Canada. The nature of the terrain was also very important – The Rock [as Newfoundland is known in Canada] was a vast, flat and virgin piece of land."

Eventually, in the late 1950s, major renovations were necessary to accommodate the ever-growing influx of passengers. The CA$3m (€2.17m) invested in the redevelopment resulted in a new 20,000 sq m terminal and modernised, extended runways. When Gander's new international terminal opened in 1959 it was the most important airport in the world. Not only because of the 400,000 passengers passing through its gates annually, mostly due to the boom in mass commercial flights post Second World War, but also for the splendour of its mid-century lounge.

"With so many jet-setters arriving in Gander, the government wanted an up-to-date terminal but also they were fighting the international impression of Canada being backward," says CEO Gary Vey of the then-futuristic project. "It was a way to claim, in front of the world, that the country was a beacon of style and a leader in airspace technology."

Gander has remained largely untouched through the decades. Today the striking "Welcoming Birds" bronze sculpture by Canadian artist Arthur Price sits undisturbed in the middle of the geometric terrazzo flooring. Seamlessly aligned next to them is seating in soft grey and navy blue from Robin

01 Commissionaire
    Jerry Cramm
02 The viewing area with
    Christen Sorensen
    armchairs and sofas
03 Mezzanine area
04 Seats by British
    Columbia designer
    Robin Bush
05 The mirrored
    powder room

Bush's Prismasteel line designed for Herman Miller.

Adding to the artistic flair, and softening the feel of the space, is the stirring 22-metre mural by Canadian artist Kenneth Lochhead. "It is bright and creates a certain liveliness to the room," says Vey of the artwork that can be enjoyed from the comfort of the Christen Sorensen armchairs in the viewing area.

A wood-panelled escalator leads to the mezzanine floor – some say it was the first escalator in Newfoundland. Currently not functioning, it rises up under the wall clocks in the lounge, which show the current times in London, Montréal/New York and Moscow. "These cities are not randomly selected; back then they were the top destinations served by the airport," explains Vey, reminded of

04 05

Gander in numbers

Gander's glory days when the airport was a pitstop not only for the planes but also their precious passengers. "I know people who still remember talking physics with Albert Einstein or sharing Fidel Castro's first encounters with snow during a layover in Gander," adds Cramm. "The locals were able to mingle with high-profile guests."

Eames's fibreglass chairs can still be found in the mirrored powder room, just next to the ladies' toilets. "A lot of important people have used those chairs," says Cramm. Indeed, hanging on the walls are photo collages of former regulars to the airport: Sinatra, Brando, Monroe, Bergman, Dean, Taylor and Burton. Those who weren't pouting in the powder room were surely at the bar: Gander airport was granted Newfoundland's first 24-hour alcohol licence.

Today the international terminal often remains empty for days at a time. With the development of aviation technology and jet fuel, stopovers became redundant and by the 1970s traffic slowed significantly. Yet Vey is optimistic: "Besides some ad hoc and seasonal destinations our international traffic remains relatively low, but domestic flights are up by 7 per cent," he says. "We're still making money – maybe not as much as we wish we made but the airport will survive, there is no doubt about it." — (M)

1938: Airport opens as Newfoundland International airport
1959: New international terminal is built
400,000: Average annual passengers in the 1950s
30 per cent: The revenue from domestic flights in 2012
CA\$7.8m (€5.6m): Annual revenues 2011–2012
3,109m: The length of runway 03-21, still among the longest in North America
20,000 sq m: The size of Gander International Airport's terminal
CA\$7m (€5m): Gander's budget in 2013
CA\$536m (€387m): Gander's contribution to the Canadian economy
4: Scheduled direct domestic routes to Toronto, Goose Bay, St John's and Halifax

Emergency landings

Gander was put back on the world's map on 11 September 2001 when 36 planes were diverted to the airport following the closure of US airspace. "We were the only airport around with the capacity to handle that many airplanes at once," says CEO Gary Vey. In the aftermath the airport and town became home to nearly 6,200 stranded passengers and 480 crew. Today, Gander often provides emergency services to airlines in cases involving mechanical issues, unruly passengers or health problems on board.

01

02

03

01 Dedicated smoking
    area in the airport
02 Mural by Kenneth
    Lochhead
03 The 'Welcoming Birds'
    bronze sculpture by
    artist Arthur Price
04 The beautifully time-
    warped mezzanine floor

04

TOTO

Brilliant for life.
NEOREST

INTRODUCING

AN ENHANCED VERSION OF
THE INTERNATIONAL HERALD TRIBUNE
NOW KNOWN AS THE

International New York Times

THE WORLD. AND WHAT TO MAKE OF IT.

EXPERIENCE INYT.COM

1
The office
A home away
from home

2
The hardwear
Our crop of fixtures
and fittings

3
The architects
The best residential
masterminds

Design ⒹⒹⓂ
Directory
2013 /Autumn
Winter

**The
furniture**
Essential
kit for your
new pad

4

The front door
The best carpentry

5

Our guide to where to
live, how to build, who
to hire and how to fit
and furnish
your residence(s)

The homes
Berlin's cutest
neighbourhood

6

The end results
The perfect retreat

8

The experts
Who to call upon

7

Lounge Chair & Ottoman, Stool Design: Charles & Ray Eames

Go to www.vitra.com to find Vitra retail partners in your area.

vitra.

Design Directory Autumn Winter 2013

Welcome and Contents

Welcome to a new instalment of the Monocle Design Directory, a blueprint for residents, architects and developers. Published as a companion to our May edition – which focuses on the product and retail side of things – this Design Directory will guide you through the nuts and bolts and the bricks and mortar to help you create a better apartment block, less pokey residence or more expansive weekend retreat.

In this guide we survey everything from the streets and neighbourhoods in which to lay your hat to the well-made things we suggest you fill your house with. Along the way we meet the experts to call upon. From the front door to the bed, this is our comprehensive guide to making a better place to host, rent or, eventually, retire.

Key to writers:
(LA) *Liam Aldous* (TAB) *Tim Anscombe-Bell* (MB) *Michael Booth* (KB) *Kimberly Bradley* (IC) *Ivan Carvalho* (ADC) *Alexandra de Cramer* (CDO) *Clare Dowdy* (ZD) *Zach Dundas* (PE) *Pauline Eiferman* (SFG) *Simon Farrell-Green* (JAF) *Josh Fehnert* (AVF) *Alexa Firmenich* (AK) *Alicia Kirby* (JZL) *Jason Li* (ETL) *Edward Lucas* (GSL) *Gaia Lutz* (RM) *Ricardo Moreno* (TM) *Tom Morris* (GR) *Gwen Robinson* (SRT) *Santiago Rodríguez Tarditi* (AES) *Aisha Speirs* (ST) *Syma Tariq* (FW) *Fiona Wilson*

Editor:
Tom Morris

Photo director:
Poppy Shibamoto

Photo editor:
Lois Wright

Chief sub editor:
Louise Banbury

Home sweet home

Global

Preface
What makes the perfect neighbourhood? Whether you strive to reside somewhere tranquil and family friendly or you look for a vibrant and dynamic hub with good transport links, we pick out the best neighbourhoods in six major cities.

01

02   03

PHOTOGRAPHER: CHRISTOPHER WISE

Best Asia base:
Soi Langsuan, Bangkok

Soi, the Thai word for "street", can apply in typically ambiguous Thai style to a tiny lane or a whole neighbourhood. Soi Langsuan, one of Bangkok's most strategically located areas, encompasses a network of small and large streets: variously vibrant, shambolic, slick, even discreet, but all with an inimitable style. With its intriguing mix of gourmet cafés and bars, street-food vendors, luxury hotels, traditional massage shops and the city's premier park, Lumphini, the leafy area is a perfect blend of residential and commercial features.

Convenience adds to Langsuan's attraction, flanked as it is by two lines of the elevated BTS Skytrain and just a 10-minute cab ride from the highway to Bangkok's two main airports. Perfect for those nipping to Hong Kong or Singapore for business meetings, or indeed beyond. But connectivity isn't the *soi's* only asset. Retail heaven can be found at one end of Langsuan, along Ploenchit road, which is dominated by Central World – one of Asia's largest malls – Paragon and Siam centres and, from next year, the Central Embassy and Park Hyatt shopping and hotel complex. At the other end lie the peaceful green grounds and ponds of Lumphini park, a magnet for dawn joggers, and the graciously retro buildings and golf course of the exclusive Royal Bangkok Sports Club.

A nearby cluster of five-star hotels offers all-day dining and nocturnal cocktails. A few blocks away on Wireless Road is embassy row, dominated by the

04

05   06

Why we'd live there

Soi Langsuan keeps its residents happy with a tempting range of local dining, recreation and shopping options. For frequent travellers occupying its many serviced apartments and hotels, the area has it all: proximity to public transport and a direct airport route and Bangkok's best shopping centres. And there's sprawling Lumphini park for those needing a quick green fix.

01 Chic Parisian chain Café LeNôtre
02 Jean-Pierre Dovat
03 David Au's penthouse
04 Locals shield from the sun
05 City street
06 Au in his house near Langsuan
07 Vietnamese restaurant, Thang Long
08 Lemon Farm at the Portico
09 The Portico complex

07

colonial mansions of the US, Vietnamese and some European embassies. Add to the mix some neighbourhood yoga studios and ballroom dancing schools, and organic store Lemon Farm in the eclectic Portico complex, and you have a compelling neighbourhood.

Among the area's devoted part-time residents is David Au, a Hong Kong-based executive with luxury menswear retailer Trinity Limited. Au has homes around the world but confesses to a "special affinity" for his penthouse apartment near Langsuan, with stunning views over the sports club. He describes Bangkok as his "haven and inspirational Mecca".

"I enjoy the spectacular views," he says. "I often go for a swim, food and gym when I'm here. I also love the nearby Central [World] department store... the area will always be special to me but most of all I love the food, culture, architecture and history of Old Siam."

For Jean-Pierre Dovat – an architect and designer who runs Project Space, a contemporary gallery, and Mekong Estate, holiday villas in Luang Prabang, Laos – a love affair with Soi Langsuan revolves around his "perfect pied à terre"– an elegant renovated studio in the stylish Hansar building. "This area feels like the heart of an evolving 21st-century city. There's a sophistication, with its great buildings, restaurants, shops and luxury hotels, yet it also has an old, authentic feeling and a vibrant urban middle class; I also love my building – modern yet simple."

The sweeping mix of lifestyles, people and businesses around Langsuan is perhaps best summed up in its grab-bag of architectural styles – from ramshackle cottages to the contemporary minimalism of hotel Luxx; from the sleek lines and vine-covered green wall of the Hansar, designed by Singaporean firm Woha, to the pseudo-gothic opulence of Hotel Muse, one of the area's newer hotels. Ultimately, as Dovat says, "there is truly something for everyone here". — GR

08   09

Why we'd live there
—

They provide a true neighbourhood feeling in one of Berlin's greenest districts. Houses are small but, unlike larger Berlin apartments, allow for maximum use of space: ceilings are not too high and rooms are not too big.

---

01 A row of houses with the unusual staggered four-paned windows
02 Peter Apel's three-storey house
03 Apel's open-plan kitchen/living room
04 Apel's peaceful garden terrace
05 Apel and his wife designed the kitchen and all the built-in features

01   02

Best first home:
Waldsiedlung, Berlin

In the heyday of the social-housing boom in German-speaking Europe in the late 1920s and early 1930s, until political winds shifted, many architects erected visionary communal housing. A case in point is Weimar-era architecture legend Bruno Taut's Waldsiedlung ("forest settlement") in the West Berlin district of Zehlendorf, built as a mini-village of terraces (plus some housing blocks) from 1926 to 1932. Amazingly these little houses are still upright and have never been more desirable for young families seeking peace within the capital.

Originally conceived as row units, most house have 89 to 105 sq m of living space plus a back veranda and garden. The outer portions of the buildings have been listed: the landmarks commission stipulates exterior facades must be in shades of green, blue, red and yellow and retain Taut's unusual staggered four-paned windows.

But owners can modify the interiors as they see fit. "We lived in the centre for 20 years but when you have kids you ask yourself other questions," says architect Peter Apel, who lives in one of Taut's three-storey houses (they also converted the attic) with his girlfriend, Carolin Senftleben, (also an architect) and two small children.

03   04

The family bought a relatively run-down house two-and-a-half years ago and restored the outdoor elements, including the roof and windows. They opened the kitchen to combine it with a living/dining area and added a bathroom on the top floor. Unlike Berlin's pre-war apartments, which have just a few gargantuan rooms, rooms here are numerous and small. "It was a shock to move to Zehlendorf," says Apel. "But it's been such a good decision. Our neighbours have a lot of kids. I was surprised at the relationship of green space to buildings. Some trees are twice as high as the houses. It's like a fairy tale." — KB

05

Best place for a sunny terrace:
Las Salesas, Madrid

Nestled between the boisterous streets of Chueca and the decidedly calmer, more traditional calles of Chamberí, the Salesas district of Madrid has long struggled to make a name for itself. Unlike the nocturnal commotion that characterises much of Madrid, its narrow streets provide somewhat of an inner city sanctum and, for many of its privacy-loving residents, that's just the way they like it.

The neighbourhood has recently started to reassert itself, particularly as

02

independent retailers and restaurants have moved to the area. New high-profile tenants have appeared this year, such as the designers from EspacioBrut, who uprooted from the more retro El Rastro with their furniture studio and designer wares store and set up shop on Calle Pelayo. Further down the street, ceramicist Guille García Hoz has opened his own eccentric shop.

"It's good to live in an area that's not just populated by bars," says Gorka Postigo who resides in a converted 17th-century convent where, he tells Monocle, prostitutes were once brought to be converted into nuns. It was transformed into 12 split-level lofts more than a decade ago and the complex boasts a central sun-filled patio. Postigo, an architect and photographer, spends much of his time working from home and savours the serenity provided by the patio's private garden.

And locals are increasingly looking upwards, rediscovering rooftop spaces. For Keiran Bowtell, an Australian who moved to Madrid in 2008, the terracotta-tiled panorama is the perfect remedy for a long day at the office. He says some of the area's older residents don't seem to appreciate what they have. "Sometimes it seems as if I'm the only one up here," he says, "but that just means more peace and quiet for me." — LA

Why we'd live there
—

With the completion of the direct underground rail link to Madrid airport's T4, Salesas residents can now easily board a train at the Recoletos station and be checking in their luggage within 20 minutes. This means the benefits of proximity aren't spoiled by the imposing roar of air traffic and residents can sunbathe – or have their siesta – in peace.

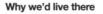

03

01

04

01 Gorka Postigo's office
02 Postigo's spacious home, which used to be a 17th-century convent
03 Keiran Bowtell relaxing on his terrace
04 Local streets
05 Bowtell's peaceful terrace

05

Best inner-city suburb:
Campo de Ourique, Lisbon

A revolutionary hotbed in the late 19th century, Campo de Ourique – a rectangular network of streets – has seen plenty of action: from congregations of artists and agitators who urged on the dying days of monarchy, to ordinary workers making it home alongside the new Republic's bourgeoisie.

The neighbourhood, designed in 1879 as part of Lisbon's expansion plan by engineer and politician Ressano Garcia, is still known as a village that is somehow separate to the rest of the capital – though it is a short walk, ride or cycle to Lisbon's centre. Families who have been there for generations, young families and artists all call this undisturbed quarter home.

"People who live here quickly get to know each other," says freelance journalist and photographer Jõao Pedro Correia, who as a former political reporter would walk to the parliament building from his apartment. "We don't need to leave the neighbourhood to go shopping for groceries, hardware, shoes and clothes. There's a traditional marketplace, a post office, good restaurants and we can buy real bread."

Small businesses surround the local park, Jardim da Parada, and one café here was a meeting place for members of the Portuguese Impressionist movement. Another purportedly has the best prego (steak sandwich) in Lisbon. The 1904 neighbourhood association Padaria do Povo ("bakery of the people") is still open for football matches and sandwiches.

"It is a neighbourhood with human scale," says designer Henrique Cayatte, who lives two blocks from his studio in the French-style cour – or residential courtyard – between the two southern boulevards. "From the arrogant Santo Condestável-tecidos church, typical of the dictatorship we had until 1974, to the buildings from the early-to-mid-20th century, there is a patchwork of styles that reflect different ways of living."

The traditional Pombaline influence on Campo de Ourique – block scales, enlarged interior living spaces and integrative decorative detailing from balconies to doorknockers – shares space with moments of adapted modernism. Joana Amaral Dias, who works for city hall on citizenship education for primary schools, had her 1940s apartment renovated by Lisbon architects RCJV.

"They retained the character of the home that was here originally, but enhanced the distribution of space, especially with their lighting work," she says. — ST

01 02 03

PHOTOGRAPHER: PEDRO GUIMARAES

04

05 06

Why we'd live there

Combining late 19th-century architecture with modernist vestiges, Campo de Ourique has the right balance of bustling life and evening calm.

01 Jardim da Parada
02 Apartments built in the 1980s
03 Local street scenes in Campo de Ourique's southern quarter
04 The corner of Rua Saraiva de Carvalho
05 A mix of 19th and 20th-century architecture
06 Engraving on a limestone building
07 A gothic-style church
08 Newer residences

07 08

Best place to raise a family:
Käpylä, Helsinki

Fondly referred to as the dimple in Helsinki's cheek, the leafy neighbourhood of Käpylä, 5km north of the city centre, offers a breath of fresh air in the Finnish capital.

As well as schools and parks, the neighbourhood is a short bike ride from the central park and Vantaa River and its wide, tree-lined streets are safe for children to play out on.

"It's an excellent place to raise a family," says Bert Bjarland, who moved to Käpylä 15 years ago when he married his wife and is now an active member of the area's residents' association. "It's not too far from downtown and it's close to nature, schools and kindergartens."

Visibly inspired by the English Garden City movement of the early 20th century, Käpylä is home to a host of distinctive, multi-storey, semi-detached wooden houses designed by architect Akseli Toivonen in the 1920s. Conceived to cater for the city's poorer families and workers, these charming, colourful properties are now divided into apartments accommodating older residents and are also increasingly popular with Helsinki's young families. "Fifty years ago, the residents were typically poor and the area was cheap," says Bjarland. "Since the 1970s, the area has undergone a process of gradual gentrification and today there are many of the old residents but also quite a few people working with media and press – as well as artists and intellectuals". — JAF

01

02

03

Why we'd live there
—
Käpylä's old-world charm, distinctive architecture and unique mix of young and old make it particularly suited to young families – without the trade-off of a long commute to the city centre. Good schools too – this is Finland, after all.

05

06

07

01 Wooden properties in Pohjolankatu, Käpylä
02 The leafy streets are a pull for young professionals
03 Käpylä church was completed in 1930
04 These colourful houses come with large yards
05 Käpylä residents
06 A building in Olympia-kylä – Käpylä's Olympic village
07 Apartments in Käpylä

PHOTOGRAPHER: JUSSI PUIKKONEN

04

Report
Where to live

01

02

03

Best place for mountains and connectivity:
Queenstown, New Zealand

"It's a great place to do thinking," says Adam Peren of Queenstown, which he and his wife Kristin O'Sullivan Peren have called home for 15 years. The couple – she's an artist, he's a tech investor – own a boutique vineyard, Two Sisters, and live on a 202-hectare sheep station in the mountains. Their home was designed by Wellington firm Architecture Workshop and is inspired by traditional New Zealand farm buildings – all the better for watching the mountains.

But Queenstown has urbane attractions as well as good weather – there are vineyards growing world-beating pinot noir, some of New Zealand's finest restaurants, good designer shopping and top-notch cafés – and an international airport. It's the size of a small town but highly dynamic. All of which attracts a globe-trotting, polyglot community.

You never get away from that landscape. Queenstown sits on Lake Wakatipu, surrounded by the Southern Alps. There is the odd sleek, minimalist compound but the most successful homes have both a sense of enclosure and a ruggedness that responds to the landscape.

For architects Pete Ritchie and Bronwyn Kerr, who live and work in an angular black house by the lake at Drift Bay, Queenstown has inspired a different sort of architecture. "We like a variety of spaces and volumes," says Ritchie. "It creates little nooks. Queenstown is very hot and very cold, and creating spaces to respond to that is important." Recent houses have included H-forms, creating courtyards on different sides. Materials are robust – concrete, plywood and timber.

"The light is so strong here," says Kerr. "That's why we like to play with sculptural forms. They're houses that would look too harsh in a suburban environment." — SFG

Why we'd live there

Queenstown has just 29,000 residents but it gets more than one million visitors a year and there are multiple flights a day to and from the international airport. Direct flights run to Melbourne, Sydney and Brisbane taking just a few hours; and Auckland – with long-haul connections to Europe and Asia – is just one-and-a-half hours away.

06

07

01 Queenstown
02 Adam Peren and Kristin O'Sullivan Peren's house, designed by Architecture Workshop
03 The view from Pete Ritchie and Bronwyn Kerr's home practice
04 Ritchie and Kerr's angular house
05 A popular café Vudu in central Queenstown
06 Adam Peren and Kristin O'Sullivan Peren
07 The Perens' home office

05

04

A tribute to light

Elliott Erwitt, 2013

Carlotta de Bevilacqua - Paola di Arianello: Empatia

artemide.com

Artemide®

01

02

DD
Report
Prefab houses

Instant home
Finland

Preface
The prefab housing market is booming in Finland thanks to its cheaper cost, versatility and eco-friendliness. And even the quality is increasingly lauded.

Writer
Josh Fehnert

Photographer
Jussi Puikkonen

Like the buildings themselves, the market for prefabricated houses in Finland is going up fast. From architect and designer Alvar Aalto's first forays into prefabrication in the 1930s to the rintamamiestalo (veterans' houses) erected by servicemen returning from the Second World War, the Nordic nation has a lengthy history with the housing type.

"According to our research, about two thirds of buyers prefer modern house designs to the more traditional style," says Mikko Kilpeläinen, president and CEO of Honkarakenne, a leading manufacturer. Although concerns about the quality and appearance of some cheaper varieties persist, a typically Finnish pragmatism has made the prefab home a significantly popular way to live.

Last year an impressive three quarters of all detached houses built in Finland were prefabricated – compared with some 50 per cent in the early 1990s. These properties are environmentally friendly, easy to build, inexpensive and, crucially, offer buyers a range of styles and finishes.

Since 2006, Helsinki-based practice PlusArchitects has made the most of the booming industry by lending a tasteful architect's eye to the prefab, creating a portfolio of sturdy, nicely proportioned homes in the process. With 100 commissions to date throughout Finland, France,

03

04

06

05

07

08

Prefab favourites

Honka, Finland
Founded in the late 1950s, this Tuusula-based manufacturer exports wooden homes throughout Europe and as far afield as Japan. Using durable pine, Honka has sold more than 80,000 log buildings.
honka.com

Archiblox, Australia
This Antipodean architecture practice is a one-stop shop for anything from bespoke beach houses to roomy extensions. With a lead time of between 12 and 28 weeks, speed and sustainability tip the scales in its favour.
archiblox.com.au

Modular System, Portugal
With options including solar panels and rainwater collection devices, the Porto-based firm focuses on creating a better environment inside and outside its houses.
modular-system.com

Germany and Russia, and a few design awards up its sleeve, the practice has trodden a fine line between precision-manufacturing preassembled components like walls and giving buyers the freedom to customise the look and feel of their commissions.

"Making a small house is quite difficult, so we tried to provide the customer with an easy way of putting up decent-looking ecological houses," Jani Lahti, the company's co-founder, tells Monocle in the practice's fourth-floor office in a converted textile factory in Helsinki. In partnership with manufacturer Honkatalot, PlusArchitects draws from 10 basic villa styles that can be tweaked and tuned to create more than 300 variations, all made from pre-cut, locally sourced spruce and pine.

The company's modern houses were by no means an obvious step in a conservative industry. "In 2006 all our competitors' houses had pitched, log roofs," says Arttu Hyttinen, another co-founder, with a smile. "They asked us, 'How can you sell these designs?' but after a few years they've changed their opinion." Ten kilometres from the studio in the leafy suburb of Länsi-Pasila, we see why. Inside Jani Lahti's spacious four-bedroomed house, the appeal of these open-plan spaces is clear to even the most sceptical. And it was all built to its owner's specifications within weeks and habitable within five months.

Elsewhere in Finland the story is the same. In the western town of Kannus, manufacturer Kannustalo has been making well-wrought prefabricated houses since 1978. Despite its healthy history, however, the mass-produced medium hasn't always been a desirable one. "People didn't think the quality of prefabricated houses was good enough, that you couldn't make alterations and they all looked very similar," explains Kannustalo's CEO Mika Uusimäki across the kitchen table of his Kosketus model house.

As one of the country's larger manufacturers, the firm's 189 staff create more than 350 houses a year. Uusimäki is confident there's room for design-centred businesses like his in a market that has more than doubled since 1995 to account for an estimated 65,000 new houses this year.

Uusimäki puts some of the negative feelings towards prefab houses down to a lack of harmony between architects and manufacturers. "There used to be

01 Outside the Honka Lumi house
02 The Lumi's open-plan interior
03 Kannustalo's award-winning
    Kosketus model
04 Inside Mikko Arevuo's country
    bolthole
05 Stepping out of the MoMA-
    exhibited Kosketus

01 02

Prefab worldwide
—

The US, Canada, the UK and Japan are the biggest import and export markets for the prefabricated house industry. Popularity is increasingly associated with the houses' green credentials as well as their cost effectiveness and convenience. Last year alone the US accounted for shipments of 50,000 prefabricated homes.

03 04

an arrogance from the architecture side. At a conference in 2003 they asked me directly, 'Why do you build these traditional houses? It's not good architecture.' So I said come and work with us and we started to work together."

What followed laid the foundations for Kannustalo's success. The manufacturer's increasingly sophisticated collections of pre-assembled homes were among the first to challenge the traditional notion that prefab meant boxy, characterless cubes thrown up by economic necessity rather than by choice. Collections such as the Lato model – a collaboration with Ulla Koskinen, editor-in-chief of interior-design magazine *Deko* and former designer at Marimekko and Artek – is a vote of confidence for a once-mocked method.

"To have someone cut all the timber specifically would have made it uneconomical," explains Mikko Arevuo, a university lecturer who commissioned his prefab in 2006. This buy-and-build culture, falling costs, environmental concerns and an increasingly design-conscious industry are all factors in the Nordic nation's growing preoccupation with prefab. Having seen the sturdy structures for ourselves, we think it's an idea worth building on. — (M)
plusarkkitehdit.fi; kannustalo.fi

PHOTOGRAPHER: NICLAS WARTIUS

05

EMOTIONS SHOULDN'T BE DESCRIBED, THEY SHOULD BE EXPERIENCED.

www.baxter.it

MADE IN ITALY

PHOTOGRAPHER: JONATHAN CAMI

DD
Report
Who to hire

Design for life
Global

Preface
Building the perfect property isn't just about the bricks and mortar. As these leaders in their field demonstrate, it's about taking into account the surroundings, appreciating the details of the materials and getting a feel for the space.

Architect
Fearns Studio, Sydney

An extension on a terraced house doesn't often lead to inspiring architecture. But Sydney's miles of tiny Victorian terraces are the perfect place to find smart solutions for converting your two-up two-down into an interesting home. Local architect Matt Fearns has been making a big impact on this old architecture.

"I don't have a desire to design buildings like airports," says Fearns. "There's enough complexity and plenty to learn in small-scale architecture. Most of my clients are in their thirties or forties and haven't used an architect before. They're outgrowing their tight urban spaces."

To find extra space in a confined structure, Fearns looks at designing the home as an object in itself. "I'm not interested in celebrating something like a door handle. The building as an object is important to me – it's something that's resolved and has its own logic. There's nothing wrong with wanting to design a beautiful object."

Considering volume, shape and light rather than texture, Fearns often uses only three or four materials, such as white set plaster, rendered brick and wooden joinery. A relationship between the interior rooms and the landscape lends warmth.

The renovation of an old beach studio in South Durras (*pictured above left*) created two bands of windows that open onto the surrounding bush while the extension of a house in Bondi sees sliding walls open up to plant-lined paths (*pictured middle and bottom left*). "In many ways, I'm not simply a style choice for clients," says Fearns. "I'm often their problem solver." — AES
fearns.com.au

Why we'd hire him:
Having worked on everything from building-regulation legalities to public art, Fearns understands issues of sculptural form as well as planning laws.

Developer
Halter, *Zürich*

"We build communities instead of just buildings," says Balz Halter, CEO of Zürich-based developer Halter Group. "In our real-estate projects, sustainability is the main issue. The office spaces, retail centres and apartments we deliver to the market take current and future requirements into account – in every sense and often beyond market standards."

The 200-strong workforce balances operations between property development and innovations in building technology to create "smart homes" and "smart working spaces". Halter also has expertise in schools and hospitals.

The company breathes new life into industrial (brownfield) sites and city centres across Switzerland. Halter works on the development of an area, such as the Hard Turm Park in Zürich (*pictured*) through a well-balanced retail/tenant mix and (semi-) public "third places" such as parks and restaurants where people can gather and interact. "It takes a clear vision, a lot of courage and most of all patience and persistence to create a great neighbourhood," says Halter. — TAB
halter.ch

Why we'd hire them:
Project solutions are found in having a closer look at target groups and their specific needs, whether it's a community hall, a shopping centre or a sports stadium. Halter keeps customers happy while creating smart, liveable environments.

Landscape gardener
Monica Luengo Añon, *Madrid*

"I've been working on one garden for eight years," confesses landscaper Monica Luengo Añon (*pictured, right*). "Working with living materials means establishing open-ended relationships with clients."

For the first time in her 30-year career she is branching out with a younger partner so she can immerse herself in each project. "You can't properly design a space without taking in the smells, sights and sounds."

Many of her clients are expats living along the Andalusian coast, who she admits better appreciate landscaping. "Fortunately this is changing. The economic situation has brought people down to earth and this means a move back to nature."

Adept at creating intimate spaces within large ones, Añon integrates both the surrounding landscape and the architecture into her gardens. "I'm not out to make a name for myself," she says. "I just want to make people feel happy." — LA
+34 91 319 0960

Why we'd hire her:
Añon's measured approach favours the creation of a garden that incorporates the landscape rather than altering it. Her Latin flair inspires creative and native solutions.

Architect
Holst Architecture, *Portland OR*

At Holst, a Portland, Oregon firm founded in 1992, partners John Holmes and Jeffrey Stuhr tailor every residential project to the circumstances of budget, site and neighbourhood. "We try to gather as much knowledge as we can, and then we bring our own tendencies to the table," says Stuhr. "We're committed to modern design, but we don't want to follow fads, either."

That means a residential portfolio notable for ambition in its context. Portland's strict urban-growth laws emphasise dense development along the city's transport lines, which has spawned many mediocre, generic flat blocks. In its multi-residence projects, Holst applies a higher aesthetic standard to the city's mandates.

For example, the Belmont district is a prim, low-rise 19th-century neighbourhood that had seen little new development when Holst embarked on its Belmont Street Lofts project in 2004. The firm needed to take the district's historic character into account without sacrificing its design ideals.

"You're walking the tightrope," Holmes says. "You look at the immediate environment and it's brick and wood. We considered stucco. And yet we don't want to do anything retro." The building's eventual tropical hardwood skin reflected the high craft and complex texture of the Victorian surroundings but stood out as a groundbreaking choice in Portland. The 27-unit's ground-floor retail spaces open directly onto the pavement to add to the high street's small-scale shops.

The city's newer Pearl District, in contrast, had become a one-note architectural environment, with faux-industrial exteriors and many shoebox-like flats with few windows. In its 937 Condominiums building, Holst created a tall, thin structure, stretching flats along the building's edges and maximising each unit's daylight. The result: a striking honeycomb of windows set in a cool, sandy-coloured skin, relieving the neighbourhood's monotonous dark brick.

"We looked at how to improve the experience of people who live in the building," Stuhr says. "But we also want to improve the experience of actually seeing it too." — ZD
holstarc.com
—

Why we'd hire them:
Besides a modernist aesthetic heavily influenced by the light and setting of individual projects, Holst's early years focused on interiors give it a hands-on perspective. "We're much more focused on the details of materials than most firms," Stuhr says.

Architect
Arbol, Osaka

With its skyscrapers, busy roads and a population of 2.8 million, Osaka is not an obvious place for contemplating nature. Yet architecture firm Arbol, and its young founder Yosaku Tsutsumi, is reclaiming the city from the grip of concrete and asphalt. Tsutsumi is determined his houses will make the best use of natural materials. "The material I feel closest to is wood," he says. "Nobody ever says they feel uncomfortable surrounded by trees."

He recently completed a wooden home in a built-up neighbourhood (*pictured right*), surrounded by tall apartment buildings. The clients, a couple in their seventies, were thinking of something conventional – two floors with a balcony for laundry. Instead they got the modern equivalent of a log cabin: one floor high and clad in Japanese cedar.

Rather than build right up to the perimeter, Tsutsumi reduced the house size, adding an S-shape of greenery that runs along the edges and through the building. "I know Osaka is urban," he says, "but I try to incorporate some form of a garden into every project, however small." Whenever he can he works with Toshiya Ogino, a landscape designer who can work wonders with a single, carefully chosen tree.

Tsutsumi added an *engawa*, the outdoor deck that runs around a traditional house, and carefully positioned the building to make the most of the sun. "It's like living on a roof," he explains. "They can enjoy the sunshine but nobody overlooks them." The interior is a flexible mix of cedar floors and tatami mats with plenty of windows, wide corridors and a practical kitchen with stainless-steel worktops. — FW
arbol-design.com

Why we'd hire him:
Arbol's beautifully designed houses using natural materals confound expectations as to what a home can look and feel like.

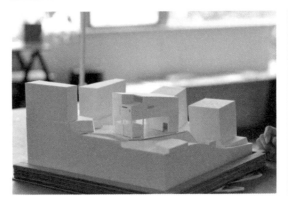

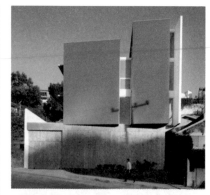

Architect
T38 Studio, *Tijuana*

Walk into either of Alfonso Medina's studios – in Tijuana or New York – and you'll find a mix of craftsmen, painters, carpenters and welders before spotting the architects. T38 Studio is a workshop where different disciplines merge to create communities from scratch. Medina's team does everything from finding the site of a project to building and developing it.

"The most important component of a city is its housing, so to have the best possible city, you need the best possible house," says the 30-year-old Texan.

Medina set up T38 Studio in Los Angeles in 2005. Focusing on property development and construction, he has built more than 30 housing projects to date. Although Medina's architectural style adapts to the conditions of the surroundings where he is building, he mainly uses concrete, steel and glass: materials that are both affordable and durable. He also uses locally sourced wood to add warmth and colour.

When asked what makes the perfect city, Medina responds: "There is a competition between cities to see who can attract more talent – cities are becoming more efficient and offering better public space and infrastructure to their residents." — SRT
t38studio.com
—

Why we'd hire him:
Medina's designs and buildings are always developed in collaboration with craftsmen from the communities he works in – we like the idea of mixing local knowledge with an international perspective.

PHOTOGRAPHER: EDGAR ZIPPEL

Landlords/developers

Stefan Karl and Angela Knewitz,
Berlin

On the border of the gentrified Berlin districts of Mitte and Prenzlauer Berg, an unusual, not-quite-finished building sits on a residential street. Among the mostly pre-war apartment houses is a grey edifice entering its final phase of construction. This is Monohaus, named for the one thing it's made of – a special concrete that not only provides solid structure but also stunning aesthetics and usability.

"The concrete is one piece, inside and out. Interior and exterior are one and the same," says Stefan Karl, who, along with his wife Angela Knewitz, has made the build a privately funded labour of love. The seven-storey Monohaus will contain a 167 sq m duplex penthouse apartment (plus roof garden) for them, three one-floor units of about 110 sq m on the middle storeys and a ground-floor duplex abutting a garden.

Why concrete? "We asked ourselves, 'What would be the purest form for a house?'" says Karl. "We wanted a place that was focused, concentrated, with no ornament. Concrete was the logical material." After finding an empty plot, and a two-year negotiation with its owner (the plot, in Berlin's old Jewish neighbourhood, had lain empty after being bombed during the Second World War), Karl and Knewitz developed the Monohaus with Berlin architecture firm Zanderroth. The couple also approached concrete manufacturer Heidelberger Beton about getting "more favourable conditions" for erecting the

first residential all-concrete building using the company's special mix of materials. Heidelberger Beton was game.

Building started in March 2013 with each storey being poured bit by bit – a careful process, as the concrete requires the right temperature to set properly. Walls are 55cm thick, and the concrete's texture is remarkably smooth, save for intentionally visible seams and occasional surface burps that reveal the tiny clay globules which add to the material's breathability and insulation capacities. Windows are vast, making the most of natural light. Interior spaces are open and airy, but the floor plans include nooks for spaces like home offices. Villeroy & Boch are developing fixtures for the units.

It all feels quietly powerful and somehow Asian. "I consider it a Japanese house," says Karl. "I did judo as a child and there's a word, *zendo*, which means meditation hall. I nearly called the house Zendo." For Karl and Knewitz, the house – whose lower units will be on the rental market in early 2014 – is a sustainable investment, as well as an almost spiritual endeavour. Karl researched the plot's past and found out who once lived here, and is proud to be part of Berlin's rebuilding process. A funny irony is that the couple recently had twin boys. Someday, the Monohaus will belong to a duo. — KB
monohaus.de

Why we'd hire them:

Karl and Knewitz are about sustainability, not just profitability. They plan to rent the units the family's not living in, the apartment layouts are both generous and practical, and their collaborations are clever.

PHOTOGRAPHER: SEAN FENNESSY

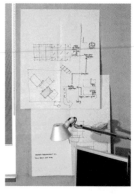

Interior designers
Hecker Guthrie, *Melbourne*

On a recent trip to Denmark, Hamish Guthrie and Paul Hecker – the two founding principals of their eponymous Melbourne-based interior design studio – stopped at the window of an estate agent. "Every house looked like it could be on the front cover of a magazine," says Hecker. "But what resonated with us were the interiors. A couple that had bought their house in the 1960s simply added to it over time. They bought well, bought once and weren't focused on the idea of being fashionable."

So, despite being one of Australia's most successful interior-design teams, it's this well-paced and personal approach that Hecker and Guthrie also apply to their many residential projects. Having met while working together at an architectural practice more than 20 years ago, the duo set up shop together in 2001. Since then, they've created some of Australia's best-known restaurants and hotels – including The Establishment in Sydney and Melbourne's Longrain – as well as hospitality spots across Asia, but nearly one third of their work is still focused on designing homes in Australia. "With residential projects, the client is very different," says Guthrie. "A restaurant design not only matters to the owner but also the people who will use the restaurant. Homes are much more personal. Ultimately, our fundamental human needs don't change; it's about intimacy, cosiness and feeling protected."

With this in mind, the big glass box style of living is out for Hecker Guthrie. Instead, its homes mix aesthetic needs with sensory experiences. In a recent residential project in Melbourne, living-room spaces can be opened up or made private through a mixture of custom-built, sliding glass doors and curtains, which not only alter the interior's sense of scale but also allow for the more intimate (and traditional) room sizes of the Victorian house to remain intact. "We're trying to show people that life could be better if you can edit your space and change it," says Hecker. "It doesn't need to be expensive – adding a plant, putting things away or bringing them out again. It's the process itself that reinvigorates." — AES
heckerguthrie.com

Why we'd hire them:
In addition to designing private homes around the country, Hecker Guthrie has worked with developers on apartment interiors for the past 10 years. From large family homes to one-bedroom apartments, the duo create warm and flexible spaces.

DISCIPLINe

Beautifully designed, consciously made

Preface
Floors, tiles, windows and doors: just some of the crucial elements that go into making a house solid and sustainable. We've scoured the globe to find the professionals and perfectionists who have made finishing touches their pride and joy.

01 Flooring

Castiglioni
Bregnano

Based south of Lake Como, Castiglioni creates made-to-measure hardwood floors from over a dozen types of trees sourced from forests as far away as Chile. "We don't sell an off-the-shelf product," says Davide Castiglioni (*pictured bottom right, on left*), the owner of the business that was begun by his father in 1968. "Every job is bespoke and we often lay the wood."

Davide and his three siblings make floorboards that have found their way into villas in Lugano, hotels in Milan and boutiques in Hong Kong. On a visit to the company's main factory, Davide and brother Eugenio (*far right, middle*) take Monocle inside a workshop where carpenters patiently work to apply a range of finishes – surfaces can be lacquered, brushed or even treated with coats of beeswax. "We age pieces in a special oven," says Davide. "In a few hours you can give larch a darker complexion, for example."

The company's panels are composed of three layers. On top there is the client's choice of wood, which can vary from teak to Slavonian oak; beneath, two more layers, often in pine, are crisscrossed to create a more stable structure than a solid block of parquet.

While modern machinery is used to saw three-metre thick trunks into millimetre-thin floorboards, staff use hand tools to shape and smooth surfaces. Finely cut mosaic patterns are often requested, with orders for deck flooring and wall panelling on occasion. Installation is included in the service to ensure panels are wedded properly.

The company has five-man teams that some weeks find themselves putting down parquet in a Tokyo apartment or South African manor house. "It gives staff a bit of variety not having to be in the factory every day – though not every job is for a villa owner on the French Riviera," says Davide. — IC
castiglioni.net

Why it works
If you are willing to pay extra for bespoke footwear to keep your toes comfy the same should apply when you are barefoot in your home. A well-laid wood floor adds warmth to a house.

PHOTOGRAPHER: LUIGI PIANO

02 Doors
Fumihiko Watanabe
Niigata

Door makers don't come better than Fumihiko Watanabe (*pictured*). Only 38, he's crammed more into his 20-year career than most achieve in a lifetime. His skills have won him commissions such as partition doors for Kyubey, one of the most celebrated sushi restaurants in Japan; he has also won prizes and been honoured by a Japanese prime minister.

Watanabe is a second-generation craftsman who can make anything a client requests, be it a wooden front door or a traditional sliding door. "I don't like to show anything unless I think it's flawless," he says. His workshop is lined with planks of wood, mostly cedar, as well as cypress and the Aomori hiba he favours for *kumiko*, the most intricate of his doors. Even his tools are works of art – some have been passed down from his father, others he made himself with blades crafted in the nearby town of Yoita.

As his technical skills have improved – his detailed pattern work involves pieces of wood only a millimetre thick – so he has become more interested in perfecting doors that are designed for every day use. "Simplicity presents its own challenges," he says. Unlike most craftsmen, Watanabe smooths even his most delicate pieces with a razor-sharp plane. "Sandpaper flattens the texture of the wood," he says. He doesn't use varnish either.

There is nothing precious about Watanabe, whose hobby is roaring around Niigata on his Kawasaki motorbike. He does admit to being a wood nerd, though: "If I see a good piece I have to have it." — FW

Why it works
Fumihiko Watanabe's carpentry skills are second to none. He is a perfectionist, too – his execution is impeccable.

Timeline

1975
Fumihiko Watanabe is born in Niigata

1993
Starts a five-year apprenticeship under his father Fumio

2003
Wins the prime minster's award for an intricate wooden screen

2006
Completes a sliding entrance door for one of Japan's top sushi restaurants: Kyubey in Ginza

2007
Awarded the title of Master Craftsman, an honour given by the Ministry of Health, Labour and Welfare to outstandingly skilled craftsmen. At 32 he is one of the youngest craftsmen to ever be given the title

2011
Another award at the National Tategu Competition for a set of delicate sliding doors

PHOTOGRAPHER: KOHEI TAKE

03 Carpentry
Connell Hull Company
Oregon

With his background in fine arts, it's not surprising that Ben Hull's woodwork is so soundly designed. He started making large-scale abstract sculptures in wood and steel while getting his degree at Portland State University. "Soon, I had to get a little creative and find something to do that was more marketable," he says.

Eight years later, Hull (*pictured*) is a versatile craftsman who has created furniture for local Patagonia and Starbucks stores, and remodelled the beautiful Bend Mountain Coffee storefront. "I really enjoy commercial work because it's an opportunity to put my work into a public arena," he says. "Whenever I come to a new space, I envision it without anything in it – there's usually a lot of unnecessary stuff so I try to take it out. From there, I'll rebuild it and add my stuff."

Hull says one of his favourite things to do is timber screens, which are perfect to divide a room without building a wall and help maintain a sense of lightness in the home. — PE
connellhullcompany.com

Why it works
Hull's skills can be applied to any odd jobs in the house, including shelves made of big ponderosa pine slabs for your living room.

Timeline

1993
Formation of parent company R&G Metallbau

2002
Installation of the first Sky-Frame system

2013
The 4,000th Sky-Frame installation and development of the Sky-Frame Arc, a curved sliding window

04 Windows
Sky-Frame
Zürich

"Sky-Frame's aim is for transparency to take centre-stage", says CEO and owner Beat Guhl. Established in 1993, the company produces floor-to-ceiling and wall-to-wall sliding-window solutions that would have Mies van der Rohe smiling.

The Sky-Frame system is designed to ensure transitions between rooms are flush and barriers to the outside are removed, allowing interiors to be flooded with light. Employing integrated locking systems and toughened anti-break glass, the windows have been used in projects ranging from the façade of the rooftop bar at London's ME Hotel to the 80-metre glass front for the VIP lounge of Zürich stadium Letzigrund. "We wanted to shift the focus away from the window to the light and the sky – a more open living environment," says Guhl. — TAB
sky-frame.ch

Why it works
Sky-Frame's windows add a feeling of spaciousness to any interior.

05 Construction tiles
Elemento V
Campo Largo, Brazil

Once a staple of residential design in Brazil, the *cobogó* – originally a cement construction with a decorative yet functional hole through its middle – has been forgotten by builders for more than half a century. However, manufacturer Elemento V is hoping to change that with a ceramic version.

The company was founded five years ago by architects Alexandre Nobre, Daniella Arruda Botelho Nobre and José Eduardo Arruda Botelho (*pictured far right, left to right*). They expect to end this year having produced about 60,000 units and plan to double the size of their factory by late 2014.

Elemento V's bricks can be used inside and out. "In addition to them being resistant to climatic variations, you can stack up to 20 metres of them without any beams," says Nobre. Brazilian architect Isay Weinfeld is already in on the act, using 7,500 bricks to create a roof parapet for a hotel project in Brasília. Around 30,000 pieces are also heading for the state of Espírito Santo, where a new football stadium is about to be built. — RM
elementov.com.br

Why it works
It is an easy way to add some tropical modernist flair to your home, as well as letting a nice breeze circulate inside.

06 Door handles
Byggfabriken
Malmö

With options for an array of building details for the home, Byggfabriken's door handles and accompanying back-plates are particularly striking. "It is the sensitivity to cultural heritage that stands at the core of the business," says creative manager Josefin Kvist. "We want to allow customers to tastefully decorate their homes in a manner appropriate to the style of the building."

Using brass and nickel handles – often with a bakelite or teak doorknob – alongside backplates made from pressed steel, the range offers classic designs. Using historic catalogues and architectural drawings from the 19th and early 20th century, Byggfabriken design engineers create a handle and plate sample in line with the original fitting. The product is then assembled to match the original in style and quality. — TAB
byggfabriken.com

Why it works
With its pared-down Scandinavian design, this range of fittings will round off any renovation project.

PHOTOGRAPHER: JOEL ROCHA

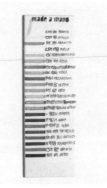

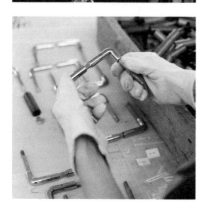

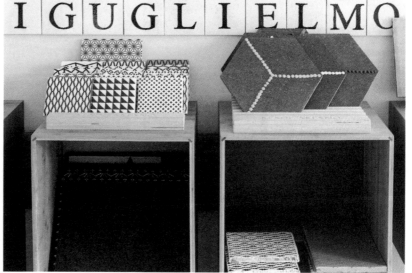

NERMEDU
YALSRHA
ECALTAC
NLKEISF
RICOLAT
NTRDEPHI AM
IVHJSLHVUA
GUSCOSMOSN
DGRGMNUCT?
IASIFLBTOS
IGUGLIELMO

07 Tiles

Made a Mano
Copenhagen

Made a Mano's tiles all share a sense of heft – unsurprising, given that they are made of lava from Mount Etna and Vesuvius. The idea for the company came to co-founder and designer Josephine Akvama Hoffmeyer while renovating her home in Denmark.

"Everything that was available in terms of tiles was mass produced but there was a very limited choice," she says. "I found someone painting traditional motifs on table tops in Sicily and commissioned them to make my first collection."

The future for Made a Mano will bring more ambitious products and sculpting. — MB
madeamano.com

—

Why it works
The glazed Christalli and geometric Cuba ranges are works of art in themselves.

08 Kitchen
Vipp
Copenhagen

The Vipp bin is a design classic courtesy of Holger Nielsen, father of current Vipp owner Jette Egelund (*pictured*). However, things have moved on from waste disposal: having gradually expanded the product range to other accessories, she decided to make the leap to an entire kitchen in 2010.

Said kitchen features three main pieces: the Wall Module, Tall Module and Kitchen Island. The 200kg stainless-steel work surface is designed to display its war wounds proudly. "Scratches are fine because our products are tools," says chief designer Morten Bo Jensen. — MB
vipp.com

Timeline

1939
The first Vipp bin is made by craftsman Holder Nielsen

1992
Nielsen dies and his daughter, Jette Egelund, takes over

2006
Ex-Biomega designer Morten Bo Jensen is hired

2011
Vipp's Jensen-designed kitchen launches

Why it works
Vipp's kitchens are designed to last for decades: there are no welds and the company even produces components that are usually outsourced.

PHOTOGRAPHER: JAN SØNDERGAARD

---

09 Trays and trolleys
Kaymet
London

The south London quarter of Bermondsey was once home to light industry but many businesses relocated out of the capital or disappeared altogether. Not so tray and trolley manufacturer Kaymet, which has stayed in the borough since Sydney Schreiber set it up in 1947.

The company has been given a new lease of life by Mark Brearley, formerly head of Design for London at the Mayor's office. Ken Schreiber (*pictured below on right, with Brearley*), the son of Kaymet's founder, has taken on the role of general manager.

Brearley is earmarking Kaymet products ripe for reinvention. "The trolleys are pieces of mobile furniture," he says. At the moment they're tea trolley height – but what about sofa arm height or coffee table height? You could put a computer on it or have it in the bathroom." — CDO
kaymet.co.uk

Why it works
Kaymet's hand-finished aluminium trolleys will add a dose of mid-century practicality to any home.

Timeline

1947
Kaymet brand is established

1959
A purpose-built factory is erected

1990s
Trolley sales shrink as fashions change

January 2013
Brothers Mark and John Brearley invest in Kaymet

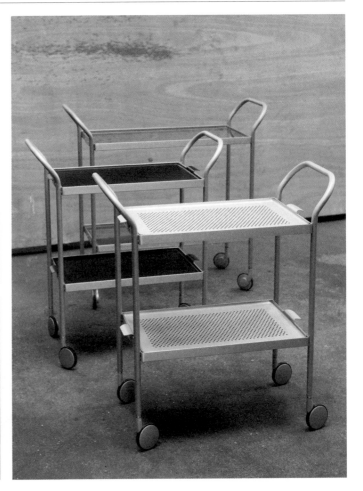

PHOTOGRAPHER: LAURA BRAUN

01 Seating area in the atrium
02 Airbnb works on many levels
03 'Et voilà': the Paris room
04 Rendezvous in the Paris room
05 Selection of working spaces

01   02

DD
Report
Airbnb

A home from home
San Francisco

Preface
With meeting rooms designed to look like rental properties, Airbnb's new office is tailor made to be a homely setting for its workers.

Writer
Alastair Gee

Photographer
Carlos Chavarria

For employees at San Francisco's Airbnb, the rental-accommodation website phenomenon, deciding where to hold a meeting is uncommonly stimulating. They can opt for the eclectic surrounds of Milan, whimsical Paris or even the tiled floors and thatched roofs of Bali. However, no air miles are clocked up in the process: at the company's new headquarters, many of the meeting rooms are close replicas of some of the company's most popular listings from around the world. It's a design gimmick but for a lodging company that doesn't actually own any bedrooms, it's a clever way of using design to give corporeality to the brand.

Airbnb's office shares a lot with its tech cousins over in Silicon Valley, long known for kooky workplaces and where amenities include on-site masseuses and gourmet chefs. At Airbnb the sentiment runs a bit deeper, with the designers seeking to create a comfortable atmosphere – in part because employees can spend more waking hours at work than at their residences, notes co-founder Brian Chesky – and a space that encourages employees to be sociable. "I liken our office to a Michelin three-star office," says Chesky.

Established in 2008, Airbnb originally occupied a three-bedroom bachelor pad in San Francisco's SoMa district. There were Eames chairs and a red-velvet Jesus on

03

the fireplace (a room from this flat, Airbnb's equivalent of the Hewlett Packard garage, is recreated in the HQ). Eventually there was so little space that staff were forced to sit on kitchen counters and the stairs outside.

The latest office is in a four-storey building with a retractable roof that used to house a jewellery centre; Chesky was entranced by the cavernous atrium. "When I saw it I had a vision of cross-sections of apartments and homes," he says. The project was conceived by Chesky and Joe Gebbia – another of the three co-founders – and realised by the Gensler architecture firm and Interior Design Fair. A key motif is the contrast between the functional central office spaces – an open-plan landscape of standing and sitting desks – and the "homey, detailed, residential and almost kitschy" meeting rooms, as Chesky puts it. This works on an aesthetic level and also meets the design goal of having a multitude of spaces for different types of work.

"I think about what type of meeting I want to have and match it to a room," says producer Gauri Manglik. With its dining table, loaded bookshelves and Smeg fridge, Paris is a good choice for leisurely brainstorming. The programmers, meanwhile, have a grotto-like room with beanbags, music and dim lighting for focused coding. However, the founders insist that employees need not have their own dedicated workspaces at all

04

05

Report
Airbnb

The story so far

Airbnb began life in 2007, when two of the founders decided to rent out airbeds in their apartment on San Francisco's Rausch Street to conference visitors. Later they won a spot with the prestigious Y Combinator – a business-development programme that has also funded the likes of Reddit and Dropbox – and honed their idea for a site where people could offer their spare rooms and homes for rent.

Rental properties currently on offer include a treehouse in California's Santa Cruz, igloo-shaped cabins in Greenland and a lighthouse in Port Washington, New York.

Salubrious surroundings

The Silicon Valley tradition of designing unusually agreeable offices dates back to the 1950s, says UC Berkeley architecture professor Margaret Crawford, when Stanford University opened the Stanford Industrial Park for technology firms. With occupants such as HP, it introduced the idea of a campus filled with amenities for workers, such as shuffleboard and badminton courts. This was not a completely novel idea in the US – there is a long history of company towns such as Hershey, Pennsylvania. Now, Crawford says, there is "an arms race of amenities" in Silicon Valley to attract top talent.

01

02   03

01 Trust and safety manager Anna Steel in the Bali room
02 Manager Dave O'Neill
03 Employees relax in the kitchen area
04 Artwork covers the cafeteria walls
05 Rausch Street room, based on Airbnb's original digs
06 Software engineer Surabhi Gupta
07 Co-founder Brian Chesky
08 Lunch is served

04

and are permitted to move about the office as they see fit. "The notion of a desk is so 20th century," says Gebbia. This sentiment is clearly not shared by everyone, as the encrustations of personal belongings around particular computers testify. For others, such as longtime staffer Lisa Dubost, it fits. "It's the most amazing feeling of freedom," she says.

Another priority in the design was fostering interaction among the staff and thus, so the founders' thinking goes, prompting new ideas of benefit to the company. It is for this reason that the toilets are located at the extreme ends of the floor: employees have to cross paths with other employees to reach them. "We make sure there are magnet spaces across the building," says office manager Jenna Cushner, referring to the coffee and food stations where colleagues meet for a bit of banter. In the cafeteria, where the on-site chefs serve lunch, there are long tables to facilitate conversation.

Employees praise the homeliness of the space, saying that the soft couches, good coffee and the dogs that people bring to work have the biggest part to play. That said, Chesky insists that his staff are anything but pampered, a familiar charge against Silicon Valley types in gleaming offices. "I view our team as special forces. I expect a lot of them. In return they get everything they need to be successful." — (M)

05

06   07

Q&A: Kassin Laverty, founder, Interior Design Fair

Monocle: What was your role on the Airbnb build?
Kassin Laverty: A cross between a set designer and a translator – because we had to translate the essence of the chosen [rental listing], their vibes and the country they are in.

M: What were the most difficult items to source?
KL: The [plush] cactus in the Milan hallway was quite the challenge. The real deal costs thousands of dollars and finding a cheaper alternative was tricky. We finally found a woman in Missouri who was up for the challenge – she sent it to San Francisco via Greyhound bus. The Copenhagen room had a knife rack on the wall but for safety reasons we didn't want to leave a set of knives out. Instead we found costume knives and cut them down to real-life size.

M: Did you utilise your creative licence in any of the meeting rooms?
KL: The sofa in Milan is actually a bed. We slip-covered it and added wheels to the front to match the listing.

08

The living is easy

Global

Preface
With the right furniture, storage solutions and utensils, your home life can be transformed. Decorate and co-ordinate your personal space with these ideal items.

Still life
Anders Gramer

1

Dining chair
Hans J Wegner

Danish designer Hans J Wegner knew a thing or two about dining in comfort. The CH37 was designed in 1962, inspired by a simple Shaker aesthetic. We'd have one of these at either end of our oak dining table, accompanied by four armless CH36 chairs down the side. — TM
carlhansen.com

2

Speaker
People People

A friendly solution for your living room electronics comes from Stockholm design company People People. The four-year-old firm's newest project, dubbed the transparent speaker, has a small wi-fi antenna that makes it eligible to connect to all electronic devices. "People don't own cars anymore so they show off with their living rooms," says Martin Willers, one of the four founders. "These speakers are the perfect way to do so." — ADC
peoplepeople.se

3

Letter opener
Plant Brooklyn

"We try to do good," says designer Bjarke Ballisager regarding his eco-friendly interdisciplinary studio. Williamsburg-based Plant Brooklyn was founded by Ballisager and his wife Holly McWhorter who share a background in architecture. This letter opener is made out of poplar while its blade is constructed from recycled paper. — GSL
plantbrooklyn.com

Drying rack
La Base

The humble dish drainer is not generally at the top of anyone's wishlist. However, if you do lust after kitchen kit have a glance at La Base, a range from Japan designed by home-cooking star Yoko Arimoto. The drainer is made from top-quality Japanese stainless steel and stands in a sloping tray coated with silicon for durability. Looks good and does the job. — FW
labase.jp

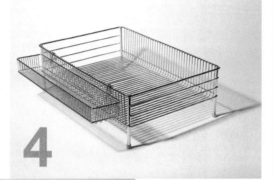

4

Tableware
Billy Lloyd

London-based potter Billy Lloyd's new "Billy" collection for The New Craftsmen consists of a bowl, plate and mug, and is manufactured in Stoke-on-Trent. It's not just the historical ceramics centre of the UK that Lloyd is aiming to put back on the map with these pieces, but also some of the more traditional craft techniques, including jollying and jiggering. Both these methods (yes, those are their real names) were used to create the distinctive ridge effect. "The ridging makes them tactile," says Lloyd. "Lots of tableware has a smooth exterior but I was interested in a profile that accentuates form and demonstrates a precision in handmaking. I'm trying to show off a bit of precision and skill that can be done by hand and not on a computer program." — TM
billylloyd.co.uk; thenewcraftsmen.com

5

Vases
Ro Collection

Danish design company Ro was established in Copenhagen this summer by Rebecca Uth and Ole Kiel, former colleagues at Georg Jensen who had long planned their own independent collaboration. They named themselves after the Danish word for "Serenity, calmness and peace of mind". Ro launches with a collection that features a lounge chair from Shannon Payton and Arunas Sukarevicius, vases from Nina Erichsen (*pictured*) and a toolbox from Aurélien Barbry. It's an eclectic selection that captures the essence of Ro: thoughtful works intended to endure. — ETL
rocollection.dk

6

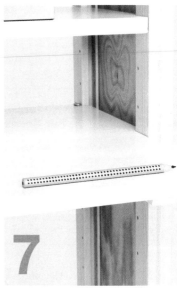

7

Storage shelves
Lundia

It's tough to come by a product as practical and versatile as Finnish design company Lundia's shelving units. Since 1948 the family-owned company has been constructing its shelves out of free-growing pine sourced from local forests, where long winters and short summers make the wood grow slowly and, most importantly, durably. "Lundia is the opposite of throw-away culture," says CEO Michaela von Wendt from the firm's main office building in Hyvinkää. "The core idea in our shelving system allows you to build, dismantle and reconstruct the shelves over and over again – without tools. It grows with the owner, from a child's room to a student's studio to an office." — AVF
lundia.fi

Cutlery
Pott

8

Although a traditional flatware firm in the 21st century may seem hopelessly old fashioned in a sea of cheap, disposable products, German company Pott stands out for all the right reasons. Dating back to the turn of the 20th century, the firm has worked with Bauhaus and Werkbund luminaries such as Wilhelm Wagenfeld, Elisabeth Treskow and Josef Hoffmann and gained a global reputation for innovation in cutlery design. Its items sit in museums around the world, including MoMA. The most popular range is the four-piece silverware set called Pott 33 that was one of the last designs by second-generation owner Carl Pott before he died in 1985. Known for the fine grooves at the tip of each handle, the utensils are also wider than average, making it easier to scoop up your food. — AK
pott-bestecke.de

9

Coffee table
Shigeichiro Takeuchi

Japanese designer Shigeichiro Takeuchi was invited by Commoc, a Tokyo furniture and product-design studio, to collaborate on the creation of a coffee table. The Tricom's most unique feature is its single powder-coated steel pipe, winding underneath a solid glass top to form three legs —a simple yet fluid design. Available in black, white or green, it sums up Takeuchi's design principle: "To find the essential function and structure of the object". — AVF
commoc.jp

Coffee and side tables
Arthur Casas

10

Ever since Oscar Niemeyer designed a rocking chair, Brazilian architects have liked the challenge of turning their hand to furniture. São Paulo architect Arthur Casas's Arquipélago's coffee and side tables, handmade by Etel Carmona, are some of our favourite end results. Available in either Freijó or Sucupira woods, they're raised off the ground by some architectural *pilotis* (legs) and are undoubtedly the best place to rest a caipirinha. — TM
arthurcasas.com

Salt and pepper mills
Normann Copenhagen

Designed for Normann Copenhagen by Royal Danish Academy of Fine Arts graduate Simon Legald, these Craft salt and pepper mills are formed from a classic white-oak mill crowned with Italian marble knobs; black for pepper, white for salt. Nestled inside the solid wooden column is a ceramic CrushGrind grinder, tested to grind for two centuries of use without visible wear. A seasoned favourite. — ETL
normann-copenhagen.com

12

Serving pot
Marimekko

13

Marimekko's autumn collection was inspired by the stirring shades of the Finnish weather. Marimekko designer Aino-Maija Metsola has produced a series of watercolour-heavy textiles and homeware with a meteorological bent to it. Not so much a storm in a teacup as clouds on a jug, this ceramic serving pot – plus a dainty milk jug – are great for serving or decoration. — TM
marimekko.com

11

Tea towels and oven mitts
Saana Ja Olli

Saana Ja Olli is a Finnish textile company founded in autumn 2008, the cherished offspring of Saana Sipilä and Olli Sallinen, a design couple from Turku. The pair work only with sustainable European hemp with printing, sewing and design all taking place near their home in southwest Finland. Just as production is rooted in their locale, so is the vision. "We love traditional Finnish folk craft aesthetics and want to keep them living with our prints," says Sipilä, rather than seeing them consigned to forgotten history. These pieces feature a repeating *Maailman synty* (the birth of the world) design, inspired by Finnish mythology and the country's traditional wall rugs. — ETL
saanajaolli.com

Garden chair
EMU

Emu has made its reputation as a leading outdoor-furniture company by combining elegant designs with weather-resistant materials. The "Shine" collection by Arik Levy is an example of the Italian company's recent efforts to collaborate with international designers; other partnerships have seen works by the likes of Jean Nouvel and Patricia Urquiola. We love this light aluminium chair in yellow with its magnificent sunshine effect. — GSL
me.emu.it

14

15

Towels
Murakami

The Japanese city of Imabari is synonymous with towels. We like the premium quality bath towels from Murakami, which has been in business in Imabari since 1927. Generously sized, they are made from cotton and come in seven colours. — FW
murakami-towel.com

16

Sofa
B&B Italia

For sofas made with a commitment to craftsmanship we turn to B&B Italia. The family-run Italian firm has pioneered injection-moulding technology using cold polyurethane foam to turn out firm but comfy sofas with a long life cycle. Standing out from the pack is the sleek-bodied Frank sofa designed by Antonio Citterio. Conceived as a modular system that can be mixed and matched with a selection of backrests, central benches and chaise lounges, it is available in leather or fabric. — AK
bebitalia.com

18

Sofa
Erik Jørgensen

A 1970s classic, the EJ 220/270 sofa by Danish manufacturer Erik Jørgensen is the perfect resting place for your new home. Last year, the EJ 220/270's back cushions were given buttons but we're also fans of the pared-back simplicity of the chrome-footed original. — TM
erik-joergensen.com

17

Blankets
Nishikawa

No bed should be without one: a cashmere blanket in classic beige from Nishikawa in Osaka. Nishikawa has been making bedding since 1566 and the cashmere blankets are still made by craftsmen in the Senshu area south of Osaka. An investment that will see you through many winters. — FW
nishikawa-living.com

19

Bench
Heerenhuis Manufactuur

Set up as an antiques business in Antwerp back in 1978, Heerenhuis Manufactur moved into manufacturing about 15 years ago and has been producing its own beautifully made furniture ever since. Run by Geert Legein and Louis van Haesebrouck, the collection is simple, comfortable and focused on using great-quality materials. This rubber-and-oak bench is a case in point. "We like to use real materials – basic, uncomplicated, non-perfect stuff," says Legein. Hence the rubber seat? "It will not stain, tear, rip, split or discolour – and it is amazingly comfortable." Distributed through London's Different Like a Zoo studio. — TM
heerenhuis.be; differentlikeazoo.com

Children's furniture
Soeta Craft

Made in white beech with a paper-cord seat, this pint-sized chair for children is made by Yasuhiko Soeta, a craftsman from Fukushima. Soeta produces original wooden furniture and accessories that he designs and makes lovingly by hand from start to finish. He chooses the wood too and leaves it unvarnished, preferring to use a light oil instead. — FW
ne.jp/asahi/fukushima/soetacraft

20

Speaker
Nixon

With a surfeit of gadgets on offer it's a relief to find something simple. The Nixon Blaster is a shock-resistant, water-resistant wireless speaker that can play for 12 hours non-stop. Light and portable, it comes in a selection of colours – olive making a change from the norm. Nothing complicated about it, it just works. — FW
jp.nixon.com/blaster

21

22

Cups and bowls
Ceramik B

Montréal-based ceramicist Basma Osama founded Ceramik B in 2007 to specialise in minimalist tableware with elegant silhouettes. These Morijana cups and Bohemian bowls come in soft natural hues and are meticulously shaped and sized to make your morning serving of tea and cereal a contemplative experience. They are available at Toronto retailer Made, which only sells Canadian designs. — JZL
ceramikb.com; madedesign.ca

23

Footrest
Coco Flip

Melbourne-based design studio Coco Flip named these quirky Puku ottomans after the affectionate Maori word for "chubby belly". Inspired by founder Kate Stokes' visit to Japan last year, the seats are upholstered in fine wool blends from Danish company Kvadrat and can be playfully mixed and matched in 15 different colour palettes. "I loved the way Japanese design so often uses anthropomorphism, giving human form or other characteristics to inanimate objects," she says. "I also love Miyazaki films, so I wanted to try and give this product a real character – cute, a bit chubby and slow but loveable." Stokes founded Coco Flip in 2010 and mostly works with manufacturers based in Melbourne. "As we usually keep to raw materials, working with upholstery and colour was an entirely new and exciting experience," she says. — AVF
cocoflip.com.au

24

Stepstool
Sarah Kay

This solid-oak step-cum-stool is the first solo piece by British-born designer Sarah Kay for London retailer and manufacturer SCP. Kay recently went it alone, having worked for years with Andrea Stemmer as part of design duo Kay+Stemmer. This A-shaped stepstool is ideal for a multitude of uses throughout the home. "I have fond memories of various stepstools in friends' homes that I would perch on while they cooked," says Kay. "Since their use is so specific but sporadic, I wanted to make sure that it could double as a shelf and side table." — TM
sarah-kay.co.uk; scp.co.uk

25

Bed
Nihon Bed

For a proper night's sleep it would be hard to improve on a mattress from Nihon Bed, Japan's oldest manufacturer of western-style beds. The company, which was founded in 1926, rarely advertises but it only takes a quick 40 winks on one of its beds to know why they turn up in Tokyo's best hotels and why everyone from sports stars to royals is using them.

The secret is not in fancy materials or new technology – it's all in the springs. Where the average bed has 600 springs, one from Nihon Bed has 1,200 of them, creating a mattress that is supportive without being uncomfortably hard. The beds are made by a skilled team led by Akio Kurosaka (*pictured*) in Nihon Bed's factory in Ibaraki. Back in the showroom, staff will discuss customers' sleep patterns, take into consideration their height (and any back problems) and come up with the best

mattress. Options include soft, regular and hard with varying configurations of the individually wrapped springs. The Silky Puff mattress is like a cocoon while the Beads Pocket is for those who like something firmer.

Also on offer to complete the perfect bed set-up: pillows, quilts and original bed linen in a range of muted colours and fabrics including Giza 45, the finest cotton in the world. None of this comes cheap, but Nihon Bed says it's an investment that will last for years. And what price a lifetime of good sleep in your new home? — FW
nihonbed.com

THE MONOCLE SHOP

The November Collection 2013

Monocle products and collaborations available at our shops and online

PHOTOGRAPHERS
David Sykes & Robert Harper

◆ **1**

Travel jacket by
Barena
£350

—

This chic travel jacket is the latest gem to come from MONOCLE and Barena's long-time partnership. It is luxurious and soft, made with washed flannel. Tailored for comfort, this navy jacket is light to wear during your flight but sharp enough for client meetings.

Colour: Navy
Sizes: 46, 48, 50, 52 and 54
Made in: Italy

"Monocle 24 News, I'm
Louise Banbury...."

Keep connected to Monocle
24 at home and in the office

Big Jambox by
Jawbone
£300

Designed for MONOCLE by San Francisco's Jawbone, the Big Jambox is a compact
portable speaker boasting a high-quality, crisp sound at any volume. Controlled by
Bluetooth so you don't have to worry about wires or docks, and small enough to fit in
your suitcase, it's perfectly compatible with an active lifestyle. It's nice to look at too
and comes wrapped in a bespoke MONOCLE outer casing.

Colour: Black
Dimensions: 256mm×80mm×93mm
Made in: USA

3

Travel blanket by *Oyuna*
£550

London-based Oyuna has created this light yet cosy travel blanket, made for MONOCLE on limited production with Mongolian cashmere. It's small enough to fit in your weekender but large enough to keep you warm on a long-haul flight. And it comes with a belt-like leather strap to keep it rolled up when you travel.

Colour: Charcoal
Measurements: 180cm × 100cm
Made in: Mongolia

oyuna
exclusively for
MONOCLE

*Monochan:
I'm all ready for
party season!*

To view the full collection
please visit monocle.com/shop

Waistcoat and cardigan by
Esk
£240 (CARDIGAN)
£200 (VEST)

—

Made with the finest cashmere and extra-fine merino, this vest and cardigan set are brought to us from Esk's woollen mills in Scotland. Details include a pencil pocket and real horn buttons.

Colour: Grey and navy
Sizes: S to XL
Made and milled in: Scotland

*Monochan:
All this cashmere is
light as a feather*

5

Leather notebook by
Monocle
£40

Produced in collaboration with our German stationery partner,
Brandbook, this elegant leather notebook is the latest addition to the
MONOCLE stationery collection. The A5 book's cover features a gold-
embossed MONOCLE logo, housing 160 pages of ruled Munken paper.

Colour: Black
Sizes: A5
Made in: Germany

NOTEBOOK

*Shibachan:
This notebook is
perfect for pawing
over*

SuperConnect radio by
Revo
£300
—

Introducing the new SuperConnect radio by Revo in collaboration with MONOCLE. An update of Revo's
Heritage model, it comes with Bluetooth wireless connectivity, meaning you can use your Apple iOS
and Android smartphones to stream music. It uses aptX™ technology for a rich, CD-quality sound,
rather than the normal below-MP3 quality of standard Bluetooth. And most importantly it has a pre-
programmed Monocle 24 button to take you direct to our live stream.

For more information, please go to monocle.com/shop

Cashmere mittens by
Flouzen
£95

—

French cashmere brand Flouzen has teamed up with MONOCLE to create these soft, cosy winter mittens. They're bright yet simple and 100 per cent cashmere – a perfect companion on a chilly day.

Colour: Navy and red
Sizes: One size
Made in: Mauritius

Wool socks by
White Mountaineering
£30
—

White Mountaineering has designed these patterned knitted
socks exclusively for MONOCLE. Perfectly rustic and cosy for the
winter months.

Colour: Navy, red and olive
Sizes: One size
Made in: Japan

SHOES by *Common Projects*

Document holder by
Tod's
£220

—

<small>MONOCLE</small> has teamed up with Italian luxury fashion brand Tod's to create this elegant brown leather folio case. Perfect for filing essential documents when you're on the move and large enough to carry your iPad or tablet.

Colour: Dark brown
Dimensions: 32.5cm×24cm
Made in: Italy

Knitted Toy by *Makers & Brothers* and *Claire-Anne O'Brien* £125 (MONOCHAN)

———

MONOCLE's favourite feathered friend has been brought to life by craft specialist Makers & Brothers and Irish textile designer Claire-Anne O'Brien. Made from high-quality wool, this is the perfect gift for a child and a must-have for a MONOCLE collector.

Material: Wool
Made in: UK

*Monochan:
Who cares if he
doesn't look so smart?
He's there to cuddle!*

The Monocle Guide to
Better Living
Gestalten
£60 (GIFT EDITION)

———

The Monocle Guide to Better Living is an informative and entertaining collection of essays, reports, original photography and illustrations over more than 400 pages. It's our own contribution to making the world a little more liveable and loveable. Published by Gestalten. This limited edition has a brown linen cover and matching sleeve.

Dimensions: 21cm×27cm
Printed in: Germany

Oliver Spencer

Made for men
Toronto [WORKING TITLE]

Just steps away from the glitzy Yorkville neighbourhood in Toronto sits Working Title, a new menswear shop for those who appreciate a little substance with their style. "There's a focus on the contemporary and the progressive," says co-owner Paul Shkordoff of Working Title's underlying philosophy.

"We work with brands that prioritise shape and form, with a nod towards subtlety." In addition to classic menswear items from Alden, Gitman Brothers Vintage and Homespun Knitwear, customers will also find pieces from more refined brands such as Patrik Ervell, Engineered Garments and Svensson. The upper floor, with its stark white walls, minimalist displays and high ceilings sits in contrast to the lower level's expertly curated bookshop and photography gallery. — MDL. *workingtitleshop.com*

Best buys

01 Unlined Chukkas by Alden

02 Chinos by Unis

03 Knit baseball jacket by Patrik Ervell

04 Round collar shirt by Engineered Garments

05 Tee by Etudes Studio x Osma Harvilahti

Make a market
Reykjavik
[FARMERS MARKET]

At the heart of Reykjavík's fishpacking district, in a former fish factory, sits Farmers and Friends – a new flagship store for knitwear mavericks Farmers Market. Established in 2005 by musician Jóel Pálsson and his designer wife Bergthora Gudnadottir, Farmers Market set out to create a modern fashion brand inspired by Icelandic roots, using natural materials – particularly the fuzzy wool of the local sheep. "It was definitely not hip to be using Icelandic wool in 2005," Jóel says. "Everything was about globalisation and taking over the world. But we wanted customers to see our products and think, this has to be Scandinavian."

Farmers Market has expanded to silk dresses, trousers and British-style wax jackets. "The first thing to do was to reinvent the Icelandic sweater but we have been building around that," says Jóel. — PP
farmersmarket.is

Retail therapy
London
[CELESTINE ELEVEN]

Working with London-based interior designer Morse Studio to create a "rough and yet luxurious" environment, Tena Strok opened her Celestine Eleven concept shop in June. The roomy modernist space in Shoreditch combines untreated plaster walls and reclaimed wood counters with sleek shelves and furniture. Dresses by Meadham Kirchhoff and Marios Schwab, tops by Rika and knitwear by Theyskens' Theory barely have time to hang on copper-plated pipes before they are snapped up. The library and apothecary sections have titles on cooking, photography and fashion or skincare by Alexandra Soveral and Sort of Coal. "We want to pair focused fashion and elements of alternate living," explains Strok, whose shop also offers alternative therapies such as Reiki massage sessions. — JZL
celestineeleven.com

Suunto
Vantaa, Finland
Established in 1936 by Finnish orienteer Tuomas Vohlonen, Suunto watches are a must for explorers. The latest Ambit2 has a GPS with a heart-rate monitor, weather functions and a battery that lasts for 50 hours.

Modern knits
Aran islands [INIS MEÁIN]

Inis Meáin Knitting Co makes luxury Aran sweaters drawing from the Irish island's generations of weaving expertise. It reinterprets stitches once used in fishermen's garments while using the softest wool and cashmere yarns; the result is a modern knitwear collection. This vibrant piece will fare you well through winter. — TAB
inismeain.ie

Majestic mud
Cordova, Alaska [ALASKA GLACIAL MUD CO]

It was after a rafting trip in the Alaskan wilderness that Lauren Padawer decided to hand-harvest mineral mud from the Copper River Delta in the southeast of the state. The composition of the substance deposed there, she says, is the most diverse in the world thanks to the region's volcanic and sedimentary rocks. Founded in 2006, Padawer's Alaska Glacial Mud skincare brand offers a line of face and body exfoliating masks and soap bars. — PE
alaskaglacialmud.com

Flash pack
Örnsköldsvik, Sweden [FJÄLLRÄVEN]

Fjällräven, a household name in Sweden, is the go-to choice for heavy-duty backpacks. Its classic model is made from strong, waxed G-1,000 fabric (courtesy of the brand) with leather trimmings and comes with pockets for a thermos and a laptop. — VL
fjallraven.com

Icy outings
Avesta, Sweden [HAGLÖFS]

Swedish brand Haglöfs has been making mountaineering equipment and clothing for almost a century. Today it is the largest supplier of Scandinavian outdoor gear. This waterproof Triton II Hood fleece comes with reinforced hood, shoulders, hem and back and is the perfect layer for icy outings. — ADC
haglofs.com

Cold comfort
Milan [MONCLER W]

Milan-based outerwear producer Moncler has partnered with Japan's White Mountaineering to produce Moncler W – a collection of signature items for the harshest winter. The line uses cotton-nylon blend chambray and jacquards and features wave-shaped padded details with woven Fair Isle wool inserts. — AVF
moncler.com

Dizzy heights
Caslano [BALLY]

To mark the 60th anniversary of Mount Everest's first ascent, Swiss shoe manufacturer Bally has launched an Everest capsule collection. It features an updated version of the Bally Reindeer-Himalaya boots worn by Tenzing Norgay in 1953. They have a double-stitch construction and lightweight molded lug sole. — AVF
bally.com

Checked out
Stockholm
[INDIGOFERA JEANS]

Mats Andersson and Johan Söderlun founded Indigofera Jeans in 2009. Specialising in denim, the Stockholm-based brand now also offers blankets, cotton shirts and T-shirts. Featured here in sturdy red and black-chequered cotton selvedge flannel, this Norris shirt will last for winters to come. — ADC
indigoferajeans.com

Wrap up
Lielax, Finland
[TJOCKT]

Tjockt's scarves are all hand-knitted in Finland using high-quality merino or alpaca wool. To keep warm during winter nights, Monocle has opted for the "Wild and Woolly" – a cosy and versatile scarf that comes in light grey, white and dusty rose. Tjockt takes pride in using all natural materials. — VL
tjockt.com

STILL LIFE: DAVID SYKES

WARM
FRONT
—*London*

Preface
It's the sound of the stud
button popped, the feel of
the collar turned up, the
bulk of the puffy down. Yep,
it's autumn. But don't get
browned off – a jolt of pink
or a dash of red will keep
your perk alert.

PHOTOGRAPHER
Robert Harper

FASHION DIRECTOR
Takeharu Sato

JACKET by *Tomorrowland*,
POCKET SQUARE by *Finamore*,
SHIRT and TIE by *Sophnet.*,
TROUSERS by *Oliver Spencer*,
BAG by *Just William*, GLASSES
by *Lindberg*

JACKET by *Barena*, SHIRT by *Ts(s)*, BOW TIE by *Hackett*, TROUSERS by *Gucci*, BELT by *Trunk*, SHOES by *Carmina*, BAG by *Oliver Spencer*

JACKET by *Maison Kitsuné*,
SHIRT by *Polo Ralph Lauren*,
JUMPER and TROUSERS by
Prada, GLASSES by *Persol*

JACKET by *Strasburgo*,
POCKET SQUARE by *Finamore*,
SWEATER by *Hermès*,
TROUSERS by *Nanamica*,
GLASSES by *Persol*, BAG by
Just William

WAISTCOAT by *Ts(s)*, SHIRT
by *Battenwear*, TROUSERS by
Massimo Alba, WATCH
by *Cartier*

JACKET by *Nanamica*,
T-SHIRT by *Blue Work* from
Tomorrowland, SWEATPANTS
by *Battenwear*, SHOES
by *Yuketen*

CARDIGAN by *The Inoue
Brothers,* SHIRT by *Gitman
Vintage,* TROUSERS by
Penfield, BAG by *Cisei*

MODEL:
Kit

MAKE-UP:
Lyz Marsden

HAIR:
Simon Maynard

Preface
'It's São Paulo. They love
the proposal but they need
the final changes in seven
hours.' Looks like it's going
to be a long night. So
stay sharp.

PHOTOGRAPHER
Mark Sanders

FASHION DIRECTOR
Takeharu Sato

FASHIONABLY
LATE
—London

THIS PAGE: GLASSES by *Oliver Peoples*, JUMPER by *Agnona*, EARRINGS by *Cartier*, WATCH by *Patek Philippe*

—

OPPOSITE: GLASSES by *Oliver Peoples*, JACKET by *Closed*, T-SHIRT by *G-Star Raw*, TROUSERS by *Penfield*, WATCH by *Parmigiani*

THIS PAGE: GLASSES by *Oliver Peoples*, JACKET by *Closed*, SHIRT by *Dušan*, TROUSERS by *Gucci*, WATCH by *Zenith*

—

OPPOSITE: GLASSES by *Oliver Peoples*, SUIT by *Ermenegildo Zegna*, SHIRT by *Alfred Dunhill*, TIE by *Hackett*, POCKET SQUARE by *Massimo Alba* from *Trunk*

THIS: DRESS by *Fendi*,
EARRINGS and WATCH by
Cartier, BRACELET by *Valextra*

OPPOSITE PAGE: GLASSES
by *Persol*, JACKET by *Sofie
D'Hoore*, SHIRT by *G-Star
Raw*, BOW TIE by *Polo
Ralph Lauren*, TROUSERS
by *Salvatore Ferragamo*

THIS PAGE: JACKET by
Dušan, SHIRT by *Woolrich*
John Rich & Bros,
TROUSERS by *Sofie D'Hoore*

OPPOSITE: GLASSES by
Lindberg, JUMPER by
Zanone, SHIRT by *Glanshirt*,
JEANS from *G-Star Raw*
by *Marc Newson*, WATCH
by *Hublot*

HAIR:
Oliver de Almeida

MAKE-UP:
Lyz Marsden

MODELS:
*Kamila Wladyka,
Tenzing, Kimberley Ann,
John Rawlinson*

ASSISTANT STYLIST:
Kyoko Tamoto

E

Inventory Nº68

01
Clancy Moore Design
Leaded Strand Lamp
Made by a family-run metalworker in Portadown, Northern Ireland, each of these sturdy desk lamps is hand-rolled from a brass bar. Every piece differs slightly in burnish and patina and is numbered and signed by its designers, who also keep a ledger recording the final homes of their wares. — ETL
makersandbrothers.com

02
Huzi Design
Wooden car
Petrolheads young and old can thank Hong Kong-based designer Mike Mak and Huzi Design for the chance to craft their own dream car. The chassis is made from sturdy poplar and the wheels are crafted from birch (selected for its smooth movement). The walnut base gives each vehicle a distinctive grain pattern and if you fancy a splash of colour, the toys can be adorned with easy-to-clean chalk. — VL
huzidesign.com

Preface
From natural bitters and handmade spirits to dainty teapots and bird books, we reveal the products that are grabbing our attention this month.

Editor
Josh Fehnert

Photographer
David Sykes

03
Oola
Spirits

Hailing from Seattle's foodie Capitol Hill neighbourhood, Oola Distillery was established in 2010 by former gallery owner Kirby Kallas-Lewis. The brand uses local ingredients to make high-quality spirits. "Our bottles are all hand-labelled, etched and sealed. This is labour intensive but it's important for us to employ people and have a community," says managing director Jeana Harrington. — JAF
ooladistillery.com

04
Asahineko
Dustpan and brush

When Japan's forest-rich Gifu prefecture decided to utilise its trees, it turned to designers Makoto Koizumi and Kazuteru Murasawa. This handy desktop brush, available in three shapes, is made of arborvitae (*nezuko*) and cypress (*hinoki*). — JT
asahineko.jp

05
Frank Clegg Leatherworks
Briefcase

New England-based Frank Clegg Leatherworks has been producing high-quality leather goods for more than four decades. Its briefcases are still top of the pile and made from 100 per cent vegetable-tanned leather. This handy bag comes with an optional shoulder strap for portability. — ADC
frankcleggleatherworks.com

06
Verso Skincare
Beauty products

Verso, (literally "reverse" in Latin) is a Swedish skincare range that focuses on turning back the hands of time when it comes to ageing skin. Its eye-catching, minimal packaging was designed by The Studio. — EC
versoskincare.com

07
AÃRK Collective
Watches

Design firm AÃRK Collective's debut watch collection has been ticking over nicely since launching this year. "We believe in reducing the elements to the essentials and we keep branding to a minimum," says the company's director Sara Su. With their aircraft-grade stainless-steel cases and Melbourne-made straps, these modern timepieces are just the beginning for this Aussie five-piece. — JAF
aarkcollective.com

08
Our Songbirds
Book

Our Songbirds is an enchanting illustrated depiction of Britain's chattiest feathered friends. It features a bird for each week of the year and artist Matt Sewell combines a love of ornithology with a dab hand for watercolours. — JAF
mattsewell.co.uk

09
Cuckoo
Teapot

Designed by Yu-Fen Lo of Taiwanese brand Cuckoo, this dainty teapot is made of stone and wrapped in a wooden heat-resistant handle to ensure a steady grip. "To be able to make a good pot of tea while travelling is an incredible luxury for the modern urban dweller," says Yu-Fen. — AIM
ditmit.co

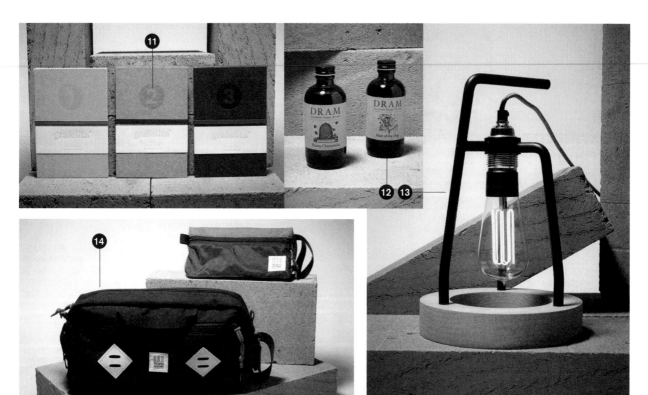

album reminiscent of the *goshuincho* notebooks found in Japanese temples. — IC
grafolita.com

12
Dram Apothecary
Bitters
Shae Whitney first came up with Dram Apothecary at food-science college while working as a bartender. "I realised most of the bitters I served were synthetically dyed and flavoured – I wanted to create something out of wild, natural herbs." Whitney attempts to bring back the ancient "cure-all" function of bitters by foraging for them herself among Colorado's alpine herbs. — GSL
dramapothecary.com

13
Ministry of Mass
Barrel lamp
Founded last year by David Braeckman and Sander Michiels, Ministry of Mass is a Belgium-based design collective with sustainability at its core. This beech-framed lamp with a rolled-steel case is ideal for illuminating large spaces and can be suspended by its hook or rested on its base. — JAF
ministryofmass.com

14
Topo Designs
Bags
Topo Designs makes colourful bags that are as at home on

the trail as they are in the city. "We wanted to bring style and simplicity back to an outdoor brand without sacrificing too many technical details," says co-founder Jedd Rose. — JAF
topodesigns.com

15
Carriage 44
Soap
After seven years in the UK, Oliver Stenberg returned to Canada in 2010 to found Carriage 44 with his wife Hannah and mother Florenda. The handmade soaps share a base of olive oil, shea butter, coconut oil and sweet almond oil, and are available in 12 scents ranging from vanilla to Stenberg's favourite – oatmeal. — ADC
cargocollective.com/carriage44

16
Bleeding Heart Rum Co
Rum
This tasty tipple was born on the island of Negros – the capital of the Philippines' sugar industry. "The idea was to create a single island rum made and aged 100 per cent on this beautiful island," says Stephen Carroll, founder of Bleeding Heart Rum Co. Distilled from the finest sugar cane and aged for seven years in American oak barrels, this smooth rum is named after Papa Isio, a lesser-known hero of the Philippine Revolution. — AIM
donpaparum.com

10
Best Made
Blanket
Founded in 2009 by Peter Buchanan-Smith, US manufacturer Best Made makes hardy objects for a life lived outdoors. We like the feel of this Lumberland Camp Blanket and nifty leather sling – perfect for a kip under the stars or a picnic in the park. — JAF
bestmadeco.com

11
Grafolita
Notebooks
Portugal's Grafolita sells a collection of notebooks made by designer Catarina Vaz. "This project resulted from my love of traditional typography and my desire to do something handmade," she says. On an old Hogenforst printing press, Vaz makes an accordion-style

Go with the ice flow
Arctic region

Preface
There was a time when a trip to the chilly climes of the north promised frostbite and, potentially, mortal peril. Now you can land at a refurbished airport, check into a boutique hotel and sightsee in a hot-air balloon.

Embrace alternative transport
Arctic Kingdom expeditions
Canada

Travelling around the extreme and isolated high Arctic north of Canada calls upon the expertise of Toronto-based travel company Arctic Kingdom, founded by Graham Dickson, a University of Pennsylvania graduate. His passion for extreme diving took him to Arctic waters for the first time in 1999, a place where he now spends most of his time taking travellers into the remote regions of Nunavut and Baffin Island. "Here it is all about logistics and knowing the right people," says expedition director Thomas Lennartz (*far left*). "Anything is possible." — DEP
arctickingdom.com

Travel options

Snowmobiles: Arctic Kingdom owns six Ski-Doo Expedition 600 ACE snowmobiles by Bombardier and has access to 10 more depending on the size of the expedition.

Dogsledding: An optional activity for guests. Trips include a private meal on top of an iceberg with delicacies such as Arctic char sashimi and caribou carpaccio.

Hot-air balloons: Arctic Kingdom has one hot-air balloon for four people in Arctic Bay and another will be stationed at Pond Inlet. Flights are made on request and allow travellers to see the Arctic sea in its gargantuan glory.

Sleep in an igloo
Hotel Arctic
Ilulissat, *Greenland*

Some 300km north of the Arctic Circle is the aptly named Hotel Arctic, its five metal igloos are perfect for those who want to stay next to the Ilulissat icefjord. Open from May to September, each igloo holds up to two people. The hotel has been awarded a Green Key Eco-Rating for being a leader in creating awareness about global warming. — ADC
hotel-arctic.gl

To find out more about the Arctic way of life, tune in to Monocle 24 this month for our series on life in the High North. Visit *monocle.com/radio*.

Get a warm reception
Puvirnituq airport
Nunavik, *Canada*

The Nunavik village of Puvirnituq completed an airport overhaul in April. Most striking is the new CA$6.5m (€4.7m) main terminal building with its shops and radio tower. The airport can now accommodate larger jets such as the Boeing 737-200C, meaning shorter flight times from Montréal.
The terminal was designed in collaboration with the local Inuit community. "The *qamutiq* [traditional sled] inspired many aspects of the building's design," says principal architect Alain Fournier, a partner at Fournier Gersovitz Moss Drolet et Associés Architectes. — JZL
+1 819 988 1530

Bunk down at basecamp
Nordenskiöld Lodge
Svalbard, *Norway*

Hidden away on a side fjord of the Svalbard archipelago, the Nordenskiöld Lodge serves as a basecamp for those hiking the glacier of the same name. Run by Basecamp Explorer, this wooden inn has all the necessary comforts. The heat for the lodge's five rooms is provided by burning wood gathered from nearby forests and drinking water is sourced straight from the glacier.

Guests can visit surrounding mining towns, go skiing or relax in the sauna. Flights from Oslo to Longyearbyen, Svalbard's hub, take three hours and Nordenskiöld can be reached by boat, snowmobile or a dog-sled trip. — AVF
basecampspitsbergen.com

Enjoy a leisurely commute
Arctic Umiaq Line
Greenland

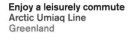

A scheduled passenger ferry has sailed this route along the west coast of Greenland for more than 200 years. Today the Arctic Umiaq Line's passenger ferry, *Sarfaq Ittuk*, also functions as a kind of back-to-basics cruise ship, sailing – depending on the season – from Qaqortoq or Narsaq in the south via the capital Nuuk to Ilulissat in the Arctic north over the course of three days.

This spectacular frozen coast is a major attraction for tourists keen to see the Arctic meadows in the south and the icy fells of the north, with plenty of opportunities to spot icebergs, whales and seals along the 1,300km route. These days the Arctic Umiaq Line is jointly owned by Air Greenland and the Royal Arctic Line, which also operates a handful of smaller ships on local commuter routes. — MB
aul.gl

Take the scenic route
Lux Adventures
Iceland

Icelandic tour operator Lux Adventures likes to get to places no other cars in the country can get to with its four custom-made 4x4 Land Cruiser 70s with monstrous 110cm tyres (*pictured*). Since 2003, the company has operated tours to places such as the Fjallabak Nature Reserve and the Landmannalaugar highlands.

"We drive on top of glaciers and volcanoes in the most intense weather conditions," says Karl Olafsson, director of development at Lux Adventures. "In the extreme interior of the country we cross fast-flowing rivers or drive through ravines over steep rhyolite rock slopes and boiling hot springs, ending up on light-coloured alluvial plains that reach the cold Arctic sea." — DEP
lux.is

Sightsee in style
Atlantic Helicopters
Sørvágur, *Faroe Islands*

For as little as €11, visitors can hop around 10 of the islands that make up this isolated Danish archipelago on board a helicopter. Since 1994, Atlantic Helicopters, a division of Atlantic Airways subsidised by the Faroese government, has been a means of getting around for both locals and tourists. The company also conducts a lot of "sling" work: dropping cranes, cars or building equipment in secluded places, filming, supporting offshore operations on oil platforms and conducting rescue missions.

The fleet consists of two Bell 412s with room for up to 11 passengers each. The subdivision works with 14 staff of whom nine are pilots specially trained to operate in extremely changeable North Atlantic weather conditions. — DEP
atlantic.fo

PHOTOGRAPHERS: DAVID DE VLEESCHAUWER, THOMAS EKSTRÖM

Strike out on a polar research ship
Akademik Sergey Vavilov
Canada

There are many expedition ships sailing around the Arctic's icy waters but few as imposing as the 117m-long *Akademik Sergey Vavilov*. Originally built in Finland in 1988 as a research ship for the Russian Academy of Science to conduct hydro-coustic tests and other studies in the world's coldest oceans, it now operates primarily as a polar expedition ship that can take as many as 92 passengers on board.

The *Vavilov*, with its highly experienced Russian crew, is operated by Canadian company One Ocean and sails around Svalbard, Greenland and the Northwest Passage above Canada. When not cruising the waters of the north, the *Vavilov* heads for Antarctica or continues with its scientific research thanks to the extra income that is generated by tourism. — DEP
oneoceanexpeditions.com

Relax in a boutique hotel
Egilsen
Stykkishólmur, *Iceland*

Two years ago, Gréta Sigurðardóttir bought an 1867 wooden house from Stykkishólmur's mayor and transformed it into the 10-room boutique hotel Egilsen, with the help of Reykjavík-based architecture company a2f. "We just kept the exterior as the skeleton and changed everything inside it," says Sigurðardóttir.

The three-storey building is home to one of the most extensive literary collections in the region, from unique leather-bound Shakespearean novels to limited-edition Icelandic children's books. "What can I say – I'm a big fan of books." — ADC
egilsen.is

Stay in a fishing village
Tromvik Lodge
Tromsø, *Norway*

Tromvik is an idyllic retreat for those seeking some R&R on Norway's northernmost tip. Evening barbecues include fish caught in the surrounding waters, with dishes such as ceviche, king crab and pan-fried halibut.

"There is such tranquillity and peace here," says owner Tore Gjert Eriksen, who runs the lodge with wife Anne. "You're so close to nature and all it has to offer: hiking in the forests, fishing for trout and salmon in the lakes, chasing the Northern Lights and whale watching." — AVF
tromviklodge.com

Catch the Northern Lights
Kakslauttanen
Saariselkä, *Finland*

There are two main attractions for visitors to Finnish Lapland: meeting Santa Claus and watching the Northern Lights. For the latter, the Kakslauttanen hotel in Saariselkä is the place to stay.

A 30-minute drive from Ivalo airport, Kakslauttanen has grown from a modest log-cabin village into a high-end destination where guests can stay in "igloos" made with thermal glass to watch the Aurora Borealis from bed. And spend some time in the on-site smoke sauna – its the biggest of its kind in the world. — MH
kakslauttanen.fi

Stay on an Arctic island
Malahorn
Grímsey Island, *Iceland*

The Malahorn guesthouse offers a tough choice between hunkering down and enjoying the view or strapping on sturdy footwear and exploring the Icelandic coastline. Nearby Grímsey is the largest island nesting sight for the Atlantic puffin; visitors can see upwards of 300,000 of them swooping into the freezing waters for fresh fish.

The guesthouse is cosy, offering accommodation from a self-catering cottage for the independent traveller to full-board for those looking to take a load off. — JAF
malarhorn.is

Effective cold relief
Canadian North

Preface
Passengers are merely one part of the equation for this Arctic airline: connecting isolated communities and ferrying food and fuel are just as high on the agenda.

Writer
Debbie Pappyn

Canadian North has been serving the Canadian Arctic for more than 80 years. The North American carrier is owned by 30,000 Inuit shareholders (the Inuvialuit and Inuit of Nunavut). An extensive network of scheduled flights and cargo services is offered throughout Nunavut and the Northwest Territories, as well as charter operations in Canada and the US.

It also does the crucial job of linking small and remote communities that are often unreachable by road or sea during the winter. Northern towns such as Clyde River, Cambridge Bay and Kungaaruk depend on its services, not just for passenger transport but also to receive cargo such as food and diesel.

But air passage to the High North is not always easy. Canadian North pilots often have to deal with poor weather, sometimes making last-minute decisions as to whether to attempt a landing. Even if they do manage to touch down there's no guarantee they'll be able to take off

again; travellers often calculate additional travel days into their schedule to be able to make connecting flights.

Canadian North is based in Yellowknife in the Northwest Territories but one of its main hubs is the town of Iqaluit in the Nunavut Province. Daily flights operate between Ottawa and Iqaluit, from where smaller Dash airplanes connect the more remote communities. The company's slogan is "Seriously Northern" and the logo is a polar bear and the midnight sun – two distinct features of the Arctic north of Canada.

"The company tries to employ as many Inuit as possible," says marketing co-ordinator Jean Vivian. "The airline also offers substantial discounts to local people. In addition we provide different sponsorships and support special events, sports teams and school activities in remote communities." — (M)
canadiannorth.com

Aircraft: Seven Boeing 737-200s, five Boeing 737-300s and four de Havilland Canada DHC-8-100 Dash 8s.

Number of employees: Approximately 800.

In-flight services: Snacks on all flights of less than an hour and light meals with free non-alcoholic drinks on longer journeys (Canadian beer and wine is for sale). Most flight attendants speak not only English but also the languages of the north, including Inuvialuktun, Inuktitut, Inuinnaqtun and French. Canadian North also publishes in-flight magazine *Up Here*.

Take a frosty flight
First Air
Kanata, *Canada*

First Air's planes, including three new Boeing B737-400s introduced in the autumn, carry 225,000 passengers on scheduled and chartered services across 30 destinations in Canada's north every year. No surprise then that the bulk of its fleet of 23 aircraft is retrofitted for icy landings.

The company, which generates CA$190m (€137m) in sales and pumps CA$40m (€29m) into the northern economy every year, has been strengthening its ties to the region. That's long been the case with in-flight magazine *Above & Beyond*, which proudly bears the tagline "Canada's Arctic Journal". For 25 years the publication has been keeping passengers abreast of the latest happenings, including everything from environmental issues to Inuit culture.

In 1990, the Inuit non-profit Makivik Corporation bought the company, transferring complete ownership to the 9,000 members of the First Nations group in northern Quebec. Today the company provides jobs for more than 1,000 people, 450 of whom live in the Arctic.

The airline transports some essential cargo to Arctic communities on its passenger planes: its two L382G Hercules aircraft are capable of carrying fire engines, among other things. In July, the airline renewed a five-year commitment with The North West Company to transport fresh produce and non-perishable food to the grocery chain's 128 shops, ensuring that the larders of Canadian Arctic dwellers are well stocked. — JZL
firstair.ca

Small is beautiful
Bergen

Preface
Nordnes, in central Bergen, is
attracting a new generation
of creative types – who don't
mind a lack of private space.

Writer
David Michon

Photographer
Kristian Helgesen

01

Half-jokingly, you might hear someone call it "the Republic", but more easily you'll get a sense of what distinguishes Nordnes by just taking a brief stroll from the city centre through this peninsular neighbourhood of Bergen. Shooting off from the town centre into the Byfjorden, the atmosphere changes as soon as you cross its threshold: from mighty stone buildings to wooden cottages, it's a village vibe now (not that Bergen is a frantic metropolis, of course).

In the 1970s and 1980s, Nordnes was all but a slum, home to drug addicts and prostitutes. Its high street may still not be quite there but cobbled side streets ooze charm and there is more than enough to justify residents' warming patriotism. Here you'll find one of two cinemas in all of Bergen, discover Norway's oldest artist-run arts centre or reach the neighbourhood's tip and be treated to the stunning 102-year-old swimming club, the Nordnes Sjøbad (a heated, salt-water bathing club with stunning views).

"This neighbourhood attracts a certain type of person," says artist and gallerist Marie Storaas, 32. Architects, artists, young, old and multicultural, they are also people who don't mind a snug living space: Storaas's three-floor wooden home, built in 1775, is only 90 sq m and fits her family of five. Thankfully this is Scandinavia, capital of cosiness, and what would feel like cramped quarters in Britain or North America here feels warm and pleasantly idiosyncratic while still being orderly.

Where private space is at a premium, more is made of what lies beyond your front door. "The entire area serves as our living room," says Storaas, who always

02

03

01 Homes on Strangebakken
02 The peninsula isn't shy of
     hills
03 View of Nordnes from the
     Fløyen Mountain
04 Marie Storaas, husband
     Snorre Saveraas and
     their family
05 Nordnes Park at the tip of
     the peninsula
06 The first floor of Storaas's
     home
07 Cottage-like kitchen at
     Storaas's home
08 Ingeborg Revheim and
     Petter Sætre
09 Nordnes's only busker

Property boom

Nordnes is characterised by its impressive collection of traditional wooden homes dating from the late 1700s and early 1800s that occupy the southern half of the peninsula. Over the hill, flanking Strandgaten, is a very different stock: post-war apartment blocks and commercial buildings, constructed after the 1944 explosion of a Dutch cargo ship, *Voorbode*, that destroyed many of the houses.

The cosy wooden homes (it's not unusual for a child's bedroom to have a footprint of under 5 sq m) force a particular lifestyle, says architectural psychologist Eirik Glambek Bøe: "It makes you reconsider your home; more of your life has to happen in public spaces."

04

05   06

07

08   09

swam at Nordnes Sjøbad as a child and moved to the neighbourhood 11 years ago. "There is more of a community vibe [compared with other parts of Bergen]. The geography definitely contributes." The architecture dictates a more socially orientated set of residents, helped by the fact that few choose to leave Nordnes after landing one of its coveted homes.

While the lifestyle of small living spaces can be recreated, the housing stock in Nordnes can't. When the oldest of the still-standing wooden homes were built nearly 250 years ago, forestry in Norway was a more considered practice. Slow-growth trees were individually selected for specific purposes: trees good for making window frames might differ from those appropriate for flooring, for instance. In Storaas's home, layers of wallpaper and treatment were stripped back to expose the now-rare quality of its wood. Today, the felling of trees is heavily mechanised and faster-growth trees are more commonly used: cheaper but not as durable.

Oddly, it's an economic crisis 30 years ago we have to thank for Nordnes

01

02

Property guide

Overview
Foreigners buying property
in Bergen must have a non-
resident personal identifica-
tion number (a D-number),
and the application takes
a few weeks. As opposed
to some regions in Norway,
you can buy here without
occupying the home, so you
can buy a holiday property.

Prices (average) for
traditional wooden home
per sq m
1 bedroom–€7,000
2 bedrooms–€7,500
3 bedrooms–€7,700

Estate agent
Dag Jonny Johannessen
DNB Property
dnbeiendom.no
+47 915 04800

03

The Local
Monica Hannestad (*left*)
Director, Design Region Bergen

A resident of Nordnes for 10 years, Monica
owns a modernised wooden home on a cobbled
pedestrianised street. "You don't ever feel lone-
some here. The people are so friendly," she says.

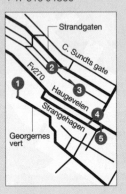

05 06

07

being as it is: slated for demolition, its
residents only succeeded in fighting back
because the city's coffers couldn't hack it
– a stroke of luck not enjoyed in Oslo.

Today, the city has clearly changed its
opinion: re-cobbling Nordnes's narrow
streets; experimenting with new waste-
management infrastructure that would
take unsightly bins off the pavement (by
putting in underground shoots, to be
expanded across the city); and, just last year
giving a facelift to Bergen's only remaining
ballast quay (and giving the residents of
Nordnes another spot to swim).

On its west shore is perhaps the
neighbourhood's best asset – the United
Sardines Factory (USF). In 1993, this
former factory was transformed into
a cultural centre to match any other: a
relaxed restaurant, gallery, jazz café and
the energy of having more than 80 artists' studios and offices occupy 12,000 sq
m. This year its 1,500-capacity concert
hall was renovated, designed to support
amplified music, and boasts furniture
designed specifically for USF by Bergen-
based studio KnudsenBergHindenes (it's
the centre's second in-house collection).

08

09

Stay

Klosterhagen Hotell ④
This 15-room hotel is located at the centre of Nordnes, a five-minute walk from the centre of Bergen. And it's got a social conscience: some staff are part of a service-training programme inspired by Copenhagen's Hostellet Vesterbro.
Strangehagen 2
+47 53 00 22 00
klosterhagenhotell.no

Gallery

Salongen ②
A charming 15 sq m gallery tucked away on a pedestrian side-street, Salongen is run by two Nordnes residents and shows their work (photography and paintings) as well as that of other artists.
Nykirkeallmenningen 7
+47 41 51 56 96
romforkunst.com

Hordaland Arts Centre
Showing both local and international artists, the gallery puts on five exhibitions a year. Enjoy a slice of the café's famous carrot cake that is worthy of its reputation.
Klosteret 17
+47 55 90 85 90
kunstsenter.no/en

Eat & drink

Kafe Kippers ①
Enjoy the sunset and dine outside on the vast terrace overlooking the fjord, opt for the cosy 80-seat indoor space or kick back with a locally brewed Hansa at the adjacent Jazz Café.
USF, Georgernes Verft 12
+47 55 30 40 80
usf.no

Bjellands kjøkken ③
Randi Bjelland's five-table restaurant is as close to stepping into your Norwegian grandmother's kitchen as you can get: homely and kitschy with traditional home-style dishes.
Strandgaten 201
+47 55 90 02 44

Shop

Hordaland Arts Centre ⑤ bookshop
With more than 500 books and magazines in both Norwegian and English, the bookshop opened last year and goes beyond monographs: you can find art commentary and novels here too.
Klosteret 17
+47 55 90 85 90
kunstsenter.no/en

A cloister of apartment buildings next to the USF complex has helped make it even more of a hub and its vast 500-seat seaside terrace is packed in warm weather. Maria Prestmo has lived in one of these apartments since 2002, the year after they were built, and co-owns the Salongen Rom for Kunst gallery with Storaas. For her, the neighbourhood's density is key to its success: "My children's school is two minutes up the hill, there's a place to play in front of my door and a place to swim in the summer."

Amenity is never more than a stone's throw away in the neighbourhood (though Nordnes could perhaps use a better grocer if you're looking to shake off the gold handcuffs and set up shop here). And its assets range from historic to contemporary, some perfectly preserved (such as the bathing club) and others smartly updated. But the real spark of Nordnes is its mix of ambitious institutions with a humble environment and how it toys with scale: how a vast former factory can seem at home next to the tiniest of houses. — (M)

10 11

12 13

La Giudecca, Venice
Women in Venetian prison La Giudecca are the unlikely producers of some of the city's finest vegetables, which they grow on the vast prison allotment. The fruits of their labours, including purple asparagus, cardoon and Creazzo broccoli, are sold outside the prison walls in a weekly market.

Örtagård Öst
Jämtland, *Sweden*

Brothers Bengt-Johnny and Jan-Anders left behind their careers, one a croupier, the other an electrician, to return home to Öster Övsjö in Jämtland. They now spend their days producing natural cordials and berry wines from wild fruits collected across the region, for restaurants including Noma in Copenhagen. Their offshoot business, Jämtlands Vingård, makes mead for the acclaimed and remote country restaurant Fäviken Magasinet, from honey collected on their property. "They are beverages that you can work with in the dining room," says Robert Andersson, sommelier at Fäviken. "They are fresh, dry and elegant in a way that I don't find in other non-alcoholic drinks." — CR
nordictaste.se; favikenmagasinet.se

Alquimie
Melbourne

Newly launched drinks quarterly *Alquimie* is dedicated to both alcoholic and non-alcoholic beverages. The tightly designed title delivers the stories behind everything from Japanese sake to Frankfurt's Apfelwein.
"We wanted to take a timeless approach rather than the hottest things right now," says co-founder Nicholas Cary, who also established graphic design magazine *Process Journal*. — AK
alquimie.com.au

For recipes, restaurant tips and some fine food banter, take time out for a tasty bite of our food and drink show, The Menu, on Monocle 24. Go to our website at monocle.com or download shows from iTunes.

Top 3
Nutcrackers

From traditional designs to modern solutions that do away with any nut debris, here are our favourites.

01 Royal VKB
Wave goodbye to flying nut shells thanks to Ineke Hans' compact nutcracker, whose design ensures any waste is contained ready for easy disposal. A simple twist is all that's required.
royalvkb.com

02 Robert Welch
Made from solid cast iron with a steel spindle, this Hobart Nutcracker was the work of late British silversmith and designer Robert Welch and is still manufactured at the same factory in the Cotswolds.
robertwelch.com

03 Normann Copenhagen
Designed by the trio who make up Ding3000, this nutcracker was launched as a solution to traditional tools that cause finger pain when cracking nuts. New to the Normann Copenhagen range, its silicone and aluminium design adds a contemporary twist to the task. — AK
normann-copenhagen.com

Erich Hamann
Berlin

They've been perfecting the chocolates here for over 100 years – and today they come wrapped in 1920s-style packaging, made on machines developed by founder Erich Hamann. In 1912, the company was one of the first to introduce dark, bitter-cocoa chocolates in a market dominated by sweeter treats. The entire production process is still housed in the 1928 Bauhaus building and is run by Erich's grandson, Andreas. Keeping faithful to old recipes and techniques, the store's dozen employees craft cocoa truffles, classic Mokka-Bohnen, fruity pralines and the house's signature creation, slim pieces of chocolate bark. — AVF
hamann-schokolade.de

PHOTOGRAPHERS: ANDREW URWIN, WESTON WELLS, LI-HAN LIN, JOHAN LIM, TINA STAFRÉN. STILL LIFE: DAVID SYKES

Q&A

**Cynthia Shan-
mugalingam**
**Founder,
Kitchenette**
London

Cynthia Shanmugalingam was previously an economist at the UK Treasury and has recently launched Kitchenette, an incubator supporting start-up food businesses.

What is Kitchenette exactly?
It is London's first kitchen incubator inspired by similar models in the US, such as La Cocina in San Francisco and tech start-ups such as Y Combinator. We aim to create platforms for people to create food businesses as it is such a high-risk area. Food is so accessible, you can make it from anywhere and it is possible for people to overcome their economic disadvantages and get themselves out of poverty by using food.

How does the service run?
Small businesses don't have to pay to get advice, they apply online with their enterprise idea; we interview them and then try the food. If they get accepted they go through a 12-week intensive programme that incorporates classes on everything from food branding to the economics of setting up. We also set them up with pitches in markets and pop-up stints in restaurants so they can get feedback and first-hand experience along with one-to-one time with industry advisors.

What's your current roster?
At the moment we are working with six people, including Kimchinary, a Korean taco maker who makes her kimchi from scratch and Co&Co Chocolates, an online chocolate business. Instead of a cash fee, we see ourselves as long-term partners in the businesses we work with, so we take a small stake in the business. — AK
wearekitchenette.com

Empire Mayonnaise
New York

Elizabeth Valleau teamed up with chef Sam Mason to launch Brooklyn's Empire Mayonnaise store, which supplies the likes of Dean & Deluca with handmade mayonnaise created from free-range eggs and non-GM oils. "My mother is of French descent and I grew up eating homemade mayonnaise," says Valleau, who counts flavours such as black garlic and white truffle among her offerings. — AK
empiremayo.com

Common Man Coffee Roasters
Singapore

The opening of Common Man Coffee Roasters in Robertson Quay in August hails a new era for coffee in the region.

A joint venture between Harry Grover of 40 Hands, the Spa Espirit Group and Australia's Five Senses Coffee, it's more than just a café serving aromatic brews. Its lofty aim is to "democratise" specialist coffee in the continent.

"We want to take down the preciousness about coffee and are going to open up the specialist coffee market in Asia by doubling as a wholesale coffee distributor using the expertise of Five Senses," says Cynthia Chua, founder of the Spa Esprit Group. From the food to the décor, no detail has been neglected and speciality coffees will be served from cups that are hand-turned by a local potter. — AK
commonmancoffeeroasters.com

Menu picks
Eggs benedict with ox cheeks and chive hollandaise.

Turkish breakfast with eggs wrapped in filo pastry.

STAR DISH
Beef tartare, Luksus
New York

With stints as a Noma pastry supremo and head of R&D at Momofuku, the culinary accolades of Halifax-born chef Daniel Burns are now being put to use in his recently opened Brooklyn joint Luksus, which features a Nordic-inspired menu.

The beef tenderloin used in this dish comes from Oregon's Painted Hills and is served with caramelised onion chip, padron pepper and heritage tomatoes; accented by the tart but sweet pickled ramp caper berries (a wild cousin of leek). Burns has turned the grand dame of French bistro fare on its head with this umami-packed pleasure. — SRT
luksusnyc.com

Super Swedes
Stockholm

Preface

Stockholm used to be a conservative culinary destination, filled with fancy restaurants and overcomplicated cuisine. That was until locals in need of a more laidback atmosphere raised their voices (and cutlery) clamoring for a place where they could grab a quick bite and a coffee to go. Luckily a new generation of food entrepreneurs have answered their call and met their demands with big-scale, clever-format enterprises.

Writer
Gabriel Leigh

Photographer
Simon Bajada

Taverna Brillo
Ready to serve

Taverna Brillo is a space of many dimensions, from low-lit corridors to a glass-ceilinged atrium with a 150-year-old olive tree. The Jonas Bohlin-designed interiors incorporate art throughout, from a commissioned carpet to sculptures.

Set in the well-heeled neighbourhood of Östermalm, the multi-function space seeks to elevate Swedish notions about food retail. It includes a bakery (chief baker Håkan Johansson represents Sweden in the international Bakery Masters competition), a ready-meals section, delicatessen, gelateria, pizzeria and a flower shop, with a larger, more formal dining room and restaurant at its centre – all open until 02.00 on most days.

"People are still changing their attitudes towards eating out and ready-made meals," says owner PG Nilsson. "The change is now picking up pace. People are very focused on quality today." — (M)
tavernabrillo.se

Top 3 dishes

Brick-oven-baked pizza with chanterelles, bacon, lardons and svecia cheese
The pizza menu revolves around seasonal ingredients – in this case chanterelles.

Blackcurrant sorbet with pistachio gelato
A combination of Nordic punch and Italian sweetness.

Sturehof surströmming
Surströmming is fermented Baltic herring.

Broms
The food bank

Anna Bauer started Broms as a catering business in her cellar seven years ago. When a property developer asked her if she could do something with the ground floor of an old Nordea Bank off Karlaplan, she leapt at the opportunity. The result is a multi-faceted food establishment with everything from fresh produce and Broms-branded dry goods at the corner entrance to a selection of top-notch cured meats, cheeses, delightful baked goods and a full restaurant too.

Bauer spent time abroad and credits the influence of London and New York. When she returned to Stockholm eight years ago, she found herself lacking a place where she could go at any hour and spend time over a late lunch.

"Sweden has been extremely conservative about food," says Bauer. "My vision is to meet the demands of everyone's lives. Chefs shouldn't decide what time people are supposed to eat." — (M)
bromscatering.se

Top 3 products

Rotisserie chicken with root vegetables and mixed salad
The chicken comes with two sauces, such as *kimchi* mayonnaise and lemon crème fraîche (pictured).

Homemade knäckebröd
Crispy bread baked in sheets of wholegrain goodness.

Cinnamon and cardamom buns
These staples of Swedish coffee breaks are baked on site.

K25
Global food

K25 is an all-new take on the "food hall" in Stockholm, a testament to the gap it fills in the market. Here customers, many of whom come from nearby offices, have access to a dozen high-quality food businesses located under a bridge crossing over Kungsgatan in the centre of Stockholm.

There are nine restaurants plus a coffee shop and a bakery – handpicked by owner Ricard Constantinou, a food-focused entrepreneur whose parents emigrated to Sweden from Greece.

Food options include sushi, Greek and Turkish food, Chinese dumplings, burgers and baked goods from renowned bakery Fabrique. "Stockholm has developed some interesting restaurants during the past 10 to 15 years," he says. "But a food hall like K25 didn't exist and I thought it was important to show you can serve food in an alternative way."

One of the main goals at K25 is to entice people to take their food to go, and many of the items for sale are packaged accordingly, for portability. They have to do that because there isn't enough space for everyone to dine – according to Constantinou, they're up to a 35 per cent takeaway rate. — (M)
k25.nu

Top 3 products

Burger with cheddar and bacon from Lilla Vigårda
Vigårda cooks up some of the best burgers in Stockholm.

Pour-over black coffee from Kura Café
The New Zealanders running Kura use Geisha coffee beans from the Hacienda La Esmeralda in Panamá.

Räksmörgas prawn sandwich from Lisapåväg
You can't go wrong with this.

Urban Deli
One-stop shop

Since it opened four years ago, Urban Deli has become an institution in Stockholm's Södermalm. It's a full-service grocer complete with a butcher counter, restaurant and bar that's a cosy place to spend time by day and has a festive social scene by night.

"We want to bring the produce and the food into focus without being pompous about it," says Jesper Konstantinov, manager and part-owner of Urban Deli. Its popularity has meant it's bustling on a Monday, when restaurants here find it tough filling seats.

"The restaurant business is all about service, it's all about the atmosphere, whereas in the food-store business in Sweden it's all about low prices and maximising efficiency," says Konstantinov.

"And none of us really enjoy going out food shopping in Sweden because you go to really sterile, boring shops. We wanted to open up a food store where we'd like to go ourselves." There's already a second Urban Deli in Sickla, and ideas afoot for variations on the theme and even an Urban Deli hotel. — (M)
urbandeli.org

Top 3 products

Steak tartare
The addition of egg-yolk cream makes this a highlight.

Tomahawk and entrecôte from the butcher's counter
Want to impress at a barbecue? Go for these giant cuts.

Half-dozen oysters
Menu choices include Fine de Normandie, Utah Beach and Gillardeau – or opt for a mix.

Like food? Like drink? Then tune in every week to our radio show The Menu, hosted by Markus Hippi. It's a global survey of the culinary world. Visit monocle.com

Youthful spirit
Rio de Janeiro

Preface
Renowned designer Sergio
Rodrigues views restaurants as
theatres, where atmosphere is
as key as food. His 'last meal'
would be a beef fillet at Gero.

Writer
David Michon

Photographer
Lianne Milton

"I'm crazy about food. And I love Gero,
it's one of the best restaurants in the city.
Even an empty plate here would satisfy
me. Whenever I make furniture for a
restaurant – like here – I don't charge, I
barter for food. Any food that is well prepared and well presented I like (though
I don't think I would eat insects). Brazilian food has a lot of specific ingredients; maybe it's a bit of an acquired taste.
When the Portuguese colonised, the food
here wasn't really to their liking, so what
we've ended up with is a fusion of European, African and aboriginal cuisines.
The rest of Latin America is much more
directly influenced by Spanish cuisine so
it's easier to interpret.

I have always loved food. When I was
nine, my uncles who were in the foreign
service were hosting a dinner – a very
formal dinner full of diplomats. I snuck
into the kitchen and there were these two
amazing puddings on the stove, freshly
made. And I ate them both! It was a huge
scandal [laughs], they had nothing to
serve as dessert.

I don't cook myself, I just eat! In a restaurant, the patrons and the atmosphere
are as important as the food it serves.
What makes for a successful restaurant
is the scenography – they are theatres. I
want there to be a lot of laughter, especially at my last meal. In terms of who
I'd invite: my wife Vera and my mother –
people who have a youthful spirit.

My wife has a theory about this. When
I was a child, I was diagnosed with lethar-
gic encephalitis – an inflammation of the
brain. The doctors told my mother that I
wouldn't die from it but that I would most
likely go crazy. That hasn't happened
yet but Vera thinks I may have just been
stuck with the mentality of a nine-year-

01

Recipe

Beef fillet cooked in red wine sauce
(Serves 1)

190g beef fillet
50ml red wine (cabernet sauvignon)
30ml demi-glace sauce
5g butter
5g extra virgin olive oil
Rosemary and thyme (to taste)
Salt, black pepper (to taste)

The method
01 Rub salt and pepper on the beef fillet.
02 Brown in a pan with extra virgin olive
oil for two minutes on each side.
03 Add the red wine and let it evaporate.
04 Add the demi-glace sauce and herbs.
05 When cooked, let it rest for 30
seconds and serve.

02

03

Profile

Born in 1927 in Rio, Rodrigues is a contemporary of Brazil's design and architecture greats: Oscar Niemeyer, Lucio Costa and Joaquim Tenreiro. His furniture kits out much of the great Niemeyer-designed buildings of Brasilia but is equally easy to spot in newer additions to the country's best interiors, such as at Rio's Fasano hotel. Initially an architect, Rodrigues has had success in interior design and lighting projects as well as his furniture. He comes from a family of artists and intellectuals, which is reflected in his approach: deeply thought out, referencing a personal philosophy of what Brazilian life is and should be.

Venue

Gero opened in 2002. The menu is designed by Rogério Fasano (owner of the Fasano hotels) and is based on classic Italian recipes such as lamb shanks and veal ravioli. The room was designed by Aurélio Martinez Flores, who also worked on Gero's São Paulo outpost.

Menu

To eat:
To start, salmon carpaccio with lemon and olive oil. This is followed by beef fillet with saffron risotto (Rodrigues can barely wait to tuck in). And for dessert, hazelnut and chocolate sorbet made by the restaurant.

To drink:
There's nothing but still water on the table.

04 05

06 07

08

old ever since and that is where my creativity comes from. I don't feel censored and I don't really care what others think – something like what a child experiences. When I design I am my own client – that is all. I used to worry more about my designs though. When I was younger I'd put drawings under my pillow so while I slept they could marinate.

It was always very frustrating for me to see certain Brazilian architecture so revered, part of the Bauhaus movement that had so little to do with Brazil, and the interiors ignored. I designed the Mole chair in 1957 but it didn't get recognition until four years later. It was a design that reflected the Brazilian way of life: relaxed. That it could eventually match the prestige of the architecture was a dream. That chair is part of the MoMA collection now. I've furnished the national theatre in Brasilia and the Ministry of Foreign Affairs. I am very happy.

That I believed so strongly in Brazilian design and made a success of it – I think it helped open doors. I think it helped others to believe in it as well and I think that may be my biggest legacy. Today, there are some very talented designers in the country. I now hope to open an institute to preserve my work and eventually open the archives to students the world over, to make the study of Brazilian design more accessible. I am very happy that my son Roberto is involved in the business as well." — (M)

EXPO
November 2013

№
68

ALASKA'S 50-YEAR-OLD, STATE-RUN FERRY SYSTEM IS NOT A PROFIT-MAKER. BUT FOR THE PEOPLE WHO USE IT, IT IS AS IMPORTANT AS THE POLICE OR FIRE SERVICE. MONOCLE CLIMBS ABOARD.

WRITER
Tristan McAllister

PHOTOGRAPHER
Roderick Aichinger

LIFE AT SEA

THE HIGHWAY THAT FLOATS
—*Skagway*

Inside a stout grey building, passengers queue at the ferry terminal in Skagway, located at the northern end of the Lynn Canal on Alaska's south coast. Today's crowd is a mix of just who is drawn here during the long Alaskan summer days. A tour group composed of retired couples takes up most of the seats inside the terminal, while clusters of young, rain-soaked adventure seekers are scattered about the floor, trying to get some dry sleep, heads rested on their backpacks. The crowd seems small but this is just the first port on a route that will take their ferry, the *M/V Columbia*, south from here to Bellingham, in Washington State. During the trip's four days, the faces will change and numbers will grow as locals, tourists and wanderers trade wheels for water at ports along the way.

The Alaska Marine Highway System – a fleet of 11 ferries that plies Alaska's waters – is the primary mode of transport, along with Alaska Airlines, that keeps the cities and settlements strewn across the state's rugged, vehicle-inaccessible and weather-challenged archipelagos connected. As novel as the name might sound, the "Marine Highway" as locals call it is simply considered a highway that floats.

The state of Alaska makes the finances of the 50-year-old Marine Highway public and it's no secret the ferries don't turn a profit. In 2012 the service generated almost $54m (€40m), but spent nearly $171m (€128m). A mix of state and federal subsidies make up the difference. Marine Highway spokesman Jeremy Woodrow says, "It's well understood that for many communities and residents across Alaska, the Alaska Marine Highway System serves as a vital link for social and economic activity." Fiscal issues aside, these ferries are part of life here and most Alaskans see it as an essential service like police and fire departments.

The people who work at the Skagway ferry terminal fill many roles. One minute they might be checking you in and the next they are dashing across the dock to tie up an arriving ferry in just about any imaginable weather condition. On this drizzly July day, terminal agent Drew Tronrud is tasked with securing the lines that *Columbia* will use to dock. He says his job is easier in the summer but that the weather is a wild card any time of year. "You could have weather where you can't fly for weeks but you can always get on the boat and make it," Tronrud says.

Once the Skagway team secures *Columbia's* lines, down comes the loading ramp. Soon a procession of travellers, cars and lorries disembark. A crew of 60 will need the next three hours to ready the ship for her trip back south. "I lower myself to scrub public toilets just to ride the ferry," jokes Anne Marie Van Wart, a retired software engineer, who says she loves her new seaborne job as a steward. Public toilets are a funny, yet appropriate, way of looking at it. After all, this ferry and others

in the Marine Highway fleet (toilets included) are all public property, owned by Alaska's taxpayers. But employees such as Van Wart clearly have out-of-the-ordinary state jobs – they're often turning down beds and scrubbing down heads (boat talk for loos) in the wee hours of the morning, as these ships can make port at any hour of the day. From stem to stern everyone knows their role. Soon passengers, vehicles and cargo are loaded and *Columbia* heads south on a 1,610km journey to seven ports between Skagway and Bellingham.

Built in 1974, *Columbia* is one of the better-known ferries in the fleet. The biggest of the lot, she stretches 127 metres, holds 600 passengers and can transport 134 vehicles. A heavy-duty machine, she was built with Southeast Alaska in mind – her shallow draft means she can clear some of the most treacherous and shallow waterways around. But don't let her sturdy build fool you, for she is as much beauty as she is brawn. Her lines are on a par with the elegance of Aristotle Onassis's yacht, the *Christina*, or the original *Pacific Princess* (made famous on TV's *The Love Boat*). While the vessel has undergone numerous interior overhauls to stay current, many of the design elements have been meticulously maintained.

Just behind the forward observation area, hidden by one-way mirror glass, the cocktail lounge is a time capsule. It even smells like a musky old bar one might expect to find on an ocean-going vessel. Original velveteen paisley panelling lines the walls and an archetypal bust of a seagoing beauty greets patrons at the door. The ceiling is adorned with hundreds of large vanity light bulbs. Standing on the dance floor, head angled to the ceiling, chief steward Emelie Karline says, "We clean the bulbs one by one when we are in the yard."

"I know, it's so gaudy," she says, but the smile on her face implies that the kitsch is what makes this boat so special. Karline, originally from the Philippines, devotes much of her time to this ship. "I spend more time here than home," the 18-year Marine Highway veteran says, explaining her two-week-on, two-week-off schedule. That's a normal rotation for most of the crew onboard, including the ship's officers steering *Columbia* from the bridge deck.

Today *Columbia* nears one of the more dangerous parts of the trip: the ominously named Peril Strait. This stretch of water on the run between Juneau and Sitka is known for its precarious position and folklore about stranded parties on the beach who were poisoned by shellfish and never rescued. In 2004 a ferry in the Marine Highway fleet ran aground on a nearby reef. While a good samaritan ship rescued all passengers and crew, it's a vivid reminder of what those who steer *Columbia* face on a daily basis. The names around Peril Strait say it

02

03

04

05

06

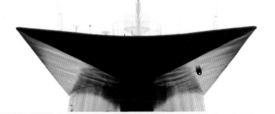

07

08

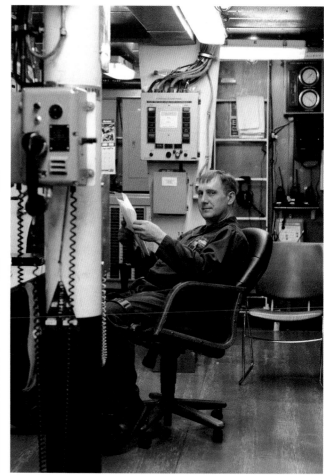

09

10

11

14

15

16

17

18

19

20

21

22

23

25

26

List of plates

all – "Deadman's Reach" and "Poison Cove" are a few of the designations on the bridge's navigational chart placed in front of *Columbia's* Third Mate, who feeds the captain real-time information. Up ahead, the Sergius Narrows can be almost impassable in the wrong tides. At its narrowest point, the waterway gives ships about 90 metres. Couple that with a ripping tide and the margin for error is hair-raisingly small. Remember *Columbia* is longer than the narrows are wide.

"We should have been here 20 minutes ago," says Captain Ken Grieser as he stands at the helm with a watchful eye forward. *Columbia* was late leaving Juneau earlier in the day and the lost time means the tide and currents aren't optimal.

Above the captain a sign taped to the varnished wood window frame reminds those at the helm: "Constant vigilance is the price of safety." The mood on the bridge isn't tense but all appear attentive. Grieser, flanked by his senior officers, has done this passage many times. "Left five rudder; left 10," he commands as the ship winds through the narrow channel. The waterway soon widens and the officers on the bridge breathe easier. "Take a break," says the skipper; they'll do a similar stretch again in 20 minutes.

Grieser, 43, a soft-spoken yet confident Juneau-born ship's master, spent five years in the US Navy and piloted frigates in the Persian Gulf before coming to the Marine Highway 13 years ago.

Pilot Gabriel Baylous, 29, is a sharp navigator who grew up in a port on the Marine Highway. At the helm for the arrival in Sitka, Baylous docks *Columbia* – longer than a football pitch – at the ferry terminal without batting an eye. Although an accomplished seaman, he says his father still sees him as the excited young boat enthusiast he once was. "Dad's surprised they let me drive this thing. He wouldn't let me drive his Bayliner," the bright-eyed officer remarks. Deck cadet Meryl Chew, only 19, also grew up in one of the small towns served

by the Marine Highway and knows these waters well. "They like hiring kids from Alaska here, so you've got a pretty good chance of getting a job," says Chew.

At the ship's aft, the solarium looks more like a campsite than a boat deck. Backpacks, sleeping bags and even tents are strewn about. A dynamic mix of locals, tourists and commuters pass the hours between ports, gawking at the misty-green fjords as the ferry sails by. These views are the stuff of legend, and they captivate onlookers scanning the water for their first look at a humpback whale or a bald eagle.

The wildlife viewing is punctuated with a thermos of coffee, a good book and even an impromptu game of cribbage between new friends. "If you come here, it would be a shame to not see Alaska this way," says Swiss traveller Ramona Zehnder, seated on a solarium cot, as she eats her picnic lunch. "There really is no other option."

This is a truth for Zehnder and the others who've forgone the staterooms for the cheaper, more scenic option of slumber in the solarium. While Zehnder is on the trip of a lifetime, her fellow passengers are just taking part in a routine voyage. This underscores a simple fact for Southeast Alaska's residents: options to get around these parts are expensive and limited. "It costs us $100 each way to fly to Juneau, which makes the lower cost of the ferry more reasonable," says Gustavus resident Karen Platt, bundled in her sleeping bag. This summer the one-way ferry tariff from Gustavus to Juneau is $33.

Platt and her nine-year-old daughter, Yarow, are on summer holiday, but most of the time their ferry trips are a means of survival. "We load the car and do dentist, eye and doctor visits all in one trip to Juneau," says the mother.

There is calm on board these ships. Maybe it's the fact they cover great distances and passengers have to be OK with the "slow boat". For extended periods mobile phones don't work and there is no internet. Behemoth cruise ships with their glitzy shows, buffets and gymnasiums dwarf *Columbia* as they pass by. These big luxury liners, with all their pomp, don't make for the more organic experience found on this ferry.

If crunchy campers, picnic lunches and throwback lounges aren't your thing, *Columbia* does have an indulgence or two worthy of world-class travellers. Inside the aft dining room, passengers sit and wait for a fresh piece of Alaskan salmon or local spot prawns. This evening's meal service is much like one on land, with one seemingly un-American exception: tips are against the law. And, as one waiter soon discovers, people don't always remember that the law says tipping a state employee is a bribe. "Aw man, these people left a tip again," he exclaims, as he dashes out of the dining room, hoping to return the gratuity. It's yet another reminder of how unique this experience is.

It's the afternoon of MONOCLE's last day onboard. As *Columbia* navigates the narrow channel leading to the port of Ketchikan, fishermen passing by in gillnet and seine boats turn and wave at the people observing from their perch on the ferry decks high above.

The air is almost electric when the ferry comes to town. Alaska's flag – eight stars of gold arranged in the shape of the Big Dipper – is emblazoned on *Columbia's* smoke stack. For locals, these ships are symbols of a state that has made the effort to keep its people connected. But when these big blue ships sail south, beyond Alaska's waters, the flag they bear reminds onlookers of the unique and enchanting 49th state and the people who keep it moving. — (M)

Observation
ISSUE 68

As the Monocle team takes to the road again, thoughts are turning to new projects for the year ahead, writes Tyler Brûlé.

Everyone likes a little expedition, particularly when it might involve propeller-driven aircraft and gravel runways, luggage tags with airport codes that raise eyebrows at Heathrow check-in desks (are you sure this is where you're flying to?), a chance of blizzards in late August and the opportunity to buy fine handicrafts made out of reindeer skin. And there's nothing our editors like more than trotting down to the basement to borrow one of our special supply of Canada Goose jackets for High North and high-altitude assignments. In case the cover didn't give it away, the handsome man in the coyote collar and the husky with the fluffy coat are representative of the current race to all points north of the Arctic Circle. As our foreign editor argues in our opener (*page 33*), there's a scramble for established players in the region to bolster their position while a host of newcomers (many with rather tenuous claims to the region) seek new partnerships and permanent seats on various councils.

While a sizeable editorial contingent spent late summer flying around on SAS, Air Greenland and Air Canada feeder services (Tristan McAllister took to the sea to report from the decks of Alaska's state operated ferry service on *page 271*), another group were on ANA, Qantas, Thai and Cathay Pacific zipping north to south, from Tokyo to Melbourne, to launch our book across the Asia-Pacific region. Having met hundreds (thousands?) of readers at various signing events for *The Monocle Guide to Better Living*, we've been busy comparing comments and collating feedback regarding everything from our roster of retail products, programme line-up on Monocle 24 and requests for new specials in the magazine.

Some time in the coming weeks we'll sit down and draw up a list of priorities for the coming year. By the time our December-January issue thumps down on desks and coffee tables (it's shaping up to be our biggest issue ever), we should be able to share our plans for new outposts and special projects for 2014.

In the meantime, our foreign editor is busy wrangling heads of state and foreign ministers to sit alongside our upcoming soft-power survey, our business editor is setting up our new bureau in Istanbul and our photo desk is deploying photographers to the plains of Central Asia, the platforms of Europe's best-designed train stations and into the offices of some the world's sharpest entrepreneurs.

At the same time we ventured out on the road the moment this issue went to press to meet more of our readers across Europe and held events in Geneva, Zürich, Stuttgart (thank you to the team at Bungalow for hosting our first ever event in the southwest corner of the Federal Republic) and Paris (*merci* to everyone at Colette for squeezing us in during a very busy fashion week). Over the coming weeks we'll also be in New York (McNally-Jackson books) and Toronto (our shop and bureau on College Street) to sign a few more copies (yes, we're already in our second print run) and listen keenly to your feedback about the various parts of our business.

As the days grow shorter, we'll be looking north again as we plan to take a whole team on a snappy four-day tour of the Nordic region. From mid November you might see some oversize Rimowa equipment cases belonging to our Monocle 24 battalion around baggage carousels as a group of 10 of us dart around the capitals to talk to mayors, architects, retailers, defence analysts and artists for a series of special programmes we'll be hosting live from Stockholm, Oslo, Copenhagen and Helsinki.

Along the way we're hoping to get back into the studio with some of our favourite performers to record a few songs for the Christmas season and also to track down some new companies to work with for our retail collaborations. Evenings will be devoted to our readers: Monday to Thursday during our trip we'll be hosting our subscribers and partners at special events combining our editors in proper cosy attire, a large line-up of MONOCLE products to help dent Christmas wish-lists, a new version of our book and a tasty line-up of food and drinks. As with all of our events, subscribers will be sent invitations over the coming weeks. We're always open to suggestions for what we might do after we've finished at our first venue and are ready for something that might involve a more intimate bar and even a tiny dance-floor to get the season properly under way.

Before I sign off, a bit of housekeeping. I'm happy to report that my trusty assistants Tommy and Isabel have now take up new posts on the masthead – Mr Seres is now part of the advertising team (with a special focus on travel) and Frau Käser has joined the Monocle 24 research desk (with a view to affairs in the Middle East). Thank you to both for their tireless service. In their place, I'm happy to welcome back Helen Pipins (we last shared a dining table when we launched another magazine back in 1996) as the mistress of logistics and diary and Kristoffer Parup as the master of business development and research. As ever, all your comments, questions and tips are welcome at *tb@monocle.com*. — (M)

For more from our editor-in-chief, read his column in the FT *Weekend.*